P.R. Hague
Captain
Dowding Shoal.

Honour Restored

The Battle of Britain, Dowding and the Fight for Freedom

HONOUR RESTORED

THE BATTLE OF BRITAIN, DOWDING AND THE FIGHT FOR FREEDOM

by

Squadron Leader Peter Brown AFC

'Red Two' in the Battle of Britain

SPELLMOUNT
Staplehurst

British Library Cataloguing in Publication Data:
A catalogue record for this book is available
from the British Library

Copyright © Peter Brown 2005

ISBN 1-86227-301-4

First published in the UK in 2005 by
Spellmount Limited
The Village Centre
Staplehurst
Kent TN12 0BJ

Tel: 01580 893730
Fax: 01580 893731
E-mail: enquiries@spellmount.com
Website: www.spellmount.com

1 3 5 7 9 8 6 4 2

Printed in Great Britain by
Oaklands Book Services
Stonehouse, Gloucestershire GL10 3RQ

Contents

Sortie to Dunkirk

On the morning of 2nd June 1940, I was in some difficulty. I was a Pilot Officer flying in a Spitfire over the North Sea trying to return to my base in very poor visibility, having been shot up by a Messerschmitt 109 high above the Dunkirk beaches. I was getting low on fuel and had not been able to make any radio contact. I was very isolated. At 4.30 am I had left Digby in Lincolnshire flying with my Squadron, No. 611, to Martlesham Heath near Ipswich. After refuelling at dispersal and receiving the inevitable and always welcome mug of tea, we met up with No. 92 Squadron led by Flight Lieutenant Stanford Tuck, with whom we were to fly on patrol over the Dunkirk beaches.

This was to be our first squadron operational patrol to attack the enemy. It was decided that as Tuck had flown patrols over Dunkirk before, his squadron should lead. We had no briefing about anything; we just took off and followed in convoy. Finding Dunkirk nearly 70 miles away was not difficult. From a long distance the smoke from the burning oil tanks could be seen as a column in the sky rising to over 10,000 feet. After patrolling as the second squadron for some time at 15,000 feet without seeing anything, suddenly, without warning, the sky was full of yellow-nosed Me109s above us, and diving down. We had been well and truly bounced. This often happened with fighter units in combat with Me109s for the first time.

A pilot's first four or five operational flights were always the most dangerous. Two of our pilots were immediately shot down and killed, and four of us received damage from the Me109s. I could feel the bullets hitting my aircraft and I knew that death was very close. It was a moment of truth! After evading the Me109 I looked around the sky and, from being full of aircraft, there was not one in sight. I decided to climb up to 15,000 feet again and patrolled on my own over the beaches for about 15 minutes. In retrospect a very unintelligent thing to do but so important to me at that time.

I then saw a large formation approaching and, remembering that my aircraft had been damaged I decided it was time to go home. I set a course that I thought would take me back to Martlesham Heath. The visibility

1

over the sea was very hazy and I could only see a mile or so ahead. I knew I had been hit many times, and hoped that the aircraft and the engine would hold together. If my course was too far to the east, I would continue flying over the North Sea until my fuel ran out, and no one would know where I had baled out to send help. I tried several times to make contact with Control by radio but without success. After what seemed an eternity, I finally sighted land at Foulness Point in Essex. I turned to the west, and within a few minutes I was over Rochford Airfield at Southend. At last I was safe, or so I thought.

I lowered the flaps and undercarriage, which fortunately came down and locked without difficulty, and knowing my aircraft had been damaged, I tried for as gentle a landing as possible. Immediately the wheels touched down my Spitfire swung badly to the left; a bullet through my port wing by the Me109 pilot had burst the tyre. Fortunately, it was a grass airfield and I managed to prevent the aircraft from ground looping and rolling over. After I taxied in, the flight sergeant counted the bullet holes. When he reached 30 he stopped and said very firmly 'You won't be going anywhere in this aircraft today, Sir.'

I had been bounced and shot up, my flight had lasted for two hours, I had just managed to reach land, and I had survived a landing with a burst tyre. I had been well and truly blooded. I do not remember suffering any emotional after effects, only chagrin at being beaten up instead of shooting down an Me109.

In one special way the fighter pilot is different from any other fighting men. Once the action has started he fights alone. He decides when to break off the combat, if he can, and whether to search for a second aircraft to attack, or to set course for home. If he is hit by enemy bullets, he decides whether to bale out, tries to force-land or attempts to reach base and save his aircraft. If he is killed he dies alone.

* * *

I have started the book with a recollection of Dunkirk because I believe that the battle over Dunkirk was the beginning of the Battle for Britain. By getting our men back to England we were still in the fight and still ready to fight.

Dedication

This book is dedicated to the people of Britain who stood alone against the threat of Nazi invasion and occupation, and sacrificed so much to protect the freedom of our great country in 1940 and for future years. They include wives and mothers, sons and fathers, our fighter pilots and aircrews, Air Chief Marshal Sir Hugh Dowding, our Commander-In-Chief of Fighter Command, Winston Churchill our great leader and Prime Minster, our well loved King George and Queen Elizabeth, and the newspaper vendor in the Strand in London who showed me how to stand firm in the face of danger.

* * *

Also to my brother Sergeant Freddie Brown RAFVR, who was killed in action as the navigator of a Wellington bomber, with all his crew companions on a raid over Viareggio, Italy on 1st November 1943. He was 21 years young.

Acknowledgements

My Special Acknowledgement is to historian and author Richard C. Smith whose continued friendship and support have helped to ensure the publication of this book. I had completed my original research and conclusions by early 1997, but had been unable to proceed to publication. I met Richard at this difficult time, and he arranged for me to deliver a thesis on my work in public, later in 1997, in time for me to protect the rights for my research and conclusions. I can now present 'Honour Restored', based on my original work, and which I trust has gained by my further research and understanding.

Dr Jack Dixon, from Canada, for permission to quote from 'Victory and Defeat', his book on the achievements of Air Chief Marshal Dowding and the scandal of his dismissal.

Steve Gleeson M.B.E., for his friendship, and steadfast and crucial support when Chairman of the Trustees of the Battle of Britain Historical Society.

Squadron Leader Chris Goss, author and historian, with his specialised knowledge of the Luftwaffe and for information from Major Molder's Luftwaffe logbook.

John C. Hewitt, author of 'Ireland's Aviator Heroes', who became a true friend in Northern Ireland.

The Imperial War Museum, Photographic Archive for permission to use images from their collection

Squadron Leader A.T.MacDonald of R.A.F. Bentley Priory for kindly giving permission for the photograph of the author with the portrait of Air Chief Marshal Dowding to be used with 'Honour Restored'.

Francis K. Mason, author of 'Battle over Britain' whose book has been a great source of information about the Battle and the pilots.

The National Archives (Public Record Office) with their efficiency, courtesy, and helpful staff making their invaluable records so accessible.

Geoff Nutkins of the Shoreham Aircraft Museum, a gifted artist and a good friend, for kindly giving permission to use 'Battle above the Clouds' for the front cover.

Dr Alfred Price, noted Battle of Britain author, for his friendly advice, and for permission to quote from the exceptional tape of his meeting with

Group Captain Douglas Bader, and to consult his figures of casualties.

Winston G. Ramsey, Editor in Chief of 'Then and Now', for his ready help and advice. Especially for his permission to use the data in his great volume to make a database of operational casualties.

David Ross, biographer of Richard Hillary, for friendship, and support when it was really needed.

Colin Smith of Vector Fine Art Prints for his tenacity and continued support in the publication of 'Honour Restored.'

Squadron Leader B.G. Stapleton D.F.C., a veteran of No 603 Squadron, for our shared memories of Hornchurch, and for kindly reading my manuscript as 'One of the Few'.

Anthony Tuck, son of Wing Commander R.R.S. Tuck D.S.O., D.F.C., for his continued and tenacious support in our fight for the truth.

Kenneth G. Wynn for his 'Men of the Battle,' which stands alone as a permanent and personal record of those who were there.

To all the others who have helped and encouraged me – my most grateful thanks.

Prologue

This book tells of a great event and great people. It is about one of the most important happenings in Western Civilisation – the victory of the British people over Nazi Germany, with its threat to engulf Europe and with it the destruction of democracy and human decency.

In the year 1940, in the skies over Britain, a great aerial battle was fought against the German Luftwaffe. It was not only the greatest battle in the air, but it was one of the most significant battles in the history of the Western World. It changed the course of history for all the European nations.

The Battle was won by the British nation standing alone, and by our young pilots fighting against overwhelming odds. We were greatly supported by our friends from the Dominions of New Zealand, Canada, Australia, and South Africa, and by pilots from other nations including Poland and Czechoslovakia, who joined us in our fight to maintain our Heritage as a free nation.

After the German 'blitzkrieg' swept across Northern France in May, our British Expeditionary Force army had retreated back to the port of Dunkirk, the last Channel port available to them, in the hopes of being evacuated back to England. Against all the odds, and with the help of Fighter Command Hurricanes, Spitfires and Defiants overhead, more than 300,000 British and Allied troops were brought back across the Channel by our Royal Navy and civilian sailors to the safety of England's shores.

By June 1940 the military machine of Nazi Germany had bulldozed its way through Europe, and now occupied the Western European coast down to the Atlantic approaches. Czechoslovakia, Poland, Norway, Denmark, Holland, Belgium, and northern France had been occupied by the German army and were destined to be enslaved by the terrors of the Nazi doctrines of the Third Reich. Minority persecution would soon be a harsh fact of life. Only Britain was left to challenge the Dark Goliath.

We faced the military might of Germany which now extended from the Arctic Circle down to the Bay of Biscay. As a precursor to their plans for the invasion and occupation of Britain, the German Luftwaffe, only 15 minutes flying time across the Channel from its new air bases in France and Belgium, had to achieve air supremacy over London and the southeast of England. To do this they had to destroy the Hurricanes and Spitfires of Fighter Command or reduce them to an ineffective force. Only our fighter pilots could prevent this and save Britain from defeat.

To enslave our people and to complete his domination of Western Europe, Hitler had to occupy Britain. He had some 2,500 warplanes in northern France, Belgium, the Cherbourg Peninsula, and Norway, ready once again to prove the superiority of the 'Master Race'. When their major attacks started, in Britain we had some 750 operational Hurricanes and Spitfires in 47 squadrons, ready to defend not only London and the south-east of England, but also 1,000 miles of our vulnerable coastline.

Although the official British date of the beginning of the Battle of Britain is recorded as 10th July 1940, the massed aerial assault on this Country was started by Reichsmarschall Hermann Goering, Commander-in-Chief of the Luftwaffe, on 13th August 1940 and named by him as 'Adler Tag' or 'Eagle Day'. The world watched and waited for the inevitable defeat of our once great nation. All countries, except those of our fighting friends, expected us to be overwhelmed quickly, and to become a vassal of Nazi Germany.

On 15th September 1940, after five weeks of daylight raids in over-whelming numbers, the Luftwaffe made two major raids on London. Their bomber crews and pilots had been led to believe by Luftwaffe intelligence that Fighter Command had been effectively destroyed, and that these were merely 'mopping up' actions.

To their dismay the German formations were beaten back with such ferocity and by so many British fighters, that their pilots and their leaders knew that the tide had turned, and that the German offensive in the air had failed. There could be no invasion of England in 1940. With this triumph the occupied countries of Europe could now see that the flame of freedom was still burning brightly in Britain. It gave hope to them that one day, as was proved, they would be free again, although at heavy cost in lives to the invading Allied forces.

We owe this great victory to our fighter pilots, the young men who daily 'scrambled' in squadron units to attack enemy formations of hundreds of aircraft, up to more than 900 aircraft on one raid. A total of 544 of our pilots and aircrew gave their lives, fighting in the sky. In addition many of our pilots were wounded or suffered from burns, but still came back to fight again. Our leader in the Battle was Air Chief Marshal Sir Hugh Dowding, C-in-C of Fighter Command. Behind us were the ground crews who served us and our aircraft, even when under airfield attack.

But of course the great strength of Britain was its people, the ordinary people, and by today's standards, the extra-ordinary people, who gave to the world and to the military strategists a new axiom: 'aerial bombardment can destroy a great city but it cannot destroy the spirit of a great people'. We all knew for certain that Hitler and his generals would never march down Whitehall. It just couldn't happen. We wouldn't let it happen.

Introduction

This is the story of the Battle of Britain as I saw it as a young fighter pilot in 1940, and as I review it today with 65 years of hindsight. I will try to give the atmosphere of the time, which proved to the world that Britain was a united country, ready to defend freedom at all costs. Led by Prime Minister Winston Churchill this was indeed to be 'their finest hour'.

I am writing this book now as I believe that the young and middle aged citizens of our Country should know more about the Battle of Britain and the great sacrifices made by our young men and our people to save the sovereignty of Britain in 1940, and giving hope to the occupied countries of Europe.

I have presented *Honour Restored* in two parts which, although both are vitally concerned with Honour Restored in the Battle of Britain, are quite different in content. The first tells of the great victory of the British people of which we can be proud, but the second, restoring honour to Lord Dowding, is a sad reflection on the behaviour of certain senior RAF Officers at a time of great crisis with the threat of invasion by Nazi Germany. This has enabled me to write each study in the style most suited to it and for the formats to be different, although the whole story is dependent on the two being linked together. To restore honour to Lord Dowding it is first necessary to prove that it was a great victory and that he and his pilots won the battle. In making this presentation of two separate studies there will be occasional duplication for greater clarity of these two aspects of the Great Battle, for which I ask your tolerance.

* * *

As a peacetime officer in the Royal Air Force, trained to be a fighter pilot, when war was declared I was posted to No. 611 Fighter Squadron in September 1939, and I continued to fly Spitfires operationally until well after the Battle was over. I flew mostly as Red 2 or Yellow 2 but was never an ace – not even nearly. But I was at readiness throughout the Battle either in No. 12 Group covering the Midlands, or in No. 11 Group protecting

London and the south-east of England. I saw action against German bomb-ers and fighters. I was shot up twice, and flew with the Duxford Wing in the defence of London. I flew at 30,000 feet in -40C. temperatures and I learned that Luftwaffe bullets and cannon shells treated us all the same whatever our rank and experience. I think I can fairly claim that 'I was there'.

Hundreds of thousands of homes throughout the country were destroyed or damaged, and our people endured many hardships. These brave citizens paid a very high price for the ultimate victory, which we achieved with our Allies five years later. I hope that with my experience as a pilot in the Battle, my wartime memories and my research, that I shall be able to take you back to the Britain of 1940 to meet the indomitable men and women of that time.

Part One of the book is titled 'A Great Victory'. It tells the story of the Battle of Britain, beginning as I believe, with the escape of the British Expeditionary Force from Dunkirk under the umbrella of Fighter Command in May and June 1940, through to 15th September, the day of Nemesis for the Luftwaffe, and on to the final battles with high flying Me109 fighter/bombers dropping bombs at random.

I shall introduce you to that special breed of young men who flew in their Hurricanes, Spitfires, Defiants and Blenheims, who faced death daily and dealt with their fears by replacing them with their special brand of self-effacing humour.

Over the years there have been those who have tried to diminish Britain's achievements in the Battle. In the book I have refuted some such misrepresentations of the reality. This is a challenging book with some new approaches to understanding facets of the battle. How crucial was the weather in enabling us to beat back the German massed formations? Was it a close-run thing? Did Hitler's decision to bomb London save Fighter Command from defeat? Was there really a Big Wing Philosophy or was it merely a Myth?

Part Two of the book, titled 'Dowding, A Man of History', is presented in three sections. In the first I deal with the Big Wing Controversy in which I have always had a special interest and have researched for many years. The Controversy was essentially a battle between RAF factions as to whether we should have changed to using enhanced wings of up to 60 aircraft to intercept the large Luftwaffe formations, or whether we should have continued with the well-tried single and sometimes pairs of squadrons used during the first two months of the Battle. Fortunately I am helped in my assessment by operational experience with both types of defence.

The conflict on this issue at Command level was both tactical and politi-cal and is a contentious issue even up to the present day. What might have been considered as a conflict in tactics in a battle already fought and won, became a political issue to be resolved at Air Ministry level. Even in times of great crisis the personal ambitions of some leaders blind them to the realities of the conflict with its day-to-day fighting and the sacrifices of their young men.

This leads naturally on to the second section, which exposes the attack on the competence of Air Chief Marshal Sir Hugh Dowding as Commander in Chief during the Battle. There was a Cabal at Air Ministry that was antagonistic to Dowding who was due to be retired before the Battle, but as there was no other officer in the RAF who knew the whole of our defence structure and its operation, the Air Ministry delayed his retirement. By the middle of October it was clear that the Battle had been won and the invasion averted.

The Cabal did not want Dowding to have the credit for his great victory and a meeting was called on 17th October 1940 to challenge his tactics in the Battle. As a result, his professionalism was challenged in front of officers many ranks junior to him. This bizarre meeting at the Air Ministry and its preparations and conclusions are presented in detail with supporting evidence. It was attended by 10 officers of air rank and must always be held to the shame of the Air Ministry at that time.

Soon after, Dowding was removed from his position as Commander-in-Chief without public honour for his great achievement in winning the Battle. I now present in Part Two what I believe is the truth of the machinations leading to the dismissal of Dowding, and I am now able to name some of those involved. Dowding's pilots have never forgiven the Air Ministry of 1940 for their actions at a time when Britain faced the greatest challenge in its history. I trust that this book will be a contribution to restore honour to all those who stood firm and kept Britain, our island bastion of democracy for centuries, safe from Nazi invasion.

Part One

A Great Victory

CHAPTER 1

The People

Those who have the least give the most

In September 1939 Britain faced up to the awful realisation that, in an attempt to save Poland from the Nazi invasion, together with the French nation we had declared war on Germany. Throughout the country on September 3rd at 11.15am we had all sat by our wireless sets to hear the solemn words from Mr Neville Chamberlain, our Prime Minister:

> This morning the British Ambassador in Berlin handed the German Government a final note stating that, unless we heard from them by 11 o'clock that they were prepared at once to withdraw their troops from Poland, a state of war would exist between us. I have to tell you now that no such undertaking has been received and that consequently this Country is at war with Germany.

We were not certain what offensive military action we could take, but we all expected that very soon we would be bombed by the largest air force in the world. We already knew that our young men would be conscripted into one of the services. They would leave home, some not to return for a long time and some never to return. Although naturally everyone hated the thought of war, there was a kind of understandable inevitability about what was happening, with an acceptance that we were making the great sacrifice because the evil of German Nazi tyranny had to be fought and halted no matter what the cost.

Among the ordinary people of Britain there were very few dissenters and pacifists. The British Communist Party denounced and opposed the war as a capitalist war to benefit the arms manufacturers and they organised factory strikes. Later, in June 1941, within a very few days after the announcement that Germany had attacked Russia, the Communists then proclaimed that our war against Germany had changed and was now a war for democratic freedom. They then outlawed strikes.

There was no feeling of panic, but rather as happened later when France surrendered in June 1940, there was a feeling of a nation bonding together to fight the problem. This bonding stayed with the Country throughout the war and was a major factor in our continued determination to carry on the fight. Britain's forces were already at readiness and air raid precautions had been prepared and were put into effect.

Many declarations of war have been challenged as being needless or even evil. I have never heard such statements made about the decision by Britain and France to take up arms against Nazi Germany, not even by the most ardent pacifist.

Even if we had not declared war against Germany, our Country would still have been in grave danger. It would have meant eventual acceptance of German Nazi domination over Europe with the ending of democracy. We would sooner have gone down fighting.

I believe that a crucial factor in this attitude was that prior to the war, the people in Britain could volunteer to take an active part in its defence. They could join the reserves of the Army, and the Royal Navy, and for young men there was a wonderful opportunity to train at weekends to become Volunteer Reserve pilots or aircrew. There was auxiliary training for the fire brigades, ambulance services and air raid defence in which women could also take a part. Above all we would be fighting to defend our own Country of which we were proud. It would be easy to refer to it as the 'people's war'.

Britain was to be the first country to prove that determined citizens cannot be bombed into surrender. The effect of the raids is first to make them angry, and then to make them even more determined to fight on. Another factor was that we had had time to make preparations for the war. Air raid shelters had been built, the blackout had been rehearsed, emergency services had been planned, and the Government had ensured that everyone, even the babies, had been supplied with a personal gas mask to be kept close at all times.

I think it is important to understand that, having with a heavy heart entered into a state of war in order to save the freedom of another country hundreds of miles away, our people believed in the cause and were united. But after this grand, sincere and defiant gesture, the Country began to pay the price. Our food was rationed. No one would go hungry but the standard two ounces of butter, four ounces of margarine, and a meat allocation equal to two chops per week would be incomprehensible to us today. People formed long queues for food that could not be obtained with a ration card, and vegetables soon became the staple diet.

I felt that the rigidly enforced blackout, especially in the winter, was one of the worst aspects of the war. It was depressing and dangerous. In our cities our young children were taken from their mothers and, equipped with their gas masks, a label on their coats, a sandwich for the unknown journey, and a bag or small case with pyjamas and personal possessions were entrained to some unknown family many miles away. The alternative was to keep them at home to risk the dangers of the air raids.

Clothes rationing followed and civilian travel was almost impossible. And then came the bombing. There was the awful stomach-sinking warning of the air raid sirens sounding the alarm, and eventually the wonderful and uplifting sound of the 'all clear' with the coming of dawn. I know that, with my two brothers in the fighting Services as well, the greatest trial for those waiting at home was the knowledge that a father, brother or son, hundreds or thousands of miles away, could be in great danger every day. The separation could last for months and years, and was only made bearable because a similar anguish was shared by so many friends and neighbours. The awful unspoken fear was of the arrival of the Post Office messenger boy with his yellow telegram to notify 'missing in action'. There were no professional counsellors to give comfort to the bereaved.

The radio or 'wireless' was a vital link for all members of the nation, and the people listened to the 'Nine o'clock' news in the evening almost as a ritual. The numbers of enemy aircraft shot down in the day, which we know now were generally rather optimistic, were a great boost to morale.

The radio speeches of Winston Churchill, who had replaced Neville Chamberlain as Prime Minister, uplifted the nation, and are just as moving for me to hear today as they were then. Churchill led the nation, cajoled and encouraged our citizens, defied the enemy, moved us and was moved himself. At all times he gave the Nation the confidence that we would win through. A very great man.

King George VI and Queen Elizabeth enjoyed a unique relationship with the people. It was a combination of great respect and affection. They toured the country and met the servicemen and women and visited the factories and hospitals. This increased the affection felt for them and led to a more personal relationship. They visited the bombed sites and met the injured and homeless. This was made even more personal when Buckingham Palace was bombed. Princess Elizabeth, their elder daughter and now our revered Queen for more than 50 years, joined the ATS (Auxiliary Territorial Service) as a subaltern soon after she reached her 18th birthday. Princess Elizabeth served as an Army truck driver later in the war, confirming the growing and important role played by women as the war progressed.

Although cinemas and theatres and other places of entertainment were closed for a while, they were soon re-opened. In the summer of 1940 cricket was still played at Lords, and the Amateurs walked to the pitch down the Members' steps from the pavilion and the Professionals came out from a side gate. The great social changes occasioned by major wars had not yet started.

In spite of the rationing, the heartrending evacuation of the children, and the misery of the blackout, followed by the night bombing, the aim of the population was always to carry on as usual, with the determination to get to work each day at all costs. Those who were there will remember the part played by the ever present British sense of humour in their dealing with these harsh conditions. Knowing and understanding such people confirms why the Battle of Britain must be called 'A Great Victory'. In October 1940 I had planned to spend my day-off from the Squadron in

London, and to stay the night at the Strand Palace Hotel right in the heart of the Metropolis. In the evening as I left Covent Garden Underground station, the nearest to the hotel, the night bombing had already started with explosions and anti-aircraft guns firing with shrapnel coming down. With several hundred yards to go I decided to make a run for it. As I arrived at high speed at the entrance of the hotel in my RAF officer's uniform, a cheerful voice called up to me 'Evening paper, Sir?' I stopped in my tracks and saw a man sitting at the entrance, his regular 'pitch' probably for many years, carrying on with his life as usual without any protection, selling evening papers in the middle of an air raid. I was supposed to be· one of our brave Spitfire pilots, and I felt ashamed. I bought a paper from him, thanked him, and then walked the last few paces into the hotel with rather more dignity than when I had arrived. How could I better typify the courage and refusal to be beaten by the ordinary people of our Country in 1940, than with this reminiscence of the defiance shown to the enemy?

The war for us in 1940 was inevitable, and to an extent, as a country we were emotionally and physically prepared for it. There was little panic and unless you were very rich there was nowhere to hide. Before the war my generation grew up accepting that hardship was a fact of life, and misfortune had to be accepted and dealt with so that we could get on with our lives. Counselling, or rather comforting, was done by the family or close friends. In the main, and by today's standards, people were poor and survival was the real objective for most. Apart from the bombing and the loss of life, they could manage to survive by sharing with neighbours.

People today are different. Affluence tends to shelter us from the ups and downs of life. We now have a culture of compensation; we have demanded rights and have abandoned responsibilities. In the event of disaster the fittest have the best chance of survival. I wonder if today our Nation could unite and fight a Battle of Britain to save our democracy. We are the products of our generation and our environment. And yet there are times when I feel that, should another great leader arise, the British Lion could be aroused again to defend our country and our way of life and our freedom.

CHAPTER 2

Hitler and German Ambitions 1938

By 1938 Hitler, supported by 80 million citizens of Nazi Germany, had started on a plan to enslave Europe, and to build up a new German empire for Aryan people – the Master Race.

In 1938 Czechoslovakia had been occupied by the Germans; then in 1939 Poland was attacked. At this stage Britain and France finally decided to halt the German aggression, and gave Hitler an ultimatum to withdraw from Poland or to be at war. Russia and Germany had by then signed a non-aggression pact which resulted in the sharing and occupation of Polish territory. The decision of Britain and France in 1939 to declare war on Germany to save the freedom of the people of Poland was a very noble one, but in the cold light of day it would be a war which we had little chance of winning. We would pay a very high price for that decision.

Hitler carried on with his programme of invasion, but the following eight months of the so called 'phoney war', without serious action over Britain, gave the RAF valuable time to build more fighters, train more pilots and install more of the secret Radio Direction Finding equipment. On the 10th May 1940, after Norway and Denmark had been occupied, the Nazis marched and drove across the French and Belgian borders, side-stepping the much vaunted Maginot Line – a fixed concrete defensive system stretching for hundreds of miles across France, but not across Belgium.

With their Blitzkrieg, the 'Lightning War', the Germans sped their armoured divisions across France and drove the British Expeditionary Force back to Dunkirk. The Luftwaffe, the largest and most experienced air force in the world, gave close support to the German army, as was their planned function. The French Army and Air Force were unable to hold the German onslaught and were forced to retreat, finally capitulating on the 22nd June 1940.

Within two to three weeks of the start of the attack, realising that the battle on the mainland was lost, the Government decided to evacuate the British and Allied forces from Dunkirk to the Channel ports in England, abandoning their heavy guns, transport and mechanised fighting vehicles on the Continent.

With the surrender of France, Hitler was jubilant. He had almost accomplished his primary aim of the enslavement of Western Europe. Now there was only Britain to be dealt with. It is reasonable to accept that Hitler did not want a war with Britain, a country that he admired. But he needed to have Britain neutralised or occupied before he attacked Russia, his ultimate challenge. Following the return of the defeated British Expeditionary Forces from the beaches of Dunkirk, Hitler may still have hoped for a treaty with Britain. If that failed then he could decide on a Blitzkrieg invasion. Time would tell.

CHAPTER 3

The Dunkirk Spirit

26th May–4th June 1940

The evacuation of British and Allied personnel from Dunkirk began on 26th May 1940, and lasted for 10 days with the last vessel leaving on 4th June.

In view of the close proximity of the German forces, senior commanders in the Royal Navy believed that not more than 30,000 troops could be taken off the jetties and beaches and transported back to England. In fact, with the combined and heroic help of destroyers, paddle steamers, and pleasure cruisers from moorings in the south of England, many crewed by civilians, some 338,000 Allied troops were rescued and brought home.

Back in Britain, squadrons were called in from all Fighter Command groups to land and refuel at 11 Group airfields, where they operated under 11 Group control. Hurricane, Spitfire and Defiant formations took off to give protection over the Dunkirk beaches and surrounding areas at 10,000 to 15,000 feet. At that height they were unseen by the troops on the ground waiting for hours and even days to embark, while enduring attacks by German bombers and fighters. Our squadrons had to fly 60 to 90 miles to Dunkirk and then home again, limiting their time of protection for the beaches. They generally flew in pairs of squadrons and sometimes in three-, four- or even five-squadron wings. This concentration of strength could be operated over Dunkirk as there was time to assemble the formations, and we could choose when to go into action. Such large formations could not have played a significant part in the Battle of Britain, which needed the flexibility and speed of single or pairs of squadrons to provide a defensive shield. What a pity that this integration and co-operation could not have been repeated in the Battle of Britain two months later.

One of the problems for Air Vice-Marshal Keith Park, Commander of 11 Group who orchestrated the Fighter Command squadrons, was the tactical decision of whether to put in large formations at intervals or smaller wings as a continuous umbrella. The action was taking place 100 miles from his control centre with little effective RDF assistance.

In the 10 days over Dunkirk 80 of our pilots were killed or captured, and 106 aircraft were lost – some 25% of those engaged. The very high losses illustrate the intensity of the fighting against the Luftwaffe. These pilots and aircraft were lost from our squadrons which were desperately needed for the defence of Britain. Some of the rescued soldiers abused RAF personnel in the streets and public houses back home, quite wrongly believing that the RAF had not provided any air defence. But it is quite obvious that if Fighter Command had not been there to give protection, then there would have been little chance of saving even 30,000 men. The German Luftwaffe could have bombed all the boats out of existence at their leisure.

The fighting was very hard for many of the squadrons. For most of them it was the first time they had been in a major action and the first time they had met Me109s. The Me109 pilots were the masters of the 'bounce' and their battle experience of three previous spheres of air fighting was of great help to them. Many of our squadrons were blooded with quite high casualties. This was the first time that Me109 pilots had 'tussled' with our Spitfires and they must have viewed future operations against them with some trepidation. To my surprise they were less worried about the Hurricanes they met, believing that they were a lesser aircraft. There was nothing 'lesser' about the Hurricane pilots however as many of the Germans soon discovered. The two-seater Defiant fighters took part in the action with good results at first but with heavy casualties later on.

When France surrendered to the Germans after the evacuation from Dunkirk, Britain was completely on her own. The whole world believed that we too would have to surrender to the irresistible might of the Nazi war machine and come to an agreement with Hitler, or be invaded and occupied like the rest of Europe. In England US ambassador, Joseph Kennedy, advised President Roosevelt that Britain would be lost within six weeks, and that there was no point in sending any help.

Most of the British forces were now safely evacuated from the Continent and Hitler would need to consider an attack on England. The British accepted the challenge. In those days in 1940, as for many centuries previously, we were still an 'Island Race' with all that implied.

When the soldiers disembarked at Dover and other British harbours, they were defeated, demoralised and felt disgraced. But then, to their great astonishment, they were received by the English people as heroes. They were cheered, fed and clothed. This was the birth of what I call the Dunkirk spirit – a bonding of the people in defiance of enemy plans to attack and destroy us. While the French capitulated, some later to collaborate with the Germans, British morale rose to the heights. We all felt 'Thank God, at last we are alone; now we can fight our own battles our own way'. There was no thought of surrender, except perhaps among the intellectuals. As far as the ordinary British people were concerned, the

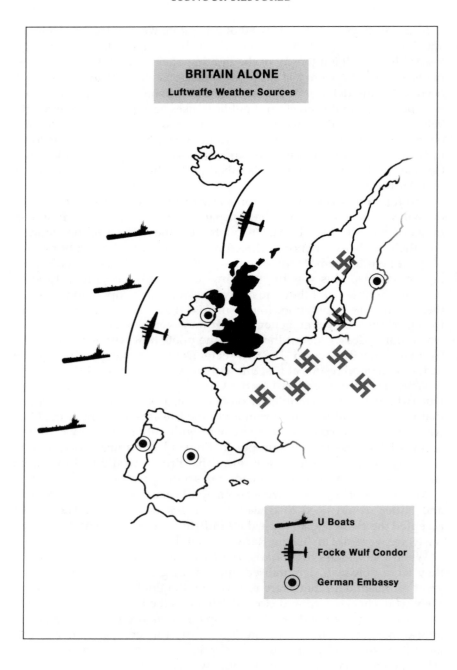

BRITAIN ALONE
Luftwaffe Weather Sources

U Boats

Focke Wulf Condor

German Embassy

only German troops that would ever march past the Houses of Parliament in London would be as prisoners of war under guard.

Our wartime leader Winston Churchill said: 'It was not I that defied the military might of Germany, it was the British people. I was just the lion that gave the roar.' It is an interesting thought that if the evacuation had been halted or failed, with over 200,000 British soldiers and airmen then held as prisoners of war on the Continent and with others captured elsewhere, perhaps our resolution would have faltered and we might have negotiated a peace settlement. Perhaps with their brave and costly action over Dunkirk, the RAF fighters had already won the first battle in the defence of Britain.

In June, when the French were close to surrender, Churchill loyally planned to send a number of our home-based Spitfire squadrons over to France to help in their fight against the Luftwaffe. After our serious losses over Dunkirk, Air Chief Marshal Sir Hugh Dowding realised the great danger to our own defence, and opposed Churchill's plans in a letter to the Air Council explaining vividly the threat to Britain. He stated that if any more Fighter Command aircraft were sent to France he could not guarantee the defence in the air of our Country. Reluctantly Churchill heeded Dowding's message and changed his mind; the squadrons so desperately needed were kept back and helped to defeat the Luftwaffe three months later.

Some historians have expressed the view that Hitler never seriously intended to invade England, but of course they weren't with us in 1940. I can assure you that everyone in England believed that they would invade if they could. So did the captured Nazi German fighter pilots, who confidently expected to be freed within a few weeks of being shot down, as they were after the Battle of France. If these writers were correct then Hitler needlessly wasted more than 1,800 of his finest warplanes and more than 2,600 battle experienced aircrews, merely to try to frighten the British people into surrender, and in so doing lost valuable months which delayed his attack on Russia with disastrous results.

CHAPTER 4

Fighter Command and the Commanders

In 1936, at the age of 54, Air Marshal Sir Hugh Dowding was appointed Air Officer Commanding-in-Chief of Fighter Command, responsible for the Air Defence of Great Britain. During the following three years he was responsible for the introduction of the Radio Directional Finding (RDF) defence system, and brought into service the new eight-gun Hurricane and Spitfire fighter aircraft just in time for the outbreak of war with Germany in 1939. Prior to this, he had been Air Member for Research and Development responsible for the design and introduction of new aircraft and technology. He was promoted to Air Chief Marshal on 1st January 1937, and was the most senior officer on the active list in the RAF – senior in service to Air Chief Marshal Sir Cyril Newall, the Chief of Air Staff. He had a quiet, dour personality, which may explain his nickname of 'Stuffy'. He was stubborn, always so in his fight for aircraft for Fighter Command – demanding the best machines and equipment for his pilots. There was a special bond between Dowding and his pilots; he deserved and received their affection and respect. He was not only an officer but he was always a gentleman, sometimes to his disadvantage. One criticism levelled against him was that he was slow to change direction in his defence tactics. Events proved him to be right in refusing to be swayed by over-rated and under-assessed Big Wing Philosophies.

In Fighter Command Dowding had one officer whom he knew he could trust to carry out his policies – his SASO Air Commodore Keith Park. With wisdom, in 1940 he appointed Park to be Air Officer Commanding 11 Group, with promotion to Air Vice-Marshal. Unfortunately Dowding had enemies at the Air Ministry and in Fighter Command. He was fighting a war on two fronts, in the air against the Luftwaffe and on the ground against air marshals and politicians. Fortunately for Britain, and indeed Europe, his fighter pilots gave the dedication and made the sacrifices that enabled him to win the battle. Dowding was charged with the defence of the Realm and it was to be a battle to defend Britain against the aerial might of Hitler's Germany. If he lost, nothing else mattered and a thousand years of our heritage and democracy would be gone forever.

In 1939 Fighter Command had been trained and organised to meet bomber attacks from Germany over the North Sea, possibly escorted by twin-engine fighters. Fighter Command was equipped with short-range, single-engine fighters, Hurricanes and Spitfires, but these were purely defensive. They flew in squadrons of 12 aircraft, flights of 6 aircraft, and sections of 3 aircraft. The squadron was identified by its own call sign and each section was identified by its colour – red, blue, yellow or green. Individual aircraft were numbered according to their position in the section; I often flew as Red 2. The German bombers flew in units of three or five aircraft. We rehearsed attacks against RAF bombers using Fighter Command parade ground techniques with attacks numbered 1–9. With the new RDF stations being completed we could plot enemy formations up to 100 miles out over the North Sea, giving us adequate warning to get our squadrons in the air to intercept them over the coastline.

Air Chief Marshal Sir Hugh Dowding had planned and built up this defence organisation over several years. The system was the only one of its kind in the world. The country was divided into groups mostly directed at Germany and across the North Sea from where, prior to 10th May 1940, the bomber threat was expected. Each group controlled several sectors, which each in turn controlled up to 4 squadrons. The map on page 26 shows the location of the Group and Sector Stations.

* * *

The largest and most important group was 11 Group commanded by Air Vice-Marshal Keith Park, a New Zealander and a WWI fighter pilot of some distinction. At the age of 48, Park flew regularly in his personal Hurricane aircraft, visiting his fighter stations. He had the heart and instincts of a fighter pilot. After controlling the Fighter Command squadrons in pairs and wings over Dunkirk, he was easily the most experienced man in the RAF in the disposition and control of fighters in action. He had 21 squadrons for the defence of the south-east of England, and London, the Capital, and a crucial target. His group had 13 Hurricane squadrons and 6 Spitfire squadrons for the brunt of the day defence. There were also 2 Blenheim twin-engine night fighter squadrons, which battled on with inadequate speed and unreliable interception equipment to fight the night raiders with great courage in all kinds of weather. We were, of course, in the early days of working with this new, exciting, exasperating and highly secret equipment. Operating in the blackout made aircraft servicing and flying even more difficult for them.

At the outbreak of war in 1939, 12 Group had the important responsibility of defending the industrial Midlands against bomber attacks from Germany across the North Sea. It was commanded by Air Vice-Marshal Leigh-Mallory, 48 years old and a very ambitious senior officer who by 1940 had already enjoyed a successful climb up the ladder of promotion

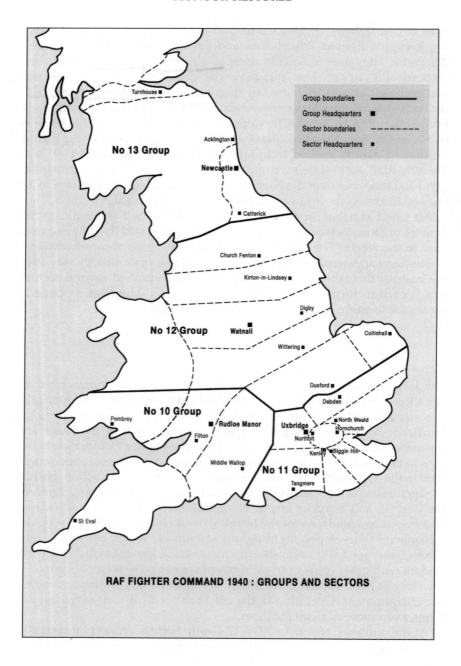

Group boundaries	────
Group Headquarters	■
Sector boundaries	─ ─ ─ ─
Sector Headquarters	■

Turnhouse ■

No 13 Group

Acklington ■

Newcastle ■

Catterick ■

Church Fenton ■

Kirton-in-Lindsey ■

Digby ■

No 12 Group   Watnall ■   Coltishall ■

Wittering ■

Duxford ■

Debden ■

Pembrey ■

No 10 Group   Rudloe Manor ■   Uxbridge   North Weald ■
Hornchurch ■

Filton ■   Northolt ■

Kenley ■ Biggin Hill ■

Middle Wallop ■   **No 11 Group** ■

Tangmere ■

■ St Eval

RAF FIGHTER COMMAND 1940 : GROUPS AND SECTORS

to take command of his Group in 1938. During WWI AVM Leigh-Mallory had been a specialist in army co-operation and continued with this specialisation in the Royal Air Force. In character, he was the opposite of Keith Park. He enjoyed the administrative side of his duties and was listed by the German Intelligence as the 'Flying Sergeant', more interested in administration than operational work. He commanded 11 day-fighter Squadrons, but had no previous fighter experience. The Group was equipped with 5 Hurricane and 6 Spitfire squadrons for day operations, and 2 Blenheim squadrons ready to defend the crucial Midlands industrial territory at night. It also had 1 Defiant squadron.

No. 13 Group in the North was commanded by Air Vice-Marshal R E Saul, also a WWI pilot, with 7 Hurricane squadrons, 3 Spitfire squadrons, 1 Blenheim squadron and 1 of Defiants for the defence of the north-east of England, Scotland and the Naval anchorages. A vital attribute of the Group was that it received battle tired squadrons from 11 Group and restored and rebuilt them up to 11 Group standards for return to the south. The Air Officer Commanding loyally accepted this role, and Park reported on the quality of the refreshed squadrons that came back to him again into the real war from this Group.

No.13 Group could have expected to have been in action against Luftwaffe bomber formations coming over the north sea from Norway and Denmark. However, with the German blitzkrieg in May resulting in the surrender of France, and with the need for Luftwaffe bombers to have Me109 protection, the possibility of major bomber attacks over the territory was greatly reduced. In fact, after the heavy defeat on 15 August of a major raid, the Luftwaffe never attacked again in full force again in the north of England and Scotland and the defence of our naval anchorages still remained. With the limited number of squadrons to cover their streched territory, the RDF system was crucial for effective defence.

Just in time for the Battle in 1940, 10 Group commanded by Air Vice-Marshal Sir Quintin Brand, a WWI night fighting specialist, was formed to cover part of the south coast, south-west England and Wales. It was equipped with 3 Hurricane squadrons, 4 Spitfire squadrons, and 1 Blenheim squadron for night defence. Later on in the Battle, facing the common enemy across the Channel, 10 Group battled shoulder to shoulder with 11 Group, giving one another a natural and invaluable support. Because of the distance of their sectors from the Luftwaffe across the Channel, the pilots would normally expect to meet Me110 long-range fighters defending the German bombers, rather than the Me109s as faced by 11 Group squadrons.

In the early days most of the battles with the Luftwaffe were near the southern coasts of Britain, where in the main the 11 Group duties were convoy patrols over the Channel, which were very tiresome, flying over the sea at 2,000 feet in continuous circuits, but which was vital work for the protection of our shipping. Other Groups had similar convoy duties and also gave protection against small coastal raids.

In my squadron towards the end of a tiring day of convoy patrols, we would turn on our oxygen to get a boost in energy and to remain fully alert. At the end of a patrol we would sometimes bid farewell to the ships in the convoy by a bridge-height fly past through the centre columns. As naval gunners had a simple and confirmed philosophy that any aircraft in range should be fired on, we were careful to prove our identification before the run in!

By August 1940, Fighter Command had a total of 28 Hurricane and 19 Spitfire squadrons, some 750 aircraft, to meet the enemy with 2,500 aircraft. Each of these fighters was equipped with eight forward-firing 0.303in machine-guns housed in the wings, and sighted from the cockpit. They had a limited range of 400 miles and could fly and fight at up to 30,000 feet. Fighter Command also had 2 squadrons of the two-seat Defiants which had a rotating turret with four guns. These aircraft had a short and chequered career. Dowding had been opposed to their acceptance as day fighters, not least because they had no guns firing forward. I think that their design and acceptance was due to the influence of World War I pilots of high rank at the Air Ministry with memories of the success of their two-seaters. However, fighter combat tactics had moved on since then. They had a few days of initial success against the Luftwaffe over Dunkirk due to their unusual design, but the German pilots soon exploited their inherent weakness in performance and restricted firepower and flexibility. After great gallantry and finally with heavy losses, the Defiant squadrons were withdrawn and used for night fighting operations.

There were 6 Blenheim twin-engine fighter squadrons for defence against night bombers. They were equipped with four guns firing forward and early and unproven RDF equipment for interception. They were not fast enough to be effective and the air interception equipment was unreliable, so their successes were few. In spite of this our night fighters battled on night after night, during which time often their worst enemies were the English weather and the nights without moon. Even when they sighted a German bomber they were sometimes not able to get close enough to engage, but they still carried on with their almost impossible task. Courage takes many shapes and forms.

With the surrender of France the Luftwaffe were in indisputable control of the western coast of Europe from Norway to Brest, and at the nearest point Luftwaffe airfields were 15 minutes flying time from English shores. The main threat now would come from the south-east and not from the east.

After the disastrous raid on 15th August the Luftwaffe accepted that German bombers could not operate over England without single engine fighter escorts. As the Me109s had a limited radius of action, it was obvious that there would be no significant Luftwaffe day activity over 12 Group.

There had been a dramatic move in the epicentre of the fighting to the south-east corner of England where most of the Battle would take place. No. 12 Group squadrons were destined for a life of convoy patrols and X raids by unidentified aircraft, with no glory or honours for Leigh-Mallory the Group Commander. This was a time when our fighter defences should have been restructured and directed, not at Germany, but at France and Belgium. All the European countries on the coast from Norway to Brest had now surrendered, and were occupied or were collaborating with the Germans. The rest of Europe was under dictatorship control or isolated. Later other countries of central Europe were invaded by the Nazis; only Britain was free from Nazi domination.

A strength of Air Chief Marshal Dowding, and also at times a weakness, was his rigid adherence to his master plan in which the Groups operated separately. No. 12 Group, instead of continuing to operate in isolation, should have pivoted to the south and acted as the reserve for 11 Group, ready to move squadrons south as the action dictated. In an emergency, 12 Group squadrons could still have defended the Midlands from their Duxford or other central England bases. This did not happen and even worse, the relationship between the two group commanders was strained, and there was a serious lack of co-operation between them. Regretfully, and with harm to the effectiveness of our defence, neither Dowding nor his Senior Air Staff Officer, Air Vice-Marshal Evill, took the early and firm action needed to deal with this vital problem.

CHAPTER 5

Defence Strategy and Operational Control

As Commander in Chief of Fighter Command, Air Chief Marshal Dowding's responsibilities were great indeed.

1. There could be no invasion of England unless Fighter Command was eliminated or made ineffective. Continued German air supremacy over the Channel and the south-east of England was essential before an invasion could start. To prevent this Dowding had to maintain Fighter Command as a powerful and viable defensive air force at least until the end of September. After that the approach of winter would inhibit invasion in 1940.

2. His fighters had to attack the invading forces by day, especially the bombers, to prevent essential targets from being bombed, including airfields, aircraft factories, ports and later London. There was no real defence against night bombing and nor would there be for many months. The crucial problem to be faced was whether to attack the German formations as soon as they appeared, in order to prevent them bombing their target, although this meant using small fighter formations. The alternative was to delay the attacks until squadrons could be given time to get above the enemy or grouped into larger formations. By this time however, the Germans could have dropped their bombs in several areas and be on the way home. Dowding and Park chose as a basic principle to attack at once with the units available. However, when the Germans finally attacked with a large formation flying on a long straight run to a target such as London, there was time to attack with two-squadron formations and even to scramble a Wing.

3. Dowding carried responsibility for Fighter Command, Balloon Command, the RDF defence system, the Observer Corps for inland tracking, and liaison with the Anti-Aircraft Command. This was a tremendous administrative burden in addition to dealing with tactical and technical matters. I believe that he should have appointed a Fighter Command deputy to be responsible for co-ordinating all the Groups and squadrons and to plan the tactics needed for the traumatic changes in events. Unfortunately he stuck to his original plans and left the Group Commanders to operate independently. He may well have decided that he did not have the right

man for such a key and immediate appointment, or more likely he felt that his system would work well with the right sense of purpose and the total loyalty of his Group Commanders. 'Therein lay the rub.'

Had he received the loyal support he rightly expected from Air Vice-Marshal Leigh-Mallory, then 11 Group could have been supported and reinforced at the critical time in the Battle. This would have made for a more effective defence with more enemy shot down with fewer losses of our pilots.

RDF plots of enemy aircraft coming in to the coast were transmitted to Fighter Command Control to be filtered and screened. They were then passed to the appropriate Group Operations Room which in turn passed them on to the designated sector station with instructions to scramble squadrons to patrol or intercept. Once airborne the squadrons were controlled by the Sector Controller who gave them vectors to fly with information such as the direction, approximate numbers and approximate height of the enemy. The controllers were also fed details of enemy aircraft locations by the Observer Corps who plotted the Luftwaffe formations once they had crossed the English coast. Although the procedure may appear on paper to be cumbersome, in fact the transmission of the plots was quite fast; indeed it had to be. With closing speeds of up to 360 mph, or 1 mile in 10 seconds, delays in transmitting information could be disastrous to the success of the interception.

Operational Control

The Operations Room was the nerve centre of each sector dedicated to scrambling and controlling our fighters on to the enemy formations. A screen of RDF towers had been built around the coast of Britain to give advance warning of the approach of enemy aircraft. This advance notice, even with the inaccuracies in the numbers of aircraft reported, was of vital value to our Ops Room Controllers. It could safely be said that it more than doubled the efficiency of our fighter defence. The plots gave information as to the approach of enemy aircraft, their position, their height and an indication of the numbers involved. A technical device enabled the plotters to record if the aircraft were 'ours' or 'theirs'. It was known as ' Identification – Friend or Foe' shortened to IFF and was highly secret. As the formations crossed the coast the plotting of them was taken over by the Observer Corps, which operated on visual and aural recording. Group and Sector Controllers of high calibre were vital to the effective operation of our fighter defence, and in the main we had them. A well known actor and World War I pilot, Ronald Adam, was one of several who established a special bond with us and were able to give support to us by voice contact, no matter how serious the situation. In times of real difficulty they were our life-line. Map on page 32 refers.

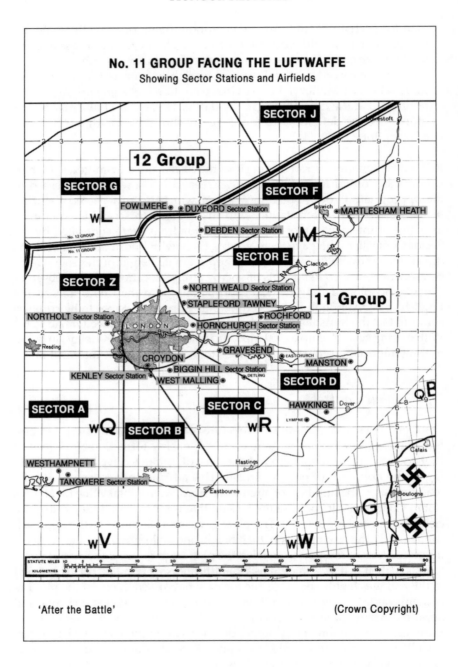

No. 11 GROUP FACING THE LUFTWAFFE
Showing Sector Stations and Airfields

'After the Battle' (Crown Copyright)

This positive control of operational aircraft was an unusual function, with at that time no real civilian or military equivalent anywhere else in the world. It could only have been possible with an integrated RDF system. Except for a period at the end of August and the beginning of September, when the squadrons were being badly bounced, the pilots had full confidence in the Controllers, who however could only pass on the plots they had received. Up to the point of contact with the 'bandits' and apart from exceptional circumstances, the Controller was responsible for the positioning of the formation. He was up to date with the enemy plots and also had knowledge of other fighter squadrons who might be intercepting. Once the squadron or flight had seen and identified the enemy, the shout of 'Tally Ho' announced the transfer of complete control of our aircraft to our flight leader. After that it was up to him how and when to attack.

It would have been wonderful if squadrons could always have been put in a position *up sun* and *above the enemy* but this was not the reality. Until the interception had been made there was no real knowledge of the challenge. Were they in front, to the side, above or below, how many, and where were the Me109s? The sky is enormous when you are looking for dots. If you haven't seen them first as dots you may already be in serious trouble.

The plots on the operations table were positioned by members of the WAAF who gave a special ambiance to the Ops Room. They were closely involved in the action 25,000 feet above them and they could hear the two-way radio messages between Control and the pilots. These young women showed great courage, staying at their posts when their operations block was bombed. Sadly some of them were killed and others were injured. The courage of some, including WAAFs at the fighter station at Biggin Hill in Kent, was recognised with awards for bravery. Women serving in the Royal Air Force were either members of the regular WRAF (Women's Royal Air Force) or the WAAF (Women's Auxiliary Air Force). In this book both parties are referred to as WAAFs.

A major problem for Groups and Sectors was how to assess the incoming enemy. Was it a real raid or a feint? Was it largely bombers or was it an aggressive fighter sweep of Me109s? Decisions had to be made on a timescale measured in minutes and ultimately based on judgement and experience and perhaps a special intuition. This was the first time ever that an aerial battle defending a nation had been fought on such a scale, at such speeds and with such technology. For Dowding and Park and the Controllers, this was a match in which the goal posts were continually being moved.

In early 1940, Fighter Command was trained and ready to meet bombing raids coming across the North Sea with plenty of warning. Precise formation attacks against bombers had been introduced and practised,

but fighting against Me109s over Britain had not been seriously visual-
ised by Fighter Command. Our Hurricane squadrons, based in France
as part of the Advanced Air Striking Force, had however already met
and 'tangled' with Me109s, but after the Invasion of France and with the
evacuation from Dunkirk, our Spitfires and Hurricanes were soon to be in
close combat with the German fighters. By mid August vast formations
of Luftwaffe bombers and fighters were flying over the south-east coast
of England from France and Belgium. Air Vice-Marshal Park and his controllers, sometimes needing minute-by-minute vigilance with changes of
direction, dealt with all these variations in strategy and tactics admirably.

The squadrons were scrambled from flight dispersals with a phone call
from the Ops Room and a loud ringing of the alarm bell. As soon as the
squadron was airborne, expected to be within three minutes, the leader
called Control to make the radio link and from then on they worked as a
team to make the interception. 'You must be able to see them,' was often
an anguished cry from the controller. 'Well, you come up and find them
then,' was the equally anguished reply from the leader of a flight whose
lives depended on seeing the enemy first!

CHAPTER 6

German Attack Plans and Relative Strengths

After the collapse of France, Hitler ordered preparations for an invasion, but I believe he still hoped that Britain would not fight and would negotiate a treaty. Soon however, Winston Churchill's speeches promising to 'Fight them on the beaches', and everywhere else, left him in no doubt about the reaction of the British people. Reichsmarschall Goering, after his successes in Europe as Commander of the Luftwaffe, was able to persuade Hitler that his air fleets could immobilise Fighter Command given a few days of fine weather, and that his bombers could then open the path to an invasion. The simple task for Goering and the Luftwaffe therefore, was to reduce Fighter Command to an ineffective force. The task may have seemed simple but it was certainly not going to be as easy as he expected.

After they started their attacks, the Luftwaffe quickly learned several disturbing facts during their battles with Fighter Command. They painfully realised that this was going to be a different war from their previous fighting over the European mainland.

1. The first major formation bomber attack against north-east England from Norway, without Me109 escorts, met with such a high casualty rate that these attacks were then abandoned.
2. Their Junkers 87 Stuka dive-bombers, although a great success with the German army against ground forces as airborne artillery, were knocked out of the sky by Hurricanes and Spitfires. After serious losses in action, they were withdrawn from the Channel zone and in effect from the Battle.
3. The Me110 twin-engine fighter known as the 'Destroyer', Goering's pride and joy, was ineffective as a fighter against Hurricanes and Spitfires and its use was restricted.
4. Bombers could only operate effectively by day with an Me109 protective screen or free flying groups of Me109s, in ratios of least two to one bomber. This meant that major bombing attacks were restricted to the

south-east of England, later to include London, by the limited radius of action of the Me109s. This area was closely contained by the 11 Group Sector under Air Vice-Marshal Park, which was continuously in action bearing the bulk of the onslaught. He shared support when needed from 10 Group to the west, fighting side by side and directly facing the enemy, but rarely with 12 Group who still wanted to fight their own war.

To carry out their attacks on Britain the Luftwaffe had three Air Fleets, No. 5 in Norway, No. 2 in northern France and Belgium, and No. 3 in the Cherbourg area. Many of the bombers and fighters of No. 5 Air Fleet had been transferred down to the Channel zone where the real battle was beginning to shape up.

Relative Strengths

What were the relative strengths of the two opposing air forces? An accurate assessment is not a simple matter. What do we mean by strengths? Numbers, serviceability, performance, aircraft reserves, and pilot calibre and replacement. What territory is to be attacked and which formations need to be protected? A rather complex formula. However, it is important that we should have some realistic idea of the basic strengths of the enemy.

At the beginning of the Battle, the Luftwaffe had some 2,500 operational aircraft made up of approximately:

1,000 Twin-Engine Bombers	Heinkel 111, Dorniers 17 and 215, Junkers 88
270 Single-Engine Bombers	Junkers 87B
800 Single-Engine Fighters	Me109
280 Twin-Engine Fighters	Me110
50 Reconnaissance Aircraft	
TOTAL 2,500	

Against this, the most powerful operational air force in the world, Fighter Command could offer the following defence when the major attacks commenced in August:

750 Single-Engine Fighters	Hurricanes and Spitfires
30 Two-seat Turret Fighters	Defiants
90 Twin-Engine Night Fighters	Blenheims
TOTAL 870	

The Defiants were transferred to night fighting duties after heavy day casualties.

The real crux is how many manned operational aircraft each side could put in the air each day. What matters is the number of immediately available pilot and aircraft replacements. The ability to maintain these numbers to deal with the perils of attrition is obviously crucial.

In July, after the loss of more than 100 fighters over Dunkirk, Fighter Command had some 650 operational Hurricanes and Spitfires with an additional 30 Defiants equipped with turret guns. By mid-August however, with low casualty rates, high production rates, and efficient repair of casualty Hurricanes and Spitfires, Fighter Command had increased its strength of day-fighters to some 750.

Our squadrons generally went into action with the traditional 12 aircraft and sometimes fewer, so that with his 19 Hurricane and Spitfire squadrons Park would rarely put up more than 228 fighters in his Group who would have to attack both bombers and fighters. Of course, in fine weather the major proportion of these defenders would need to be available at readiness throughout the day. However, the Luftwaffe squadrons could assemble their whole serviceable strength at any time for massive attacks, or have periods of rest and maintenance as they chose.

At times of very heavy attack, reinforcement from other groups was essential. It worked with 10 Group who were facing the enemy on the French coast, but unfortunately not with 12 Group in the Midlands who did not need assistance themselves as there were no significant German bomber attacks inland by day.

For the controllers in Fighter Command Ops rooms it was like playing chess with the pieces moving in three dimensions at 150–200 mph.

Even if on paper the opposing fighters had been equal in numbers, Fighter Command still had to attack the enemy bombers as well as their fighters and so the relative combat strength against the Me109s was reduced even further. A major disadvantage for the German single-engine fighters was their limited range which restricted their time over England, although they could disengage and return to base when their fuel was low. Perhaps even more important was the fact that should they be forced to land or bale out, their pilots were taken as prisoners of war. Under similar circumstances ours would normally be able to return to their squadrons to fight another day, crucial in view of our shortage of pilots.

It was not the number of bombers that were the major problem, as locked in formation they were basically defensive and were aggressive to pilots only when attacked. The crucial problem was the almost certain presence of a larger number of German Me109 fighters, visible or invisible at that moment, which presented the real threat that had to be dealt with, or allowed for, when making an attack on the bombers, the prime target. For every British fighter that attacks a bomber there is one less to engage against the German fighters. When the leader divided his force into two components, as was usual, one to attack the bombers and one the enemy fighters, he was forced to concede a great advantage to his Me109 opponents.

From the statistics it is not difficult to understand why Goering felt able to promise Hitler an easy victory over Fighter Command.

CHAPTER 7

Outnumbered and Tactics

In assessing battles on land, at sea and in the air, the relative strengths of the combatants is always one of the key factors. At Rorke's Drift in South Africa in 1879, 150 British soldiers beat off and survived the attacks of some 3,000 Zulu warriors, renowned for their great fighting ability. Numbers were obviously not the only factor.

In 1940 at 25,000 feet, in a moment of mental aberration, I attacked 8 Me109s on my own, shot one down and attacked a second. I was saved from disaster because, as I now believe, the other 7 pilots were far more concerned with searching for the other 5 Spitfires of my flight that should have been with me, rather than concentrating on attacking me. I was saved by 5 Spitfires that were not even there. Battles in the air are very much more than simple numbers.

Historians have examined English and German official records and publications to try to establish a numbers comparison with an accuracy needed for fair comment.

In calculating how many Hurricanes and Spitfires were available at any one time it is necessary to know how many aircraft there were at the start, how many have been shot down, and how many have been lost in non-combat activities; also how many replacements have been provided, both of new manufacture and those that had been repaired to combat standard. Then a simple calculation of addition and subtraction gives an up-to-date figure of squadron strengths remaining.

A fighting unit is made up of one serviceable fighter aircraft and one serviceable fighter pilot. At the most dangerous time in the Battle, it was becoming clear that our fighter strength was a function not so much of how many aircraft we had, but how many fit and trained pilots we had to fly them.

There have been variations in the relative aircraft numbers and casualties published over the years. Although this book is not intended to give extended details of victories and casualties, I have needed to have access to authentic figures to make my own assessment of battle activity. From sources that are now generally accepted, and gratefully acknowledged by me, I have prepared my own statistics, which I believe represent a fair picture of the action. As I am painting with a broad brush in this field, small differences compared with others' figures should not affect the validity of my findings.

For the Fighter Command aircraft losses I have referred to *The Battle of Britain – Then and Now* by Winston Ramsey. For the Luftwaffe figures I have used data from the records of the Luftwaffe Quartermaster General, also from *Then and Now.*

These figures can be assessed in two ways. Firstly we can extract the operational or combat casualties which can be used to compare fighting efficiency and give figures to show how the battle in the air was going, enabling us to assess our total achievements by squadron, by days, by weather, or by type of aircraft. However, whether a Spitfire is lost by being shot down over the Channel or simply disappears on a night training flight, it counts equally as a loss in a battle of attrition. Secondly therefore, we can add these non-operational figures to our operational figures to give total losses that need to be replaced. Our calculations show that Fighter Command non-combat losses were some 11% of their total. The Luftwaffe non-combat losses were some 15%. Unfortunately, the inevitability of over-claiming presents serious problems in such assessment. Both sides should have accurate figures for their own losses, but in the Battle enemy casualties were seriously over-claimed by both sides. If tactical or strategic decisions are made on the basis of these high over-claims, then disaster is almost inevitable as the history of the Battle has shown. See graph on page 129.

The Spitfires and Me109s were technically comparable, but although the Hurricane was performance inferior, it had other fighting qualities that compensated for this. In general, our controllers treated them as equal, but Spitfire and Hurricane pilots would defend to the end their claims that their own aircraft was the best fighter in the Battle. Ideally, the aim would be for the Spitfires to engage the Me109s because of performance and for the Hurricanes to attack the bomber formations as a better gun platform. Unfortunately, the Germans refused to co-operate with our ideals, and until the interception had actually been made, no one could know the composition of the enemy formation or the relative positions of the fighters and bombers, generally too late to be selective.

Fighter Command would normally have some 40% of its strength over 11 Group territory to meet the total Me109 strength available in that area. The remainder of our squadrons were at readiness to protect the rest of Britain. The Luftwaffe formations could come over whenever they chose. They could attack several targets at one time, or put all their squadrons into the air in one specific raid with hundreds of aircraft. On one occasion nearly 1,000 Luftwaffe aircraft were sent over against London. Even with RDF warning we could initially only send up single or pairs of squadrons to go into the attack. There was no time to assemble wings unless the raid was targeted against London. With 60 fighters going into action against such numbers, they would still have been outnumbered. Even worse, the

Me109s were already in position and at height. They were nearly always above our fighters, the key to success, certainly until October.

The Blenheim twin-engine night fighters were used solely for night defence and had no part to play in the defensive fighting by day, and are not included in the figures. Nor are the two Defiant turret fighter squadrons included.

With the standard 12 aircraft per squadron this meant that the maximum number of fighters that we could put up would be 564 for the whole of Britain. Under extreme pressure the 11 Group maximum of 228 could, with help from 10 and 12 Groups, be significantly increased. On 15th September 12 Group sent in support with a 5-squadron wing of 60 aircraft.

On the first major Luftwaffe raid on London on 7th September, their 348 bombers were escorted by 617 fighters. There were 965 enemy aircraft to be intercepted and attacked by our 252 fighters from 11 Group and nearby support from 10 and 12 Groups, a ratio of more than 3:1. These were very heavy odds on paper and in the air.

Another aspect of relative strengths to be considered is how it appeared to our fighter pilots as they flew the controller's vector and first sighted the enemy formations. Most of the interceptions made in 11 Group were made by squadrons with 12 aircraft or flights of 6. The average German formation over England could be made up of from 30 to 200 bombers with from 60 to 400 fighters, often with Me109s sitting high. Although these raids were generally intercepted by several squadrons, most squadrons were scrambled on their own and always met a much larger number of enemy aircraft which they had to attack. Our pilots had no doubts that they were being heavily outnumbered. They were able to reduce the odds if they could select an unprotected section.

Tactics

I am sure that from the beginning of the Battle until the end, and later, the Luftwaffe were ahead of us in fighter tactics. Their squadron commanders in the main had had battle experience in three earlier wars, in Spain, Poland and France. Practice attacks over England were no substitute for fighting live enemies with live ammunition. Because they were not flying in a defensive role, except for a while as close bomber protectors, the Me109s had greater freedom of operation and greater flexibility than we had. They realised the significance of height and used it to the fullest extent. After their first diving attack, they tended to return home to France at high speed. The German fighter pilots were flying independently and made their own decisions. We, on the other hand, were controlled up to the point of interception, often too late to affect the outcome.

I cannot ever remember tactics being seriously discussed in my squadrons or with visiting experts from Group HQ or with other 11 Group squadrons. In reality we fought on a 'catch as catch can' basis. We were unable to appraise the enemy formation and so make attack plans until we had intercepted them. Our leaders only had sufficient time to make a quick assessment and give simple basic orders. This is why the Air Ministry philosophy of pre-planning battle tactics was a non-starter.

The Me109 pilots were basically trained as hunters as all their previous operations had been offensive. They had developed their formation of four fighters as their basic unit of two pairs flying in a loose formation. On the other hand, Fighter Command pilots had been trained as defensive pilots whose main function until May 1940 was to attack German bombers, which were flying in defensive formations of three or five aircraft. We did not need to use hunting formations, and three fighters in formation attacking three German bombers in very tight formation seemed practical. Later in the Battle, when the Luftwaffe came over in mixed squadrons, which was the correct formation to select? Three German bombers in close formation could bring all their guns to bear with dangerous frontal deflection shots. It was essential for three fighters to open fire at the same time. When attacking experienced bombers in tight formation, there was always the risk of fighter collision, and more than 100 of our pilots were shot down and others wounded by German air gunners, including a number of our most experienced pilots.

A major problem affecting the planning of tactics was that the Air Ministry and indeed many of the other Commands were still thinking in peacetime terms. In times of peace an officer of Squadron Leader rank could be posted to command a squadron without special qualifications. It was on the job training. There was time to learn. And so sometimes officers from Training Command and other non-operational and administrative units were posted straight into combat squadrons. Wise new squadron commanders let their flight commanders or other experienced pilots lead for a period, but it was often not enough.

Even the move of an experienced operational squadron to 11 Group in the south after being rested in the north, could be traumatic with high casualties until the leaders and pilots had re-acclimatised. Luftwaffe pilots were not taken out of the battle in this way.

Basically in a combat situation such as the Battle, the squadron and flights should have been led by battle-experienced pilots, irrespective of rank. Our squadron was sometimes led by a pilot officer; previously a very experienced sergeant pilot, who as the leader held the respect and confidence of all the pilots including the flight commanders. All our pilots and especially our squadron leaders needed battle awareness; it was experienced leadership that mattered. The Air Ministry had not yet caught up.

CHAPTER 8

The Stakes

If Britain lost the Battle, then invasion would be inevitable and the Nazis would occupy Britain. Orders had already been printed in Germany for all British males of age 17–45 to be sent to the European mainland, probably as slave labour. Ethnic, religious, and handicapped minorities would be in peril. Hitler would then attack and occupy Russia. The black cloak of Nazi evil would spread over Europe for a century. No other country in the world could help.

The fate of Europe rested in the hands of the young fighter pilots. We were heavily outnumbered, and fighting against the elite pilots of the German Luftwaffe. Had our pilots failed or faltered, Britain would have been lost, and the occupied countries of Europe would have been doomed without hope to total German occupation and enslavement. Winston Churchill wrote in one of his volumes, *Their Finest Hour,* that 'Our fate now depended upon victory in the air'. Our Prime Minister could send battleships and armies anywhere in the world, he could make grand political plans, but when the great battle started, he could only watch and wait. During the fighting he sometimes visited the Operations Room at 11 Group. He was there for the great battle of 15th September. Churchill wrote later of his feelings at that time. 'The odds were great; our margins small; the stakes infinite.'

However, the cost to the British people of fighting and beating back the German Luftwaffe to retain our Freedom was very high indeed. For years, until the cessation of hostilities, we endured the horrors of the bombing of our towns, ports and factories, attacks by the winged self-propelled bombs known as the 'doodlebugs', and finally the terror rocket attacks on London, from which there was no warning and no defence. Young men were called up and taken away from their homes, many for years; the alternative was selection by ballot to serve in the coal mines. Many were killed in action, and many were incarcerated in prisoner-of-war camps for years in Germany, Poland and Italy. The rationing of food, clothes, sweets, petrol, and the lack of domestic items for sale lasted throughout the war and for up to another five years afterwards. Hundreds of thousands of homes were destroyed or damaged, and people slept for months or even years in primitive or brick air raid shelters. In London many thousands of families bedded down on the platforms of the Underground stations only a few feet from the passing trains. The years of the blackout made life even more difficult and dangerous. This was the terrible price that the ordinary people paid in our fight to stay a free country. And then we fought our way back into Europe with the forces of the United States and our other Allies, with heavy casualties, to defeat Germany and to release the occupied European countries from Nazi domination.

The German scientists were working on atomic energy. With victory over Britain and Russia, they could well have been the first country to develope the atom bomb. They were already developing the rockets. World domination would have been within their grasp.

It has been written that we were never really in danger of invasion by the Germans. Certainly the people of Britain believed that the Germans would have invaded our Country had they beaten Fighter Command. I remember very clearly the seven days starting on 7th September when our squadron stood-by at 'readiness' with our Spitfires half-an-hour before dawn, awaiting a 'scramble' to fly to the south coast to meet the invasion. It was a time of high expectation and high adrenaline. In 11 Group, Park had issued an order to his squadrons that in the event of an invasion pilots could expect to carry out eight sorties a day, landing mainly just to re-arm.

Some writers claim that had the Germans tried to invade Britain after the destruction of Fighter Command, then the Royal Navy battleships and cruisers would have blown the invading forces out of the water. I think that this is not at all certain bearing in mind the effect of newly laid minefields, submarines, the total German bomber force including their fearsome Ju87 dive bombers, and additional Me110 fighter/bombers free to attack the naval forces within easy range in such a confined area. The Royal Navy would have been reluctant to seek action in the shallow seas with no protection by our fighters. The Germans could certainly have landed gliders, parachute battalions, and troop transports without serious hindrance in Kent or even over London. The Me109 fighters could have been used for ground attack against the British defenders.

But it wasn't essential for England to be invaded immediately after the defeat of Fighter Command. The Germans could have achieved their purpose of neutralising Britain without landing on English soil. With total air supremacy they could then have attacked by day every crucial target with great accuracy. Unmolested except by A/A guns they could have freely attacked our airfields, and munition factories, oil refineries and storage tanks, and major ports. In particular the essential convoys from the USA could have been under continuous attack and sunk as they arrived in home waters. Britain could have been in danger of being starved into surrender. Combined with the undefended daytime terror bombing of London, Birmingham, Manchester, Liverpool, Glasgow and Cardiff, Britain could have been neutralised. Such a policy would almost certainly have resulted in a non-aggression pact with Hitler. Victory by our pilots in the Battle of Britain was more important than just the prevention of an invasion; it kept Britain in being as the base from which Europe could later be freed.

With Britain no longer a force to be reckoned with perhaps Eire and Spain could have been 'persuaded' by Hitler to provide airfields for German bombers to attack the Atlantic convoys. This would have advanced the capitulation of Britain.

Winston Churchill was right. 'Our fate did indeed depend on victory in the air.'

CHAPTER 9

Channel Combats

10th July–10th August

The Battle of Britain is officially deemed to have commenced on 10th July 1940. After the French surrender, the Luftwaffe re-grouped and re-equipped their squadrons. They were established on existing and newly built airfields in Belgium and the Pas de Calais. Many of their fighter squadrons were concentrated in this area.

We continued to send convoys through the Channel with fighter escorts, and the Germans soon attacked them with Junkers 87 dive-bombers protected by Me109s. There was considerable fighting over the Channel with their fighters but, due to the heavy loss of ships from the bombing, the convoys were eventually cancelled by the Admiralty. The Germans were forced to withdraw their much-vaunted 'Stuka' dive-bombers from the action, due to the high numbers being shot down by our fighters. The Ju87 was certainly a precision bomber but it was highly vulnerable to attacks by the Hurricanes and Spitfires.

This fighting between the Germans and British fighters over the Channel for 32 days was crucial for us for a number of reasons. Firstly, it gave our pilots in 11 Group a chance to get battle experience so badly needed to compete with the seasoned German pilots. Secondly, the German pilots heavily over-claimed their victories thus misleading Goering and his Air Commanders into a false sense of achievement. The Luftwaffe aircraft lost in this period numbered 195 with 105 aircraft lost from Fighter Command, an overkill of almost 2:1 in our favour. In fact, the Germans believed they had shot down some 300 British Fighters, a serious misjudgement, and so they erroneously believed that Fighter Command could only last a few weeks.

The third and most crucial factor of this period was the weather. Most of the 32 days had given poor flying conditions with rain, low cloud and mist. We averaged a loss of 3.5 aircraft per day, a low figure, but with the output from our aircraft factories and repair units, Fighter Command was able to substantially increase its strength, which was crucial to beat off the

Luftwaffe attacks, and to make an increase in numbers of aircraft held in reserve ready for service. The Me109 replacement rate was less than that of Fighter Command. The Germans had not felt it necessary to increase their factory output of fighter aircraft after the Battle of France as they considered victory to be certain and relatively quick. Their thoughts at that time were more concerned with the production of heavy armoured vehicles.

The weather had a profound effect on the progress and outcome of the Battle. On fine days our casualties could be five times higher than on bad weather days. Fine weather thus favoured the Luftwaffe in their need to eliminate Fighter Command as quickly as possible. However, there were just sufficient periods of bad weather in the Battle to enable Fighter Command to rest and rebuild to squadron strength.

Although well over a hundred books have been written about the Battle of Britain, I have never read one that seriously considered the close daily relationship of the weather to the outcome of the Battle.

My research has shown that the effectiveness of our defence was critically influenced by the pattern of the weather. A wet and cloudy summer and there could not have been a Battle of Britain. The low and heavy cloud would have prevented the sending up of large formations of German bombers with their protective Me109 fighter squadrons. A glorious summer however, with continuous blue skies from the beginning of July through to September in 1940, might have resulted in defeat and invasion.

In 12 Group, sunshine was welcomed for easier convoy patrols, and hopes of action. On the other hand, in 11 Group blue skies meant heavy fighting with high casualties. I believe that the effect of weather patterns on the Battle were so crucial that they deserve a separate study, and this is presented later in the book.

CHAPTER 10

Courage

The pilots in the Battle of Britain have been described as courageous, and rightly so. The *Concise Oxford Dictionary* describes courage as 'the ability to disregard fear'. My own definition has always been 'the ability to go forward or stand firm in the face of danger'. To discuss courage we also need to discuss fear, a complex subject.

Fear was never, or very rarely, spoken of by the pilots. A pilot's fear was personal, and although it was something we all felt at times, mostly it was hidden behind the fighter pilots' brand of humour. I was naturally anxious to avoid being killed, but in our killing environment it happened or it didn't happen; but I avoided dwelling on the possibility of being badly burned. My real fear in battle was of being made a prisoner-of-war and of being 'caged' for years and years. Actually being 'bounced', as I was on my first operational sortie over Dunkirk, was a very frightening experience, definitely not to be repeated. But after a few days it served mainly to remind me to keep my eyes wide open at all times in the air.

Fear is personal, it is variable, and so our reaction, or courage, is unpredictable. The only common characteristic of the holders of the Victoria Cross is, I believe, their modesty.

For the male of the species, physical courage is a badge of honour and so fear must be overcome, or there is dishonour. For me to climb a rock face 500 feet high would require very great courage – to the climbing enthusiast it would be no more than a challenge. We are all frightened of different things.

I can only write about my own experience of fear and courage as a fighter pilot, but I expect that my feelings, in the main, would have paralleled those of my squadron comrades. One day, on the first scramble, my undercarriage wouldn't retract after take off and so I left the squadron and flew back to base. Inspection in the maintenance hangar showed no fault and it retracted perfectly. I took off on the second sortie and again it failed to retract. I flew back to base a second time. Again it showed no fault. Of course retraction on the ground and in the air climbing at 160 mph imposed different loads on the mechanism. The maintenance men gave me peculiar looks. Two failures in a row. I took off on the third sortie and I prayed desperately that the undercarriage would retract so that I could go into action with the squadron. I had a greater fear of being thought a coward than I had of fighting Me109s. To my great relief the wheels retracted with a welcome thud. All was well.

At readiness in 12 Group I know that the fear level for me was not as high as when I was in 11 Group, as the personal danger level was much lower. In 11 Group at the end of August, when squadrons were being bounced with high casualties, the fear level would be much higher, and the growing tiredness of the pilots would have been a further accentuation of the pressure. So much greater would have been their courage.

With 544 of our fighter crews killed in action and many others injured in the Battle, I can only look back with great admiration at their achievement, not in disregarding fear, but in containing it and going forward into the attack. Once the attack had started each pilot was fighting as a separate individual. All other combatants in war fight side by side with their companions in arms.

People have asked how did you feel the first time you went into action? This must have varied enormously for each pilot. If it was against bombers without fighter escort and with time to get into position, there would have been high levels of adrenalin which would have overshadowed any fear of the action. As I have written previously, my first contact with the enemy at 15,000ft over Dunkirk was quite different and I reported the action as follows:

All of a sudden the sky was full of aircraft with black crosses on them. It was terrifying. I realised for the first time that there was somebody up there, trying very hard to kill me. It was my 'moment of truth'. Although badly shot up, I was angry at not gaining my first victory, but I was relieved that I had brought my Spitfire home to a safe landing in spite of the damage I had received.

I have also been asked what it felt like to shoot down a German bomber and almost certainly kill the crew. My reply was simply that they were Nazi German bombers flying over England, intent on dropping their bombs to destroy our people, our homes, our cities and our fighter stations. Unless we stopped them we would be invaded with all the horrors of Nazi occupation. I had no qualms then, and none today, about pressing the button to fire eight Browning guns when I had the enemy aircraft in my sight. The evil machine had to be destroyed to save our Country. My sole concentration was to put the centre spot of the reflector sight on a critical part on the aircraft and open fire. I am sure I kept my head well down but as I am small this was not a problem. It seems strange, but I had no emotional feelings other than to shoot down the enemy aircraft. Please remember that when over Dunkirk on my first engagement I was shot at without mercy by a German pilot.

When I attacked a bomber I was not conscious of return fire, even though my aircraft was being hit by the enemy gunners. I have since learned that it was the norm for most of our fighter pilots to aim only to destroy the enemy aircraft. Obviously I had great pleasure with any success, but in those days personal feelings of achievements were kept under strict control, and others had certainly achieved rather more success. In retrospect, I believe that the best feeling I had after combat was collecting the life jacket from an Me109 pilot I had just shot down, to take back to our flight dispersal. I then felt that I really was a proven member of my squadron.

I was never wounded, or crashed, or had to bale out. I had a number of narrow escapes but near misses don't count in war. Put simply, I like to remember that I was an RAF Spitfire fighter pilot very privileged to go into action to defend the Country I loved. The only regret I had was that I was denied the chance to attack more German aircraft.

As the Battle continued with increasing Luftwaffe attacks, the stress on our pilots built up. However, when close to exhaustion, and having suffered many casualties, squadrons were taken out of 11 Group to be rested and brought up to strength in 12 Group or 13 Group on more routine and less hazardous duties.

Undoubtedly at the times of the fiercest and continuous fighting, some of our pilots were taken very close to the limit. Because of their code it would be rare for a pilot to report this and ask for a rest. It was the responsibility of the squadron CO and the medical officer to be alert to the levels of stress in his pilots. Most of them, but not all, understood this responsibility. If a pilot had fought well, most of his colleagues had no difficulty in accepting his release from active operations and were not judgemental. Unfortunately, some senior RAF officers, safe from the dangers and stress of combat, devised a category called LMF – Lack of Moral Fibre. Pilots who lost their nerve could be assessed as LMF, taken off flying and humiliated. It was used in Bomber Command where even pilots and aircrews who had already completed a full tour of 25/30 bombing missions and were then unable to carry on, could be removed from the squadron and disgraced. I have always believed that as a broad generalisation, the bomber crews were at a higher risk than we were as fighter pilots in the Battle, with a higher casualty rate and with little chance of baling out to safety. I take this opportunity to salute their special bravery.

The Royal Air Force was different from the other Services in that only a small proportion of its force actually went into action, daily risked their lives, and became casualties. The further people are from the reality of war the easier it is to be judgemental and condemn actions beyond their comprehension. So it is today.

In retrospect I realise that we had an important advantage over the Luftwaffe pilots in that, in our fighting, we had a special dedication to defend our Home Country. After being shot down, many of our pilots were able to bale out to safety or managed to force land in England, living to fight another day. German pilots shot down were either killed or captured, and a Luftwaffe bomber could have a crew of four that would be lost.

Our pilots undoubtedly showed great bravery. But who is the bravest of them all? The squadron commander leading his squadron into action with 11 aircraft at the back of him, or the young pilot flying as top rear cover, in position on his own at 500ft above and behind the squadron, as the look-out against surprise attack by Me109s?

The pilots never talked about courage, or bragged about their achievements in battle. They would however often tell about their disasters in the air to the great amusement of the rest of the pilots.

There was no distinction as regards courage. Who would know or understand?

CHAPTER 11

Eagle Day and Sunshine

11th–23rd August

Reichsmarschall Hermann Goering had decided to start his pre-invasion attacks on England on 13th August 1940, his 'Eagle Day' ('Adler Tag'). On the 11th August the weather gave clear skies and it continued fine for six out of the next seven days. This was the sort of weather and time that he had told Hitler he needed to subjugate Fighter Command. He believed, wrongly, that by then the Luftwaffe had already shot down 300 of our aircraft.

From their airfields in the occupied countries from Norway down to the Cherbourg peninsula in France, the Germans launched their very heavy attacks against our coast, from northern to southern England and then to the west. In the eight days including Adler Tag, they lost 317 operational aircraft against our 148, a win ratio to us of better than 2:1. Due to over-claiming by their pilots, they believed they had shot down far more of our aircraft. The outstanding day of this period, and indeed of the whole Battle, was the 15th August when we shot down 79 Luftwaffe aircraft for only 31 of Fighter Command, a victory of 2.5:1. This was the largest number of Nazi aircraft destroyed in one day during the whole of the Battle. It should have been a warning to Goering, but presumably he felt that in a war of attrition, and based on his pilots' erroneous claims, Germany must win. On this day the Germans also sent a very large raid from Air Fleet No. 5 against the north-east coast of England, across the North Sea from their bases in Norway. It was a very long sea crossing, some 400 miles, and so there was no Me109 protection, only twin-engine Me110 fighters. They lost 20% of their aircraft in this raid and never attacked again with any major formation from Norway. They must have realised by then that effectively the whole of Britain was being actively protected by Fighter Command squadrons.

Most of the fighters and bombers from Air Fleet No. 5 were then moved to Belgium and France to strengthen the attacks against the south of England, where the bombers could be given Me109 protection. Goering had eventually learned that against Fighter Command his bombers had to be strongly supported by at least twice their number of single-engine fighters.

On 21st August, I was flying in a section of three Spitfires when we intercepted three Dornier 17 bombers over the North Sea, a few miles off the coast near to Mablethorpe in Lincolnshire. As soon as they saw us they turned away for home and closed up in a very tight formation. We attacked in a classic Fighter Command echelon formation, coming in together from astern. This meant that we were each subjected to crossfire from the rear gunners of the aircraft we were not attacking, as we could only fire straight ahead at our individual target. We shot one down into the sea, and claimed a second as probable, which was later confirmed.

We landed at North Coates Fittes, our forward airfield on the Lincolnshire coast, and as soon as the wheels touched the grass my Spitfire swung badly to the left but I managed to keep control. By a strange coincidence, once again a German bullet had burst my port tyre when it was retracted into the wing. There were hits in the propeller boss, the wing, and several hits in the tail very close to the control wires. Any one of these bullets might have caused me to crash into the North Sea. The other pilots in my section had also received hits, so that we might have had more casualties than the Germans. The tight flying of their pilots and the accuracy of their gunners made them formidable opponents. An important factor was that at the same time the other section of our flight attacked a similar formation of three Do17s and two of the bombers crashed on the coast. To lose four out of six bombers above the Lincolnshire coast should have confirmed to the Luftwaffe that the whole of the English coast was well protected by Fighter Command. They should also have realised by then how crucial the RDF system was to our defence.

As the Me109 had a limited range of action, so therefore, did their bombers. This meant that fighting in the Battle was mainly concentrated in the south-east of England within a radius of 100 miles of the Pas de Calais and including London. This limit on German operations overlapped almost precisely the sector territory of 11 Group. This was under the command of AVM Keith Park, who as a result, controlled the majority of the day-to-day fighting.

We should remember that when talking about losses a proportion of the German casualties were bombers, so that our higher total victories only kept us on a par with their fighter losses and our fighter numbers stayed roughly equal. In that eight-day period of intense and exhausting fighting, we had lost 148 aircraft. Another eight days like this and we would be getting low on aircraft and worse still, even lower on pilots who were much more difficult to replace. But we were still very much alive. Fortunately, we then had five days of rain and low cloud. This major change in the weather stopped the onslaught and reduced casualties to an average of less than three aircraft a day. Fighter Command was able to have some rest and replace the aircraft and some of the pilots lost in the action.

CHAPTER 12

Our Pilots at Readiness

To reduce the risk of damage from German bombers, the squadrons operated from dispersal sites around the airfield. These housed the serviceable aircraft, pilots, ground crews, petrol bowsers and electric starters, and were located on the opposite side of the airfield from the main buildings – a long cycle ride around the perimeter track in either direction. There were wooden or corrugated huts for flight offices, rest rooms and storage. Some dispersals had hard standings for the aircraft, but later, protection bays were built. Aircraft servicing and repair was carried out in the standard hangars on the main station side of the airfield.

As pilot officers we were paid £5 a week, about £300 per week at present values. The tea boy for the contractors working on our airfield received the same pay as us, but we were amused to be told that his wage included a special payment as he was working in a danger zone. We concluded that the contractor's men must be paid rather more than we were. I know of no time when operational aircrew received extra pay for the dangers of combat. Perhaps it is not possible to put a price on this aspect of service.

All aircrews in the RAF carrying out operational sorties against the Germans received a special allowance. This was a real egg for breakfast each day, as opposed to dried egg from the USA, and a small bar of chocolate and an orange once a week.

When based at a permanent station, pilots ate in their Messes – transported there and back from dispersal in open trucks. These had the advantage of permitting us to jump out on three sides speeding up the exit. At forward bases the sandwich and coffee lunches were delivered to the dispersal. Welcome guests to the dispersal were the NAAFI, the 'Sally Alley' (Salvation Army) and other church-gifted vehicles arriving to dispense tea and cake for the ground crews and the aircrews.

The pilots passed their waiting time at dispersal in many different ways. Some read, some played cards or chess, and some just slept on one of the standard RAF beds with three 'biscuit mattresses'. The popular card game in my first squadron was 'whisky poker' in which all could play with a once only basic stake of sixpence. That was the limit of the loss, but the final and sole winner after two hours or so took the jackpot worth six shillings, the price of two bottles of whisky – if you could get them. If the alarm bell was sounded followed by a scramble to interception, all bets were off. My favourite game in 41 Squadron was solo whist. With so much practice the high standard of the play forced us to keep the school to a rather select membership!

Originally the scramble order came through by the same phone as was used for flight administration. When the bell rang it could be a complaint from the Assistant Adjutant that the daily return for the previous day had not been submitted, or it could be 'SCRAMBLE!' Needless near-heart-attacks were caused until another system was substituted for the admin. phone. When the alarm bell was rung, everyone ran to their aircraft at high speed. By the time we had jumped into the cockpit with the parachute and helmet already inside and radio lead and oxygen tube previously plugged in, the ground crew were ready to strap us in. The engines were started with that wonderful comforting Rolls Royce roar of power and reliability; and then 'chocks away', thumbs up and taxi out ready for full throttle for take off. How many did they say? 50 plus. Well it's 100 plus now!

Sometimes it was for an interception at 25,000 feet and into battle; some-times it was cancelled by an instruction to return to base after 5 minutes, a false alarm. Whichever it was the adrenalin was high. A scramble take-off was always thrilling – a clarion call to action. With grass airfields we could take off in threes in the most convenient direction, forming up into a flight or squadron as we climbed. The CO calls up on the radio 'Mitor Squadron airborne'. We must remember to check our oxygen, we could be going high and we have lost pilots due to oxygen failure. I had a near death experience at 20,000 feet on one sortie, having forgotten to turn on my oxygen. In the scramble fear was not a factor, we were part of an elite team going into action to fight the enemy.

Brevity on the radio was an essential discipline and code words were used for instructions and a response. I feel that the choice of words fitted in well with pilot ethos.

SCRAMBLE	Take off for action.
VECTOR 175	Course to steer in degrees.
ANGELS 15	Height in thousands of feet.
BANDITS 100	Enemy aircraft. Best estimates of aircraft numbers given.
BUSTER	Full engine power. Emergency.
ROGER	Message received and understood.
TALLY HO	Enemy sighted.
PANCAKE	Return to base and land.

Under very trying conditions additional and more expressive words might be used by the pilots!

In August in 12 Group we sat at dispersal for days waiting for a scramble. I feel that we were not so much bored, as frustrated, in that we were not allowed to be part of the serious fighting that was taking place in 11 Group. We had been allowed to fight over Dunkirk, why not over England? I felt so strongly that we were being deliberately held back, that I formally asked my CO if that was true. He replied that we all wanted to help the squadrons down south, but he could give me no reason why we just stayed at readiness in 12 Group and took no part in the action. I know the reasons now and they still cause me much regret.

In contrast, the life of a pilot during the heavy raids over 11 Group was one of more continuous strain, camouflaged by the pilots' special brand of humour. We rested at readiness in the pilots' room or on the grass, with ears half-cocked waiting for a call to scramble, with the possibility of being in action within a few minutes. It has often been said that a fighter pilot spent 90% of his time at readiness being bored stiff and the other 10% of his time being scared stiff. I am sure, however, that during the period of heavy fighting in 11 Group there was very little time for boredom.

The action in 11 Group was intense and exhausting. At the end of August squadrons were suffering heavy casualties and their replacement pilots were new and inexperienced, often with minimal fighter training. Here they came face to face with the real war, the war to the death. It was crucial to see the enemy first, but it took four or five sorties for the new pilot to adjust to the high speed of the action especially against Me109s. In my squadron we had a pilot, Pilot Officer E P Wells, with outstanding eyesight and known of course as 'Hawkeye'. He could see dots when we could see nothing; he could recognise Me109s when we could see only dots. We always felt safer when Hawkeye was flying with us.

Fortunately we were spared the unhelpful and possibly harmful attentions of counsellors. We had our own procedures. One of our pilots arrived back late at the airfield, having valiantly struggled home with a badly damaged Spitfire after being attacked by Me109s. He had obviously had an unnerving experience, and expected at least the 'well done' hand on his shoulder by his flight commander who was waiting for him. Instead he was told:

What the hell have you done to my new aircraft? I told you to be careful with it when I lent it to you this morning. Right, get yourself another aircraft and then get some tea and cake at the NAAFI wagon. We are taking off again in 30 minutes.

I asked him what he did about this unsympathetic treatment. He replied:

Well, I got myself another aircraft, I went to the NAAFI wagon and had a cup of tea and a piece of cake, and then I took off again with the squadron 30 minutes later.

We both laughed at his response, but realised the wisdom of our flight commander. The pilot's trauma had been displaced and removed – there could of course be an even worse experience waiting for him on the next trip. Imagine being greeted after a traumatic combat by a professional counsellor with a hug and a promise of six weeks' leave for post-traumatic stress. Our flight commander's technique was effective and necessary. Stress at this level was an inevitable facet of being a fighter pilot and it had to be contained.

There was little introspection, and death, although always on the horizon, was not a topic of conversation. Most of my memories are of great humour and comradeship, with exceptional people, always to be treasured.

CHAPTER 13

The Great Challenge

24th August–9th September

And then we entered the most dangerous phase of the Battle, from 24th August up to 9th September with 17 days of almost continuous fine weather and fighting. Whatever the policy, whatever the tactics, fine weather was going to take a very heavy toll on Fighter Command. The Germans attacked our airfields, aircraft factories and ports without cease. The pilots in 11 Group were in action day after day, sometimes flying several sorties in one day; in many of the sorties they intercepted and fought the enemy. They were always outnumbered and frequently still climbing for height, when they were attacked by the Me109s generally from above. They always challenged; they were defending England and the British people. They were not going to allow Nazi aircraft to fly over Britain, with or without bombs.

Inevitably squadrons became exhausted and depleted. Replacement squadrons were flown in from 13 Group and 12 Group and some immediately took heavy casualties. Whatever their previous flying experience, all pilots were in the greatest danger in their first few actions against the enemy. Men cannot be trained on courses to the ultimate limit of action and death in war. A pilot's 'moment of truth' cannot be programmed in training – it can only be experienced. RAF rank and general flying hours in the logbook mean nothing in the air at 25,000 feet with approach speeds of more than 360 mph and an enemy you haven't yet seen. Only battle experience can sharpen the senses, improve vision and speed up reaction times for split second response. My analysis of pilot casualties at RAF Hornchurch showed that you had a slightly greater risk of being shot down if you were a squadron leader than if you were a sergeant pilot. All Spitfires looked the same and Me109 cannon shells and bullets were equally effective against all aircraft.

My first squadron – No. 611, in the comparative safety of 12 Group – often flew south to Duxford or Fowlmere airfields near Cambridge for the day, where we spent hours waiting at readiness, with occasional and uneventful patrols over 11 Group sector stations. A fighter pilot needs to be part of the action – it is a function of his being. All the 12 Group squadrons felt humiliated at being left out at this time of great crisis. Our squadron later flew with the three- and five-squadron Duxford Wings. Whatever the merits or demerits of Big Wings, the Duxford Wing at least gave some of the 12 Group squadrons a chance to take part in the real battle.

In those 17 days from 24th August to 9th September, Fighter Command shot down 429 German bombers and fighter aircraft against our own losses of 298 fighters. Fighter Command was being stretched. This was a ratio of 1.4:1, a lower success rate compared with our previous successes in the region of 2:1. We were getting low on pilot strengths, and pilots had to be transferred from other commands without adequate training.

In a battle of attrition with continuous fine weather, we might eventually have had to move our squadrons to north of the Thames, but time and the weather were on our side. We had to meet the Luftwaffe whenever they came and hold on until the end of September. But the Germans too had lost a lot of aircraft with very experienced crews, and they were beginning to feel the strain. Buoyed up by their heavy over-claiming, their pilots had no doubts that victory was close at hand.

CHAPTER 14

To Be Bounced

With the heavy fighting at the end of August our pilots were getting tired and squadrons were under-manned, but Park continued to follow the policy of attacking immediately at all costs. Enemy formations moved at up to three miles a minute and delay could be disastrous.

Records of this time and pilot memories show that our single squadrons were being 'bounced' with serious losses because they had not had time to achieve adequate height. Being bounced means being attacked without warning by enemy aircraft, diving from above or coming from behind. When, or indeed if, you see them, it is too late, and members of the flight will have been shot down and the enemy will be on their way home, diving at high speed to cross the dreaded Kanal (English Channel). Eventually to defend our pilots, the squadron and flight leaders ignored the vectors given by the controllers, and flew on a reciprocal course to gain height to ensure that they were at least level with the enemy when they finally intercepted. This action was crucial for survival even if it was to be interpreted by higher authority as disobedience of orders. To have adequate height gave the chance of victory; to be caught climbing up to Me109s presented the almost certainty of disaster. The prime responsibility of Fighter Command was to stay in being. To prevent the enemy from dropping their bombs was in fact the secondary responsibility of the squadrons and not one to be carried out at any cost. When it was realised that even the cumbersome Me110 twin-engine fighters were bouncing our fighters, drastic action was needed and our flight leaders took it.

If a squadron was seriously bounced they could lose three or four pilots and aircraft on one sortie, an unacceptable casualty rate for the squadron and morale could be affected. The shout over the radio of 'Break – 109s above' was the most feared event for pilots, except actually being bounced. Contrary to popular belief, after the fighting over the Channel convoys there was not a great deal of 'dog fighting' in the Battle. The Me109 philosophy was to dive down, open fire, and then dive at high speed to the coast. There was no merit in staying after the attack; they had limited fuel and if shot down would be captured.

Of course, the shout 'Achtung Spitfeuer' caused the same fear in the hearts of the German pilots. But they had the additional fear of the appearance on their instrument panel of the red light warning them of low fuel. If they were not on their way home and over 'Das Kanal' when this happened, they might have to ditch in the sea, but the Germans were well equipped to save their pilots baling out or ditching into the Channel. They had fluorescent dye packs on their 'schwimmvests' to stain the sea around them with an easily recognisable fluorescent dye. They had habitable floating refuges in the sea, and floatplanes to pick up their pilots. In August, September and October they were crossing the Channel twice on every sortie and not always at the narrowest point; an efficient air/sea rescue service was essential for them. Such a service for our pilots would have saved valuable lives. The RAF had no comparable air/sea rescue service at the time, and pilots shot down over the sea relied on their 'Mae West' life jackets to stay afloat, hoping that they would be spotted by searching aircraft and picked up in time. Most were not. We did not have inflatable dinghies attached to our parachutes until after the Battle.

Air Chief Marshal Dowding, aware of the additional dangers to our pilots of ditching in the sea, had given strict instructions that pilots should not pursue enemy aircraft over the Channel on their way back to France, as we could not afford to lose pilots in this way. I am sure that when attacking an enemy aircraft close to the Channel, most pilots would have found it difficult, if not impossible to disengage until all their ammunition had been spent.

Our pilots were authorised to shoot down the German He115 rescue floatplanes. Before we become judgemental, we must remember that we were fighting to the death to save our Country and its people from a terrible fate. The Me109 pilots, if rescued, could have been at 25,000 feet over England the next day, ready to bounce our squadrons and to shoot us down. However we may view it, in time of war our young men are charged by the Nation to kill or be killed, with official approval, but without option or appeal. How can actions in war, on land, at sea, or in the air be judged fairly and with honour by non-combatants, distanced safely in offices and law courts, who have not experienced the personal traumas and the desperate fights for life associated with them.

If the norm is to intercept a raid of 100 enemy aircraft with a squadron of 12 aircraft, then our pilots would always be outnumbered. But if the Me109s could be avoided it was still possible to attack a major bomber formation successfully. What really mattered in the battle was height, height and height. This gave the fighters the ability to initiate their attacks to the best advantage, so crucial when outnumbered and to minimise the chance of being bounced. One squadron above the enemy was worth at least two squadrons below. I am not sure that our Commanders and Controllers realised this until rather late in the day.

CHAPTER 15

The Duxford Wing

30th August

In 1931 Pilot Officer Douglas Bader, a young RAF fighter pilot, was demonstrating his flying abilities in his squadron biplane over an airfield when he misjudged his height and crashed. His life was saved but his very serious injuries resulted in the amputation of both of his legs. His career in the RAF was ended and he commenced life as a civilian. He never gave up wanting to fly and on the outbreak of the war he applied to become a pilot again. The medical officers approved, and with his artificial legs he passed his flying tests and was accepted. He flew in a Spitfire in combat over Dunkirk, and in July 1940 he was given command of a squadron of Hurricanes, a great achievement.

On 30th August, Squadron Leader Douglas Bader had led No. 242 Hurricane Squadron 65 miles from his base at Coltishall in Norfolk, to be at readiness at Duxford, near Cambridge, a 12 Group Sector Station close to the 11 Group northern boundaries. There were three other squadrons, including my own, at Duxford and its satellite Fowlmere. During the afternoon 60+ Heinkel He111 bombers with their Me110 twin-engine fighter escorts came in over the coast north of the Thames on their way to bomb the Vauxhall works at Luton and the Handley Page aircraft factory at Radlett. The 12 Group Controller despatched only one squadron out of the four available to intercept a raid of some 100 enemy aircraft. He chose 242 Squadron, led by Bader who had never taken a squadron into action before.

The raid was intercepted and a number of combats took place. Bader's pilots claimed to have shot down 12 enemy aircraft with a further 8 probables and with no casualties. These results were astonishing and far exceeded any combat results of 11 Group. Later intelligence has revealed that they shot down only 4 German aircraft; there were, in fact, other Fighter Command squadrons also attacking the raid on its way in, and on its way out to the coast.

On the telephone Bader discussed the outstanding results he claimed with a very pleased AVM Leigh-Mallory, commander of 12 Group. He

THE DUXFORD WING

told Leigh-Mallory that if they had had more aircraft they could have shot down more of the Germans. Of course every fighter leader in action in Fighter Command could have made the same comment. Leigh-Mallory was so impressed with these results, as he might well have been, that he gave Bader two of the squadrons based at Duxford and Fowlmere to form into a wing, and to go into action with that formation. It was an ad hoc decision; there was no planning or rehearsal. A few days later, in time for the battles of 15th September, Leigh-Mallory gave Bader two further squadrons to sortie as an independent, five-squadron wing to operate over 11 Group. This act, without close consultation with Fighter Command and based on the vastly exaggerated claims of an inexperienced squadron commander, led ultimately to the Big Wing Controversy.

CHAPTER 16

Backs to the Wall

1st–6th September

Some authors have written that Fighter Command was almost beaten by the beginning of September, and was only saved by the Germans transferring their day bombing attacks away from 11 Group airfields to London on the 7th day of the month. This is unproven and is an unfair reflection on the squadrons. In a boxing match, taking punishment in one round does not mean defeat. On 15th September, in reply to a question by Prime Minister Churchill, who was visiting 11 Group operations room, AVM Park said that there were no more reserves – a sombre statement. He was in fact saying that *he* had no more reserves in 11 Group that *he* could send into the action. This has been mistakenly interpreted by some historians to mean that there were no more reserves left in the rest of Fighter Command that could be brought into action.

Conforming with his overall policy, Dowding had left Park to fight the Luftwaffe attacks on his own in a self-contained 11 Group, and he was thinking on that basis. Park had 19 Squadrons in his direct command but there were a total of 47 Hurricane and Spitfire Squadrons at readiness in Fighter Command. Many of these could have been flown in as replacements or to fight side by side as squadrons with 11 Group. No. 10 Group squadrons were already giving support. Certainly another 10 squadrons could be found for action within a few hours and 2 or 3 squadrons, led by battle experienced fighter pilots, could have been sent in from the Operational Training Units.

On 15th September my squadron was scrambled at 11.30 hours from Digby, 100 miles and 35 minutes north of London. We joined up with the Duxford Wing in the air already en route to London, as the fifth and last squadron. When we arrived a great battle was taking place and the Wing circled around overhead waiting for a suitable place to attack the enemy formation. There was no shortage of fighters over London as the Luftwaffe pilots found to their dismay. After first being detailed to act as top cover to the Wing, my squadron belatedly joined in the action. After

COR · No one below Dowding.

returning to Fowlmere, the satellite of Duxford, we landed and refuelled, ready to be scrambled for the second raid over London. This shows that once the Group isolation policy had been eradicated, and the black lines on the plotting tables ignored, squadrons could be flown direct into an interception in the London area from within a radius of 100 miles. This encompassed a vital number of additional squadrons, but would have needed the provision of refuelling and rearming services and radio communications to enable them to land in or near 11 Group after the action, to be re-armed and refuelled ready for the next scramble.

As the German bombers and their escort Me109s had to form up before flying to London at a slower speed than our individual squadrons, there would have been time to bring them into action to protect London and the environs.

To build up our day-fighter defence, the two Defiant Squadrons could have been re-equipped with new Hurricanes, which were instantly available at the maintenance depots, and could quickly have been brought to operational standard. We were never seriously short of aircraft, but our pilot losses were of great concern. Furthermore, of course, at any time Dowding could have moved the squadrons to north of the Thames, which would have nullified the bombing of our operational airfields but would still have enabled us to protect London and most of the south-east. We were never close to 'backs to the wall'.

The failure of 12 Group under AVM Leigh-Mallory to give ready and unconditional back-up support, and to effectively defend 11 Group airfields and sector stations when requested, was dishonourable, and may well have caused higher casualties in 11 Group. The offer of support to 11 Group by Leigh-Mallory to be only as the Duxford Wing of five squadrons, confirmed by Bader in a tape recording documented later in this book, is difficult to understand and is quite unacceptable. It seems that at a time when his Country was in great danger, ambition had replaced the loyalty expected of a senior commander.

A major weakness was that there was no one in authority in Fighter Command immediately below Dowding to co-ordinate overall battle tactics, and to utilise all the squadrons to best advantage to meet the very heavy and concentrated Luftwaffe attacks at that time.

Air Vice-Marshal Evill, the Senior Air Staff Officer of Fighter Command, Dowding's nominal second-in-command, and senior to all the group commanders, might have done this, but appeared to stand on the touch line and let things happen. It is almost certain that Dowding would have obstructed an intermediate appointment between himself and his Group Commanders.

CHAPTER 17

Attacks on London

7th–30th September

In early September 1940 a German night bomber dropped bombs on London by mistake. Until then there had been tacit agreement between the combatants that the capital cities would not be bombed. In retaliation, Churchill sent a token force of bombers to bomb Berlin by night. In an important speech to the German people on 4th September, an enraged Hitler promised that he would now start to bomb London. For every kilo of bombs we dropped on Germany, he would drop a thousand kilos on London by night. He would have found it difficult by day but certainly we couldn't stop him at night. By Hitler's emotional decision, Goering not only had the authority to bomb London by night but he was also free to bomb London with his great formations by day. Hitler's previous restrictions preventing this had been removed. Many of the Luftwaffe commanders were convinced, after the exaggerated claims of their pilots, that Fighter Command was now virtually beaten. But it was still necessary to force the last few remaining Fighter Command squadrons into the air for their final destruction. The only way to achieve this was by the bombing of London by day.

The Capital City with eight million citizens, the Royal Family, Parliament, factories and docks, would have to be defended to the last Spitfire or Hurricane, and so Goering authorised, and planned, a series of raids on London. This proved to be a disastrous decision for him and the Luftwaffe.

On 7th September the Germans carried out their first major daylight raid on London, and also their first planned night attack on the Capital. The Luftwaffe maintained their night attacks on London every night except one until the end of October. They carried on with a campaign of night bombing London well into 1941. These night raids were intended first as retaliation and then as terror bombing, but they could not seriously damage Fighter Command in its defence against an invasion. This could only be done by day attacks on London, with the full support of their Me109s. To do this the Germans were to be faced with a 70-mile (25 minutes) flight over England in a straight line within easy reach of most of the fighter stations in 11 Group.

On this day a massive formation of German aircraft advanced on a front of 20 miles en route to London. It was stepped up from 14,000 feet to 23,000 feet and covered an area of 800 square miles. There were nearly 1,000 aircraft, 348 bombers and 617 fighters, and 21 squadrons of Spitfires and Hurricanes, some 250 aircraft, were scrambled to intercept. The Controllers were taken by surprise by this first massed raid on London and our response was disappointing.

The Germans lost 40 aircraft and we lost 23. They believed erroneously, however, that they had shot down 70 of our fighters and that our reduced response confirmed their views that Fighter Command had very few aircraft left.

The Luftwaffe daylight raids set the City of London on fire, and the London Docks and the East End of London were savagely attacked. These burned through the night and acted as a beacon for the German bombers on their first night raid on London.

On 9th September they bombed London again by day with a much smaller force and lost 25 aircraft against our loss of 17. Another attack was made on London by day on 11th September; a fine day when we lost 29 aircraft but only destroyed 25 German aircraft. Goering now had no doubts that Fighter Command was finished.

Several days of mainly poor weather ended this continued series of major attacks and gave Fighter Command badly needed respite.

On 15th September, another fine day, the Germans set up two great attacks on London, which were intended to force up the 'remnants' of Fighter Command to complete its destruction. Their leaders and the German pilots were convinced by their intelligence reports that this was to be the 'Coup de Grace'. On the previous day Hitler had postponed his decision to launch the invasion, known as 'Sealion' (see appendix III), until 17th September. He may still have believed in Goering's promises and the exaggerated Luftwaffe reports of British casualties.

To get to London, German bomber squadrons with their Me109 protection had to fly a long and direct route, so that AVM Park now had the time, first to group and then place his squadrons in position and at height. The Germans were in for a quantum shock.

From the moment they crossed the coast, they were attacked and harassed by pairs of squadrons all along the route until they reached London, where they found many more squadrons waiting for them. Suddenly they were astonished and appalled to see the Duxford Wing of 60 fighter aircraft circling in formation above them, waiting until there was an opening to come down and join in the attack. A total of 21 squadrons went into action against them, and they were shot up on the way back. How could this be? Their commanders and intelligence officers had told them that Fighter Command no longer existed as a viable fighting force.

There were so many Hurricanes and Spitfires in action that sometimes as many as two or three fighters were queuing up to open fire on a single bomber. After weeks of being outnumbered this was almost unbelievable to our pilots. The effect of the battles on 15th September on our pilots was a great and immediate uplift in morale. We knew then that the Germans could be defeated. The same surprise awaited the German aircrews when they returned in a similar raid on London in the afternoon. Again our 5-squadron wing of RAF fighters arrived in formation ready to attack. The Germans were harried and beaten up again, and their morale was broken. They now knew that they could not win in 1940, and that the invasion of England was only a pipe dream. The Luftwaffe, for the first time in their battles in Europe, had met their match. They painfully realised that their colleagues, shot down and captured during the battle, would not be back within a few weeks as they had expected, but would be prisoners of war for a long time; it must have been a very sobering experience for them. They had let down Hitler and the great Reich and had suffered high casualties among their best crews for nothing.

I flew with my Squadron, No. 611, in the Wing twice on this day, and managed in spite of all the confusion to attack a Dornier 17 and a Heinkel 111. By the end of the day, the RAF claimed to have shot down 185 German aircraft, which although far from accurate, was still very exciting and uplifting. In fact, it is more likely that the total was 56 aircraft destroyed, but many more must have arrived back at their airfields in France and Belgium badly shot up. We lost 28 aircraft, reverting back to our ratio of 2:1. Two days later, after the news had reached Hitler, he cancelled his planned invasion for 1940.

* * *

September 15th was indeed a victory day for Fighter Command, Britain and Europe. On that day the German aircrews realised that they could not defeat Fighter Command, and so had lost the battle. The Invasion could not take place. On that day the British pilots knew that they could contain the Luftwaffe and that Britain was safe in 1940.

As pilots in the squadron, we did not know at the time of Hitler's decision, and the Luftwaffe attacks continued but lacked an all-out effort, and the relentless pressure was reduced. However, as far as the squadrons in 11 Group were concerned, the fighting was still intense with high casualties on both sides.

But Goering still wanted to prove the superiority of his air force, so that as far as our pilots were concerned the Battle was still very real with

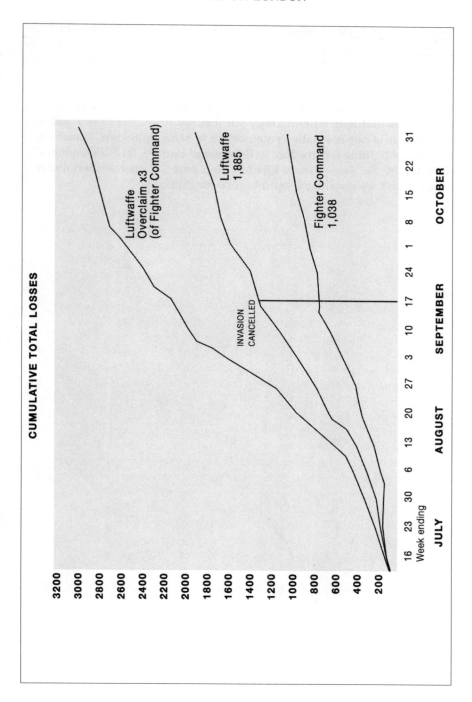

CUMULATIVE TOTAL LOSSES

Luftwaffe
Overclaim x3
(of Fighter Command)

Luftwaffe
1,885

Fighter Command
1,038

INVASION
CANCELLED

Week ending

3200
3000
2800
2600
2400
2200
2000
1800
1600
1400
1200
1000
800
600
400
200

16 23 30 6 13 20 27 3 10 17 24 1 8 15 22 31

JULY   AUGUST   SEPTEMBER   OCTOBER

three major raids on London by day at the end of September, in which the Germans lost another 111 aircraft against our 64. These raids could have no strategic value, but resulted in high and needless casualties for both sides

For some years after the war, 15th September was celebrated by our Country as 'Battle of Britain Day', but it is not now part of our national calendar. It is not normally remembered in schools as part of our great heritage of fighting for freedom in Britain and Europe. It is still shamefully regarded by the 'New Britain Liberals' as a part of British Imperialist history, which they consider should best be forgotten.

CHAPTER 18

Aces and Heroes

In the fighter squadrons, first in France and then in the Battle of Britain, a tradition grew up of the status of an ace fighter pilot, which was based on having shot down five or more enemy aircraft. It was also generally associated by the pilots with the award of a Distinguished Flying Cross. Although this belief may not have represented official Air Ministry policy for the award of the DFC, there was obviously a correlation between the numbers of aircraft claimed as shot down and the award. The main function of fighter squadrons is to shoot down enemy aircraft. Unless we use the yardstick of the number of victories, then how do we assess the achievement? Undoubtedly the CO of a squadron would put forward his recommendation, but it would certainly carry more weight if it listed a number of aircraft destroyed. Most lists of outstanding pilots published after the Battle are numerical ones based on the scores.

This confirms my view that some of the best squadron and flight commanders had not received their due honour for leadership. Often their leadership was exceptional but their claimed victories were fewer than those of their pilots.

In WWII the Luftwaffe had their own system of rewarding aces who built up scores in the hundreds, but we now know that the Germans heavily over-claimed their victories over England by 3 to 1. The numbers of their victories had been exaggerated but of course their courage in battle is not challenged by this information. Our own pilots over-claimed at an average of 2:1.

Among themselves, the pilots in Fighter Command never referred to aces or heroes except in jest. They generally knew who in the squadron were meticulous in their claims.

There was a major problem in making a decision as to whether a victory had been achieved. An enemy aircraft last seen diving away into cloud with black smoke was more likely to be a sign that the Me109 pilot was returning to France at maximum boost and could get back to base, rather than that his engine had been badly damaged and that he would crash over England or in the Channel. However, if white smoke was streaming from his engine, then it probably meant that his cooling system had been damaged, and that the engine would seize up and a successful return across the Channel would be unlikely. I believe that very few pilots claimed victories dishonestly, but optimism sometimes prevailed over unbiased judgement.

The fact that our pilots claimed twice as many German aircraft as are now accepted as actually having been shot down, shows how easy it was to be mistaken in the heat of battle. In their first major attack, 242 Squadron led by S/Ldr Bader claimed 12 aircraft shot down, 11 of them reported by the pilots as either being seen to crash or to be set on fire. Later, substantiated figures reduce this number to 4, much more in line with 11 Group scoring and way below the magical figure so readily accepted by AVM Leigh-Mallory commanding No. 12 Group. Other more experienced squadrons, such as No. 603, the top scoring and a very experienced squadron, claimed only 1.5 for every single victory finally confirmed, compared with the 3:1 aircraft over-claimed by Bader's pilots. Duplicated attacks in Big Wing and other large formation actions commonly led to over-claims with 2 or even 3 pilots making attacks on one aircraft at the same or even different times.

Although the Air Ministry did all they could to substantiate the claims, only the 'kills' over land or those close to shore could generally be confirmed. There was a second classification of 'Probable' for aircraft which were not seen to crash, and the crew were not seen to bale out, but which were so shot up that it was unlikely that they would escape home across the Channel. It has been reported that one German bomber reached its base with more than 200 bullet holes. This classification was taken seriously during the Battle, but as actual figures have now been obtained it has less significance, although some probables have since been confirmed.

Decorations

Most pilots believed that the Air Ministry honoured day fighter pilots largely on the basis of the number of kills, but at the same time we were instructed not to follow the victim down merely to confirm the kill, as it was dangerous to do this. We should stay high and look for another target. This made it difficult sometimes to claim a 'confirmed'. On one occasion I ignored the instruction when I shot down an Me109, and having seen the pilot bale out I landed at a nearby airfield. I returned to my base with the pilot's life-jacket (*Schwimmvest*), commenting to the intelligence officer 'Well you can't say this one was only a probable!'

By far the most dangerous position in the squadron was the 'Tail End Charlie' flying behind and above the squadron to search for, and warn of attacking Me109s. Sadly too many failed to return to base and no one had seen what had happened to them. No decorations were awarded for this duty.

Only one Victoria Cross was awarded to a fighter pilot throughout the whole war and this was during the Battle of Britain. A major requirement for a recommendation for a VC is that it must have been witnessed. Recommendation for this award to a fighter pilot is difficult as they fight generally high in the sky without a witness. Anyone near enough to see the action would probably be too busy fighting for his own life to watch and record other pilots in combat. This award was made to a Hurricane pilot mainly based on his combat report, and it was not precisely witnessed. It was for an act of great courage, but more than 500 of our pilots were killed in action in the Battle, many of them sacrificing their lives with comparable courage. There was a feeling among some of the pilots of the time that perhaps the one Victoria Cross should have been awarded to Fighter Command to honour all of its courageous pilots, rather than just to single out one as the bravest of the brave. The medal was later auctioned, and was purchased by the Royal Air Force Museum at Hendon. Perhaps its real resting place should be with the Roll of Honour in the Battle of Britain Chapel in Westminster Abbey. There is a precedence for this. After withstanding continuous raids by the German and Italian bombers with continued courage over a long period, the British Parliament honoured the people of Malta with the George Cross in 1943.

Winston Churchill felt that the pilots and aircrew who had fought in the Battle should be given a special award, which was in the form of a bronze 'Battle of Britain' clasp attached to the ribbon of the bronze '1939–1945 Star'. When ribbons only were worn, a silver gilt rosette was mounted in the centre of the ribbon. It is probably fair to suggest that this award is one of the most treasured of all decorations in the RAF. The holders of the clasp formed an association after the war known as The Battle of Britain Fighter Association with a recognisable dark blue tie with a pattern in gold of the British Isles and the rosette. The Association continues to hold annual reunion dinners and other functions, keeping originally young comrades, and now old comrades, in close touch. We were honoured for many years to have Queen Elizabeth, the beloved 'Queen Mum', as our Patron. We are honoured that the Prince of Wales has since become our new Patron.

CHAPTER 19

Different Wars

On 28th September I was posted from my Squadron in 12 Group to No. 41 Squadron at Hornchurch in 11 Group, which I was delighted to find was equipped with Spitfires. Hornchurch was close to the Thames, a few miles to the east of London and three miles from the outskirts of the London balloon barrage. Fortunately the river gave us a safe guide to the airfield at times of poor visibility.

As Hornchurch was to the east and so close to London, the station shared with Londoners the unpleasant experience of air raid sirens at dusk followed by night bombing. Now I had entered the real war and my life and fighting had undergone a traumatic change. Fortunately I had joined a wonderful Squadron with exceptional people with considerable battle experience. My time with them is still very vivid and my service with them is the most memorable part of my life.

No. 41 Squadron is credited by author John Alcorn with the fourth highest order of kills – 45, and the second highest number of Me109s shot down – 32, which indicates the intensity of their part in the fighting. The squadron was led by Squadron Leader D O Finlay, who had been an Olympic hurdler and silver medallist in 1936.

Among the pilots was Flight Lieutenant Norman Ryder, my flight commander with whom I flew as Number 2. He ensured my survival during my dangerous first flights in the 'real war'. Ryder was a great leader who received no decoration for his outstanding service in 11 Group in the Battle. Pilot Officer George Bennions, formerly a regular sergeant pilot, often led the squadron and was a real 'ace'. Sadly he was shot down in October by an Me109 and was seriously wounded by a cannon shell. Pilot Officer Eric Lock, a Volunteer Reserve pilot, was an exceptional shot and is now recognised as the top British scorer in the Battle. Sadly he also was shot down by an Me109 and badly injured on a sortie in November.

The Squadron had fought over Dunkirk and had served two full operational tours in 11 Group at Hornchurch. They were battle honed and had suffered many casualties. It was a highly professional and very friendly squadron with integrity as the common bond, and it was a great privilege to have flown with them.

There was a tremendous difference in the war in 11 Group compared with 12 Group. In 12 Group the Luftwaffe rarely appeared, and life was very much sitting at readiness and flying convoy patrols over the North Sea. There were very few casualties and squadrons never needed to be rested; they always operated at full strength. The airfields in 12 Group were in little danger of being bombed as they were outside the range of Me109s, which meant no German bombers by day. This was largely routine readiness. Action was only really possible over 11 Group and 10 Group, and towards the end of August our contribution consisted mainly of patrolling in single squadrons defending 11 Group sector stations north of the Thames. With the introduction of the Duxford Wing on 7th September, and the attacks on London, the pilots at Duxford and its satellite airfield were at last able to get into the action over 11 Group territory.

In 11 Group the tempo was entirely different; this was the real war and death was commonplace. The day after I joined 41 Squadron at Hornchurch, I was in action against the bombers. The next day I took part in five sorties. In fact, in the month of October with 41 Squadron, I did more sorties than in the whole of the previous two and a half months in 12 Group. The speed of action with Me109s needed vastly improved eyesight, and a quick and immediate reaction to events in order to stay alive. These qualities could only be learned in action. It was the 'Real War' with the possibility of engaging the enemy any day.

A third war was the active participation in September of the Duxford Wing of 12 Group led by S/Ldr Bader. As there was no enemy activity by day over their own Group, then they had to find it over 11 Group. Although AVM Park had requested the help of single squadrons for the protection of his sector stations north of the Thames, the 12 Group pilots felt that they were being kept out of the action. AVM Leigh-Mallory gave Bader two squadrons and, soon after, another two squadrons for him to lead as a five-Squadron Wing on his patrols over 12 Group. Bader then seized every opportunity to fly his Wing as an independent force trying to search out the enemy. He had no radio contact with 11 Group controllers who were therefore unable to exercise any control over his operations.

The Duxford Wing was at readiness for most of September and the whole of October but only intercepted the enemy on seven occasions during this period. The Wing was in action over London twice on 15th September.

The basis of Fighter Command defence was the detailed control and precise intelligence of the position of our aircraft and the enemy formations. As far as 11 Group was concerned the Wing was a loose cannon and could have been mistaken by the Observer Corps for an enemy plot.

CHAPTER 20
Me109s High

1st–31st October

In October there was a major change in the weather and there was only one fine day in the whole month. The Germans were forced to alter their tactics, as their massed bomber raids had proved to be too expensive, and the weather patterns were unsuitable with cloud at low and medium heights.

The Luftwaffe tactics changed to sending over fast and high-flying formations of Me109 fighters escorting other Me109s converted to carry bombs. They flew at 20,000–30,000 feet and were more difficult to intercept. Their bombs were not dropped with any accuracy and were mainly of nuisance value. The fighting at this stage was basically between fighter aircraft, in which unusually we had the option to attack or not. Needless to say, we always attacked if we saw them in time at a reasonable height. During this period I took part in many sorties to intercept formations of Me109s at high altitude, and shot down two of the fighters. Both of the pilots baled out and were captured. Earlier in the month I had attacked a German bomber formation at a lower altitude and had shared in the destruction of a Dornier 17.

At this stage in the Battle we had run into a serious and unpleasant problem. In the design phase someone had forgotten to put heating in the cockpit of the Spitfire and around the guns. At 25,000 feet and above, it was very cold. The outside temperature could be as low as -40F or -40C. As our cockpits were not sealed, the temperature inside was at about the same level. Apart from the personal discomfort, some of the guns froze up and did not fire. If guns failed on one side, then when we opened fire the aircraft slewed to the other side. It is difficult to shoot down the enemy with a slewing Spitfire. In addition, sometimes when we dived down into less cold air with more moisture, the windscreen froze up. This led to us being unable to open fire on the enemy even when we had the rare advantage of height.

Although the danger of invasion in 1940 was over, the battle was still fought over the south-east of England with casualties on both sides. There was no strategic or tactical benefit for the Germans in these spasmodic raids with their unnecessary casualties, other than possibly expensive battle training for their pilots. Perhaps Goering was still trying to find a way of restoring his lost honour.

In all sorties in the month of October, the Germans lost a total of 293 aircraft against 156 aircraft of Fighter Command, mainly in 11 Group, and with a win ratio to us of 1.9:1. In this fighting, basically of fighter versus fighter, we had achieved a success of almost two to one. The 31st October is officially recognised as the last day of the Battle, although fighting continued at a reducing pace into November and December. It was rather more of a calendar decision than an abrupt cessation of the fighting.

During October the Duxford Wing made 15 patrols or sorties, but shot down nothing, and indeed made no contact with the enemy, although the squadrons had been kept at readiness. In view of the fighting that was taking place in 11 Group, the squadrons would obviously have been better employed as single or pairs of squadrons elsewhere in the south. There is no doubt that even with the interception of the five massed raids over London in September, a Big Wing philosophy had no responsible or beneficial place in the defensive war over England and was an ineffective use of pilots and aircraft.

This was later proved in an air exercise the following year organised by AVM Leigh-Mallory, the advocate of Big Wings and by then the Commander of 11 Group, to prove that Dowding's defence policies had been wrong. This live exercise showed that the use of the Big Wing philosophy as a major means of defence would have been disastrous. The 'bombers' had bombed their targets and were on their way home before the defensive wing had been formed up!

CHAPTER 21

After the Battle

London, the big cities and the towns were now relatively safe from mass bombing by day, although small hit and run raids continued. However, we had little defence against the German night bombers, and England had to suffer continued night bombing for some time. It was many months before we could operate any real defence against the bombers. Even so, the numbers of the attackers lost were not enough to halt or significantly reduce the bombing, and the destruction of homes and civilian casualties continued well into 1941. In 1940 our defence at night consisted primarily of Blenheim twin-engine night fighters equipped with airborne RDF that was never really effective. The Blenheims were underpowered and even if visual contact was made they could not always catch up to the bomber on its way back to the Continent. It was only with its replacement by the new twin-engine Bristol Beaufighter in 1941, much faster, better armed, and with more efficient air interception equipment, that we were able to inflict significant casualties on the German night raiders. Bearing in mind the problems of night interception and the number of Luftwaffe bombers available for the attacks, Britain could expect to be bombed at night for some time.

The night bombing of London was followed in 1944 by the V1 pilotless 1000lb aerial winged bombs known as 'doodle bugs'. These flying bombs coming fast across the sky at 300 mph sounded like noisy motorbikes. This unusual noise, getting nearer and louder, heralded the explosive threat it carried, and was very frightening, but the silence after the motor cut as the fuel ran out was even more frightening. It meant that the V1 was diving into the ground in your vicinity and would explode within a few seconds. As long as the engine kept going and it flew past then you were safe, although others would take the impact. Then came the V2s fired from the Continent, rockets which exploded without warning in the streets of London, so that people had no time to take shelter. Their landing velocity exceeded the speed of sound, and people couldn't hear them coming.

As a point of history, before, during and after Dresden was bombed by the Allies, the Germans continued their relentless daily terror attacks on London's civilian population with their V2 rockets, from which there was no protection. War is war and war is total. The Germans knew and accepted this in 1940 when they held the upper hand.

The years of bombing, the V1s and the rockets did not force the surrender of the British people, but it left a contempt for the Nazi Regime still remembered by the generations that lived through those terrible years.

CHAPTER 22

Assessment

I cannot guarantee to present precise establishment and battle casualty figures, but the figures listed below are offered as reasonable and supported estimates of operational losses on which to make an assessment.

There will never be an absolute certainty as to the exact German losses, but there is evidence that they lost some 1,600 aircraft on operational flying in the Battle and many more were badly damaged. The Luftwaffe lost a further 285 aircraft in non-combat flying or accidents giving a total of 1,885. We lost 917 aircraft in combat or other operational flying, from which 384 of our pilots were saved, many to fight again. In addition we lost a further 121 aircraft in other activities giving a total of 1,038. On a numbers basis alone this is clear evidence of our victory.

The 544 aircrew who gave their lives are remembered on a Roll of Honour in Westminster Abbey. In this year 2005 there will be erected a fine memorial commemorating the Battle, and recording the individual names of the aircrew who fought in the action. It is being built on the Embankment near Westminster Bridge, in the heart of London, and will be a fitting tribute to our fighter pilots of 1940. It is overlooking the River Thames, close to the Houses of Parliament, and below Big Ben, the beacon of freedom for us and the sound of freedom to the enslaved countries of Europe. This bronze memorial, the inspiration and achievement of the Battle of Britain Historical Society, has been funded entirely by public subscription, without help from our government or the National Lottery Fund. There is already another memorial to the Battle of Britain aircrews at Capel le Ferne near Folkestone in Kent, with a fine sculpture of a pilot in flying kit scanning the skies over the Channel towards the French coast. Its symbolic location gives it great character. The memory of our young men is honoured by this monument for their great sacrifice in saving Britain, and indeed Europe. This monument was entirely subscribed for by 'the Friends of the Few' – pilots, relatives and supporters. Once again there had been no financial help from the Government or National Lottery Fund.

The loss of their aircraft in battle, and even more important, the loss of their experienced Luftwaffe aircrews was disastrous for Germany. They had not only lost the Battle, but also the crucial time needed for their attack against Soviet Russia, with nothing gained. There was a further serious strategic setback, in that Britain was now confirmed as a live and active enemy in the west, and the enslaved nations could have hope for the future while Britain was still free. Hitler was going to be faced with war on two fronts, which he had always feared.

Every night in occupied Europe people listened in on their secret wireless sets for the sound of Big Ben and the 'V' for Victory messages transmitted to resistance groups by the BBC after the Nine o'clock News. With its courage and sacrifice Britain kept the hope for freedom alive for millions of people in the countries of Europe. Have these countries forgotten – or have their people never been told?

If the Luftwaffe strength lost in the Battle had been transferred to eastern Germany and Poland in 1940 instead, the Germans could have attacked Russia months earlier and with an extra 1,800 warplanes flown by experienced pilots, they could have been in Moscow before the snow fell. The Nazi victory with its associated terrors would then have been total. By fighting and losing the Battle of Britain, the Germans failed in their attack on Soviet Russia. Their aircraft losses in the Battle, and the delays caused, resulted in their ultimate defeat, which prevented the planned Nazi German domination over Europe.

The achievement of Fighter Command in the Battle of Britain can be seen in its true perspective when it is realised that it needed the combined strength of Britain, the USA and Russia, to finally bring the German military forces to total surrender in 1945. And yet five years earlier Britain's Fighter Command squadrons, on their own, had halted and turned back the aerial armadas of the great German Reich.

The Weather: The Decisive Factor

Man proposes – God disposes

Effect of Weather on the Battle

A dominating factor in the Battle of Britain of 1940 was the pattern of the weather. The Germans had to beat Fighter Command within a specific time frame, and their ability to do this was dependent not only on their many bomber formations protected by hundreds of fighters, but on the freedom allowed them by the weather to form up and operate their massed formations over Britain.

The weather has been a deciding factor in military and sea power battles between nations for centuries. In 1588 the Spanish Armada sailed up the Channel to Calais to collect a large army from the Netherlands with which to invade England. Although outgunned, the English attacked the Spanish fleet with great courage. When the Armada anchored at Calais the English sent in fire-ships. The Spanish panicked and cut their cables to escape to sea. Gales and storms blew up in the Channel and the Spanish Fleet was forced by adverse winds into the North Sea, struggling against damaging weather. Their ships were immediately harassed by the English and driven north, and later were broken up on the rocky coasts of Scotland and Ireland. There was no safe haven for them, and less than half of their numbers managed to struggle back to Spain. Against heavy odds Britain was saved from invasion by the appalling weather.

When Hitler gave the order to invade Britain, Goering predicted that with only a few days of fine weather, his Luftwaffe would be able to destroy the air defences of southern England. He was obviously unaware at that time of how important the weather patterns would be to the success of his 'Operation Sealion'.

As attackers, the Luftwaffe needed advance knowledge of fine weather to plan and form up major bomber formations. Fighter Command on the defensive, however, had to take each day and each attack as it came and deal with it. Only very bad weather would permit squadrons to be released from a state of readiness.

In the summer, the weather movement over England is mainly from the south-west across the Atlantic. With their occupation of the western coastline from Norway down to the Bay of Biscay, the Germans could collate a mass of weather data for their forecasts. Their long-range reconnaissance aircraft could cover the Western Approaches and the North Atlantic from France and Norway; and their submarines could report on the weather coming in from the Atlantic. The weather data over the whole of mainland Europe was available to them in detail for further plotting on their weather charts (see page 22).

To win by 17th September the Germans had to send large formations of bombers with Me109 escorts to fly over the Channel coasts and the south-east of England, to bring Fighter Command to battle. They needed clear skies or acceptable cloud conditions over the Pas de Calais and the Channel to assemble the unwieldy formations of 100 to 900 aircraft, to keep together, and finally to see their targets. The days with low cloud were fine for low-level reconnaissance and surface attacks by small formations. These latter attacks could, however, have no significant effect on the outcome of the Battle.

The German Air Commanders needed an efficient meteorological service. But they could still only make use of the weather that arrived, even though they had advance warning of changes.

Effect on Casualties

I have analysed the day-by-day fighting in the Battle specifically in relation to the patterns of the weather.

Using figures of *operational* casualties and with a broad brush, I have made two simple classifications, which I have used to show the effect of weather.

The assessment of weather suitability for action is of course judgemental, but the relationship between patterns of weather and operational casualties is clearly established.

Fine: Days of weather, fine or suitable for large formation activity.

All Other: Variable weather including periods of poor weather, days and periods of mixed weather with little chance of continued massed formation attacks.

EFFECT OF WEATHER ON AIRCRAFT OPERATIONAL CASUALTIES
1940

	JULY		AUGUST			SEPTEMBER		OCTOBER	Total
DATE	10 - 24	25 - 10	11 - 18	19 - 23	24 - 9	10 - 22	23 - 2	3 - 31	
PHASE	1	2	3	4	5	6	7	8	
DAYS	15	17	8	5	17	13	10	29	114
WEATHER	POOR	MIXED	FINE	POOR	FINE	MIXED	FINE	POOR	
TARGETS	Channel convoys	Channel convoys & ports	Adler Tag	Airfields and ports	Airfields and London	London and airfields	London factories	High Flying ME109s	
DAILY AVERAGE									
F/C	3	3.5	18.5	2.5	17.5	7.5	10.5	5	
L/W	6	6	40	5.5	25	13	18.5	9	
PHASE TOTAL									
F/C	48	57	148	13	298	99	105	149	917
L/W	93	102	317	28	429	166	186	273	1594

F/C - Fighter Command
L/W - Luftwaffe

The days of fine weather in the Battle of Britain totalled 43 out of a possible 114 with total losses for Fighter Command of 653 giving an average loss of 15 per day. This figure for fine weather days would have been higher but for the fact that the Luftwaffe failed to make full use of them, particularly in the period 23rd September–2nd October. The German losses on fine days averaged 22.7, some 50% higher than Fighter Command.

In the remaining 71 days of poor and mixed weather our casualties averaged 3.7 a day, 25% of those recorded for fine days. The Luftwaffe average casualties for poor weather were 8.7 per day, equal to 38 % of their fine days.

As the chart on page 84 shows, during the Adler Tag period of hard fighting the Luftwaffe losses were 40 per day, more than twice that of Fighter Command's 18.5. The Luftwaffe needed fine weather to win, but the fighting was punishing for both sides.

It is obvious from the above figures and the chart that the weather had a decisive effect on casualties on both sides in the Battle. It is hardly surprising that casualty figures were so much higher on fine days. Many more aircraft were in action and were in large formations, which were more easily seen and intercepted. Fighter Command aircraft were more vulnerable to attack by Me109s on fine days with good visibility, whereas Luftwaffe bombers had little or no fighter protection in bad weather.

The Fighter Command aircraft replacement rate averaged 13.5 per day, reduced to 12.5 by replacement of non-operational losses. On fine days we could have **net** losses of up to 6 aircraft per day, but when very heavy fighting took place with losses of up to 30 aircraft in one day, then our **net** loss could be 17.5 aircraft for that day. However, on poor weather days we could have **net** gains of up to 10 aircraft per day. We started in mid-July with 650 Hurricanes and Spitfires, and by mid-August our numbers had increased to 750 with increased reserves. This was a valuable improvement in our defensive strength so that at the beginning of the Battle the weather had already exerted its powerful influence. Presumably the Me109 strength increased in this period but the Germans were not expecting heavy losses in the forthcoming battle and were not operating at full manufacturing output. It is clear that if during the period of 10th July–30th September there had been only poor weather then there could have been few, if any, major air battles, with no possibility of the defeat of Fighter Command and no possibility of an invasion. However, continuous fine weather during this period would have seen Fighter Command seriously damaged within weeks, and it could have been forced to withdraw to north of the Thames in order to stay in being. The south-east coastal area would have been relatively unprotected against Luftwaffe dominance in this area. Fine weather resulted in high casualty rates for Fighter Command, well above our aircraft and pilot replacement capacity.

There were two periods of continuous fine weather of 11 and 8 days, and several days of fine weather for the Adler Tag offensive, one of which was not exploited by the Germans. Fortunately, these fine day periods were separated by poor and mixed weather – spells which allowed Fighter Command pilots in 11 and 10 Groups respite from their maximum efforts, and for replacement aircraft to build up the squadrons. I refer only to aircraft replacement. The problem with pilot availability was far more serious. With a more helpful Air Ministry, Dowding would have been better able to deal with this problem with closer co-operation with the other Commands.

Weather Phases during the Battle

Most authors have divided the Battle into phases based on patterns of fighting activities. My phases cover similar periods, but are based on patterns of the weather. The overlap of our patterns must be considered significant, as the chart on Page 84 shows.

Phase I of 15 days, from 10th–24th July, gave generally poor weather with activity mainly against convoys and shipping, especially in the Channel. Fine weather would have led to greater activity in the Channel. We were able to make a significant build up of our aircraft numbers. F/C average loss – **3** per day. L/W average loss – **6** per day [F/C – Fighter Command, L/W – Luftwaffe].

Phase II of 17 days, from 25th July10th August, was a period of mixed weather, with some poor weather days and some separate fine days. Again the attacks were mainly against shipping in the Channel and against Channel ports. The Germans still needed time to restore their squadrons after their losses during the Battle of France and to prepare for Adler Tag. If there had been continuous fine weather in this period the Luftwaffe would have been much more active over the south coast with more Fighter Command casualties. This time fortunately permitted a further build up of our fighters. F/C average loss – **3.5** per day. L/W average loss – **6** per day.

Phase III of 8 days, from 11th–18th August – Adler Tag. By the beginning of this period three crucial things had happened. Because of the previously low casualty rate, Fighter Command had built up its operational strength, putting them closer to the Luftwaffe's 800 Me109s. Secondly, Goering was ready to start his Adler Tag mass attacks on Britain, the 'Blitzkrieg', to pave the way for the invasion. Thirdly, the weather pattern changed to a period of fine weather – perfect for his bomber formations.

The Germans used the period to make very heavy attacks on Britain, especially on the 15th, 16th and 18th August, with very high Luftwaffe losses. In this phase Fighter Command lost 148 aircraft against the 317 of the Luftwaffe. Those extra aircraft from Phase I and II were to be invaluable.

Fortunately, the weather broke from 19th–23rd August and stopped the Adler Tag assault in its tracks. Although the Luftwaffe had shot down 148 of our aircraft, in fact their pilots claimed more than 400 victories. Set against their own known losses of 317 and their vastly superior numbers of fighters and bombers, they were convinced that they were on a winning campaign. F/C average loss – **18.5** per day. L/W average loss – **40** per day.

Phase IV of five days of poor weather, from 19th–23rd August, was a short but invaluable period to rest our squadrons. We lost 13 aircraft and the Luftwaffe lost 28. During this quiet break we made crucial gains in aircraft stocks to offset against our losses in the previous period. F/C average loss – **2.5** per day. L/W average loss – **5.5** per day.

Then started the most dangerous period in the Battle.

Phase V of 17 days, from 24th August–9th September, when there was a virtually continuous period of fine weather, with just one poor day, in which our fighter airfields were extensively attacked. This phase included two massed assaults on London. This was the great opportunity for the Luftwaffe to break through.

Both sides were receiving heavy casualties, but the German casualties were shared between their bombers and fighters. Luftwaffe aircraft casualties in this period were 429 against 298 for Fighter Command. We were at our lowest ebb, but at the end of this period we still had some 650 fighters and only a week to go to turn back the Luftwaffe, did we but know. F/C average loss – **17.5** per day. L/W average loss – **25** per day. The numbers of aircraft available were kept up by replacement from depot reserves and repaired aircraft.

Phase VI, of 13 days, from 10th–22nd September stopped the German aerial Blitzkrieg. The weather changed to mixed/poor with four fine but separated days including 15th September. The Luftwaffe lost 56 aircraft on this day, with two attacks on London, compared with Fighter Command losses of 28. Total losses for the period, which included attacks on factories, were Fighter Command with 99 and the Luftwaffe with 166. With this change in the weather to last for almost two weeks, the Battle could not be lost! The aggression of the British fighter squadrons on 15th September broke the morale of the Luftwaffe with the shock realisation that they could not defeat Fighter Command, and that there could be no invasion in 1940. The Luftwaffe made no further major raids on London until the last few days of September. F/C average loss – **7.5** per day. L/W average loss – **13** per day.

Phase VII of 10 days, from 23rd September–2nd October, with a change to fine weather. Although there was that 'wished for' period of continuous fine weather, the fire had obviously gone out of the Luftwaffe. They made no real attempt to press on with the battle although there were some attacks on factories. German casualties were 186 against Fighter Command with the loss of 105 aircraft. However for some reason they made three major raids on London at the end of the period, losing 111 aircraft against our losses of 64 with nothing achieved. F/C average loss – **10.5** per day. L/W average loss – **18.5** per day.

Phase VIII of 29 days, from 3rd–31st October. Poor or unstable weather for almost the whole of October prevented any major bomber attacks on England. Fighting was limited mainly to high-flying formations of Me109 fighters and Me109 fighter/bombers. These caused little damage, but there were still high casualties in the air. The Luftwaffe lost 273 aircraft and Fighter Command 149. The total Luftwaffe casualties including training and weather accidents for this period was 379, a formidable figure and just acceptable to the Luftwaffe as they believed they had destroyed more than 400 of our aircraft.

This was basically a period when our Hurricanes and Spitfires fought it out with the Me109s at high altitude without the involvement of the Luftwaffe bombing force. F/C average loss – **5** per day. L/W average loss – **9** per day.

Goering believed he could win on the basis of his previously successful Blitzkrieg aerial warfare over Europe. An increased number of sunny days could have made it more difficult for us if the Germans had been strong enough to continue the pressure. However, they paid the price for taking the risk of attacking our island in an English summer with its known reputation for weather vagaries.

Weather Controls the Pattern of Fighting

Most authors rightly set out the phases of the battle on the different patterns of action that took place. My weather patterns superimpose and so there must be a causal explanation. As the aerial activity could not have affected the pattern of the weather over a period of 114 days, then the weather must have had a powerful effect on the pattern of the battle. There were not enough fine days for the Luftwaffe Blitzkrieg to command victory in the air. Bad weather periods broke up the inertia of the German attacks and enabled Fighter Command to rest, recover and rebuild its strength.

It confirms my view that the progress and the outcome of the Battle was ultimately dictated by the pattern of the weather. It appears that most of the time the Luftwaffe were ready and able to use the periods of continuous fine weather. They could achieve little in the poor weather, which however was of great benefit to Fighter Command.

The most important effect was with Phases I and II, when continuous poor and mixed weather helped us to build up our strength to a formidable fighting force and reserve. With the overall pattern of the weather, the grim determination of our people, the courage of our pilots, the effectiveness of our interception system and our aircraft replacement strength, the Luftwaffe could never have eliminated Fighter Command. We were still a powerful fighting force at the end of the Battle and we were never short of aircraft.

We had lost many pilots and it had become difficult to replace them, both in numbers and experience. This could indeed have become our Achilles Heel but we were saved by the crucial change in the weather.

A Close-run Thing?

In war things are never quite so good or quite so bad as are first believed.
The Duke of Wellington

It is widely believed that by the first week of September 1940, Fighter Command was in danger of losing the Battle and that we were saved only by Hitler's revenge decision to attack London from 7th September onwards. This diverted enemy attacks away from the airfields and, in theory, gave 11 Group the chance to recover. The inference from this belief was that we did not win the Battle, but rather that the Germans could have won but lost it by this disastrous change of tactics. This inference, which might make good media presentation, is unfounded and it denigrates the achievements of Dowding, Park and our pilots. In fact the pressure on our squadrons continued with attacks on London resulting in 23 of our aircraft being shot down on 7th September, 17 on the 9th and 29 on the 11th. The losses in the first three days over London totalled 69 aircraft, equal to the loss of several squadrons. Following this change to attacks on London the reality is as follows:

Fighter Command Operational Casualties, September 1940

Col I			Col II			Col III		
Sept		A/C lost	Sept		A/C Lost	Sept		A/C lost
1	Fine	15	7*	Fine London	23	13	Poor	3
2	Fine	14	8	Fine	5	14	Poor London	12
3	Fine	13	9	Fine London	17	15	Fine London	28
4	Fine	15	10	Poor	1	16	Poor	1
5	Fine	20	11	Fine London	29	17	Poor	5
6	Fine	20	12	Poor	0	18	Fine	13
	Total	**97**		**Total**	**75**		**Total**	**62**

Av. for 6 Fine days 16 Av. for all 6 days 12.5 Av. for all 6 days 10

Av. for 4 Fine days 19 Av. for 2 Lon days 20

Av. for 3 Fine Lon days 23 Av. for 4 poor days 5

* Start of attacks on London.

The following figures clearly show the impact on casualties resulting from Goering's decision to commence day bombing of London on 7th September. On the surface the casualty figures show an immediate and continuing reduction. The reality, however, is against the accepted belief and was, in fact, harmful and not beneficial to Fighter Command, which fortunately was relieved by the change in the weather.

Column I

This is a period of six days in which the Luftwaffe attacked airfields in continuing fine weather with an average for Fighter Command of 16 casualties per day immediately before Goering started to bomb London.

Column II

This details the first six days following the decision to bomb London by day. The average daily losses have dropped to **12.5**. Crucially in this period the weather changed with two poor days compared with the continuous fine weather of Column I. However, the attacks on London on fine days gave an increased average of casualties to **23**. The two poor weather days averaged less than **1**.

It is clear that the change in the weather has significantly reduced the casualty rate on our hard-pressed fighter force, whereas the attacks on London significantly increased our casualty rates.

Column III

During the next period the number of poor weather days increased to four, further reducing casualties to a column average of **10** per day. However, the attacks on London for two days gave 40 casualties, an average of **20** a day, whereas the other days averaged **5** casualties a day. I suggest that this is clear evidence that Fighter Command was saved from Luftwaffe attacks by the breaking of the weather on 10th September, thus alleviating the increased damage caused by the Luftwaffe high casualty attacks on London, and giving time to our squadrons to rest and recover.

Fighter Command was clearly not saved by Goering's decision to bomb London by day, which in fact made Fighter Command's situation more precarious. The day bombing of London was purely tactical – a measure to force up what Goering wrongly believed to be the 'last remnants' of Fighter Command.

When the weather was fine, Fighter Command incurred very high losses. So did the Luftwaffe of course. In poor weather, aircraft losses were generally minimal. The weather was now showing its control of the battle.

By 10th September the long spell of fine weather had come to an end, crucially reducing the impact of the Luftwaffe attacks. The Germans had failed to meet the charge. Fighter Command was very much 'in being'.

Although the most important factor was the change in the weather, there were also other significant changes in 11 Group and 12 Group which strengthened Fighter Command resistance in the south-east. At the end of August and the beginning of September, 11 Group were undoubtedly under very heavy pressures and were being bounced with high casualties. Our formation leaders finally took their own action to ensure adequate height, and Park wisely ordered his controllers to rectify interception procedures.

On 7th September the 12 Group Duxford Wing of three squadrons was formed and went into action in the Battle giving support to 11 Group, although not directly requested by Park, and continued to do so. On 15th September 12 Group despatched a five-squadron Wing which intercepted the main formation, much to the relief of 11 Group squadrons in action, and to the dismay of the Luftwaffe aircrews. There were other squadrons in Fighter Command that could also have been called in.

The result was ensured by the termination of the long spell of continuous fine weather, which had enabled the Luftwaffe to test 11 Group near to its limit. But 11 Group was only a part of Fighter Command. The weather broke on 10th September with only three separated fine days in the next 12 days. The strain on 11 Group was eased and it recovered its strength. On the 15th, a fine day, the Luftwaffe carried out two major raids on London. These were attacked with such aggression and high casualties that the Luftwaffe realised that they had met their Nemesis only eight days after Fighter Command had reportedly been 'on its knees'. The change in the weather had set the seal on the Battle.

Even with the continuous fine weather from 24th August to 9th September, Goering had failed to meet his promise to Hitler. This shows that Fighter Command had outmanoeuvred the Luftwaffe. Then the weather changed sides and Britain had won through.

Park expressed his view that the simple and emotive decision by Hitler to attack London instead of his airfields saved Fighter Command and Britain from defeat. Neither Park nor any other person has given direct evidence for such a simplistic statement. The available evidence is to the contrary. Park's view of the Battle embraced the whole of his 11 Group territory, and the battles fought by his squadrons. He may have felt that if his Group was close to the limit then so was Fighter Command. This was not the true position as events proved.

The Reality

From time to time over the years, there have been those who have depreciated the great victory and have proposed that there was nothing special about the achievements of Fighter Command and our people. I have listed below and refuted some of such harmful and unfair allegations. Our pilots and aircrews deserve a true and honoured memory.

In his biography of Winston Churchill published in 2001, the late Lord and Liberal/Labour politician Roy Jenkins wrote that the Battle of Britain resulted in a draw between the British and the Germans. It is incredible that the defeat by Fighter Command of the German aerial attacks over this country with more than 2,000 enemy aircraft to pave the way for a German invasion a few weeks later, could be described by Jenkins as a *draw*. How could he have made such a statement in a biography of Winston Churchill? The planned invasion was abandoned and Britain remained a free if battered country. His statement that the Battle of Britain was a draw is clearly untenable.

He makes a reference to fighting against Me109s as 'knightly jousting', which bears no relationship to the reality of so many young men being shot down in flames by an enemy they had not even seen. The principles of jousting are that the opponents start the combat facing each other at opposite ends, with equal mounts and weapons, and commence the attack together at a given signal. It is a sport with no intention of destroying the opponent. He was obviously out of touch with the Battle.

In 1940 the Nazi Germans attacked England as a preliminary to invasion, and were the harbingers of death and destruction to our citizens. In the event they were beaten back, having lost more than 1,800 operational front-line aircraft and more than 2,600 of their best battle trained pilots and crews. With our losses of 1,038 aircraft and 544 aircrew, it could hardly be referred to as a draw on a simple statistical basis. The previously victorious Germans had been bested and they had lost three crucial months in their attack on Russia, sufficient for them to fail there as well.

Our squadrons, although heavily outnumbered, forced back the Luftwaffe bomber formations and so prevented the invasion. In its simplest form the German target was the destruction or immobilisation of

Fighter Command by mid-September. They totally failed in the task set them by their Führer. Failure cannot call itself a draw. The Germans could not conquer our nation as they had others in Europe, and they were forced to withdraw their aerial armadas back to the Continent, where Reichsmarschall Goering accused his pilots of cowardice because they had failed to defeat Fighter Command. Certainly Churchill, our fighting services, and clearly the people of Britain did not regard the Battle of Britain as a draw. The Battle was won by Britain in 1940, but the war could not be won until 1945 and then only with the crucial support of our allies.

On one television programme on the Battle of Britain, the producers appear to have set out to show that there was a serious rift between officer pilots and newly arrived Volunteer Reserve sergeant pilots, who were reportedly badly housed and given the most dangerous jobs in action against the Luftwaffe. Not surprisingly, in 1940 most peacetime RAF stations were overcrowded and many personnel were billeted out. We all had to do the best we could, from which was coined the well worn phrase 'Don't you know there's a war on?' In the same TV programme, one of the pilots interviewed said that his squadron had lost four of its squadron commanders in one month. His statement confirmed the truth that it was more dangerous to be an officer squadron leader than to be a VR sergeant pilot. I am afraid that some viewers may have believed the misleading picture that was presented. They were obviously unaware that many VR sergeant pilots were commissioned before and during the Battle and later on many of them achieved high commissioned rank in the post-war RAF. Their achievements in the Battle as fighter pilots were recognised and honoured. We certainly had officers and sergeants in the squadrons and rightly so, but in the air we were Red 1 or Blue 3. We all flew the same aircraft with the same number of guns and met the same enemy.

One writer has suggested that the Germans lost the Battle because the Me109 factories were producing fewer replacement aircraft than the British factories. Surely it is to the credit of Fighter Command that the much-vaunted Me109s were being shot down in higher numbers than the Germans had expected and had planned for.

There are others who have claimed that we weren't really outnumbered by the Luftwaffe and that the Me109s were at a major disadvantage in their combat against our fighters. They argued that as the German fighters had only a limited range of operation, they could only spend a restricted time over England. But during September Me109s were able to fly with their bombers up to London – 70 miles. If their aircraft specification was unsuitable for their war plans over England, then this surely is a condemnation of the operational planning of the Nazi high command, and should not be used to detract from Fighter Command achievement.

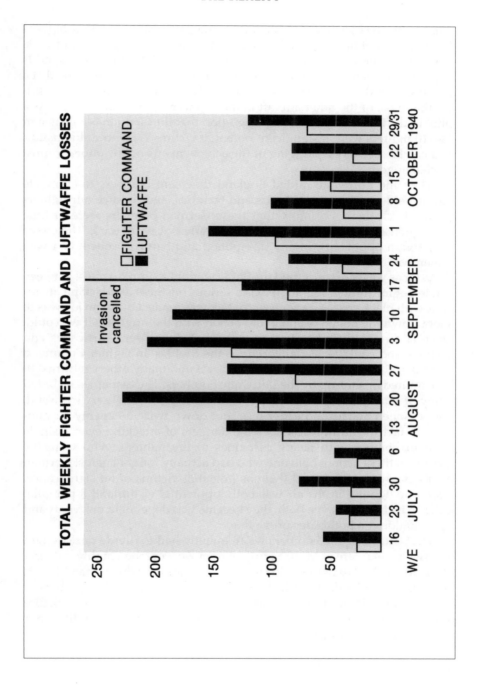

One author has written in his book on the Battle of Britain that our 754 Hurricanes and Spitfires would be pitted against 1,464 fighters and 1,808 bombers of the Luftwaffe, a ratio against us of 4.5:1. However, he adds that the Hurricane and Spitfires, comparing like with like, would really be battling with the 1,107 Me109s, a much reduced ratio of 1.5:1. He considers that most of the other aircraft in the sky were 'potential victims'. As a pilot in the Battle I find that his suggestion that the German bombers and Me110 fighters were insignificant potential victims is far from the reality, and can be seen as disparaging of the achievements of our pilots. It must be challenged.

When the Luftwaffe raided England they sent bombers to eliminate our airfields, attack our harbours and factories, and to force our fighters up to attack them. To imply that these German bombers were of little consequence in our battles with the Luftwaffe is way off track. They were very tough opponents, highly disciplined and battled trained, as I well remember.

As far as we were concerned the Battle was not a simple contest between single-engine fighter aircraft, it was a serious business of attacking all aircraft with black crosses as soon as contact was made. Our main job was to shoot down the bombers and avoid action with their fighters if we could. Over 11 Group their bomber gunners shot down our Hurricanes and Spitfires and could be as dangerous as the Me109s. In Fighter Command more than 100 of our pilots were shot down and many others returned to base injured or shot-up by the Luftwaffe bombers. The casualties included many of our most experienced pilots, including S/Ldr Peter Townsend; one seasoned Squadron Leader was shot down twice by enemy air gunners. In fact the author describes the dangers of attacking even a single German bomber with heavy casualties to the fighters. Who were the victims in these actions? No one who had actually fought against German bombers could ever regard them as potential victims of no significance. Everyone fighting in the air was both a potential victim and a potential killer. Which one, or even both, they became was dependent on events and the casualties on both sides prove this.

When attacking the bombers we frequently had to divide our strength into two to take care of Me109s, from whom we were then highly vulnerable to attack. Me110 twin-engine fighters were less of a threat than Me109s but still had to be dealt with. In action and statistically, the numbers of bombers and Me110s must be added to the Me109s to get the true picture of our being greatly outnumbered, and to give honourable credit to our pilots for their achievement.

CHAPTER 26

Our Leaders

It would be difficult to talk about any aspect of war in 1940 without referring to the greatest leader of Britain in the 20th Century. Whenever we could, our fighter pilots, with the Nation, and many other people in occupied Europe in secret, listened to the wireless to hear Winston Churchill, our great Prime Minister. His speeches were inspiring and moving as they still are today.

Winston Churchill was certainly a great man to our fighter pilots. Without him there would not have been a Battle of Britain, and instead there would have been all the horrors of Nazi occupation that we and Europe would then have suffered for decades. Without Churchill we would not have been inspired and led to victory. He loved Britain and the British people. He was an exceptional man of great stature. Sixty-five years later it would seem that the mould for such a man has been broken.

Air Chief Marshal Sir Hugh Dowding, known affectionately to the pilots as 'Stuffy', led Fighter Command in their defeat of the Luftwaffe. There is no question that Dowding was the Architect of Victory. If there had been anyone else of his stature, he would have been replaced before the Battle commenced. Bearing in mind their great need for him to lead Fighter Command, the Air Ministry treated him with little respect at this critical time, and indeed he was under formal notice of retirement with a specific date just before the Battle started. This inexplicable decision was made at a time when he was to be charged with the defence of Britain against the aerial might of Germany. The Air Ministry appear to have been more concerned with getting rid of him, rather than giving him their fullest support at this time of great threat to the Country.

Sadly, there was a Cabal of politicians and senior officers at Air Ministry, including Air Vice-Marshal Douglas, Deputy CAS, who planned to have Dowding removed from office, in spite of his great achievement in winning the Battle.

A very senior meeting of officers of Air rank was called at the Air Ministry on the 17th October 1940 and chaired by AVM Douglas. I have called this meeting the 'Meeting of Shame'. Ostensibly it was called to discuss fighter tactics with special reference to the extension of the use of

Big Wings in the defence of Britain. One would have thought that it was the responsibility of Fighter Command to deal on its own with tactics. It is difficult to imagine what contribution on changing tactics could have been made by armchair Air Marshals whose operational experience related to biplanes in World War I. It is now clear that the real purpose of the meeting was to impugn Dowding's policies and tactics during the Battle, and with the implication of unnecessary casualties and delays in winning the victory. A major criticism and a key factor claimed was his failure to use Big Wing formations in the battle and to provide adequate defence against night bombing.

In the second part of this book I review this Meeting of Shame in detail and present the evidence for my conclusions, based on official documents. I expose the shameful behaviour at this meeting and afterwards, and also the activities of the Cabal and others who were involved. I also reveal the real and dishonourable reason for Dowding's dismissal, which in fact serves to accentuate the greatness of this man.

Soon after the meeting, Dowding was ignominiously dismissed without promotion or suitable honour and with no public statement commending his great contribution and leadership. He was replaced as Commander-in-Chief by Air Vice-Marshal Douglas, a member of the Cabal that planned his removal from office. Church bells were rung across Britain at Christmas 1940 to celebrate that the dangers of immediate invasion were past; Dowding was not present in Britain to hear the celebration. He had been sent to the United States, to a position not of his choosing and for which he was quite unsuited.

Dowding loved his fighter pilots, his 'chicks' as he called them, and cared and fought for them as he had done for his fighter pilots in WWI, for which he had been criticised and removed from operational command. To him the word 'casualties' always meant pilot losses. Other senior officers saw the word as applying to aircraft losses. Our pilots knew this and never forgave the Air Ministry and its Air Officers for their cavalier and grossly unfair treatment of their Commander-in-Chief. They felt it carried with it an implied reflection on their achievements in the Battle of Britain. Air Vice-Marshal Park directed the fight against the Luftwaffe from 11 Group Headquarters at Uxbridge. Throughout the Battle, and at the time of Dunkirk, he controlled the disposition of his 19 squadrons, and set the tactics of interception, which involved instant decision.

He carried the responsibility for the success or failure on a day-to-day, hour-to-hour basis against the Luftwaffe. He must rank as one of the most outstanding tactical Commanders in aerial warfare history whose daily decisions were to affect the course of British and European history. There had been no previous experience of such warfare on which to call. His achievement deserved high honour, which he did not receive.

Within a month of Dowding's dismissal, Park was summarily removed from office by the Air Ministry and downgraded to command a Group in Training Command. Park's removal from his command was inevitable. Park's place as the Commander of the valiant 11 Group was taken over by AVM Leigh-Mallory of 12 Group, who had failed to co-operate with him in the Battle, and had set up the myth of the Big Wing Philosophy in the attempt to belittle Dowding's competence as C-in-C of Fighter Command. Thus did the politicians and senior officers at the Air Ministry reward the victors of the Battle.

The Air Ministry antagonism against Dowding was clearly made public in an official Air Ministry booklet on the Battle of Britain published in 1941. Dowding's name was not mentioned even once, although Goering was referred to on 12 occasions without any reference to his status as the Commander in Chief of the Luftwaffe offensive. When Churchill found out about this, he ordered the booklet to be withdrawn, and reprinted, telling of the part played by Air Chief Marshal Sir Hugh Dowding.

CHAPTER 27

Our Fighter Pilots

And now to honour our Fighter Pilots with their assumed, unauthorised, cherished, and guarded right to have their top tunic button undone, and to wear flying boots in the Mess.

We were helped to withstand the pressures on us by our relaxed attitude to life, and by our always present special sense of humour. We needed a loose rein and most of our station commanders understood this.

Many historians have already written of the courage and the sacrifices made by our young men. Even at the worst time in the Battle, they never failed to attack the bombers, though heavily outnumbered, and despite the casualties in their squadron. Whatever were their personal fears, these were never discussed but were held in check. There were no professional counsellors for us at dispersal, fortunately, but I believe that there was a bond or spirit within the Flight that gave the pilots mutual support for the next scramble. When I write about our pilots I include of course the aircrews of our Blenheims and Defiants, the air gunners and the AI operators, who flew with the pilots and showed the same courage and made the same sacrifice.

The German pilots and aircrew were all full-time professional officers, NCOs and airmen with previous service in real wars, and with tactics based on their battle experience. By contrast, Fighter Command was made up of regular officers from Cranwell, Short Service Commission officers, regular sergeant pilots, volunteer pilots in the Auxiliary Air Force and Volunteer Reserve, commissioned and NCOs, who had civilian jobs and trained at weekends. There were also some pilots from University Air Squadrons and from the Fleet Air Arm. A total of 2,936 pilots of Fighter Command flew on operations in the Battle.

All of these pilots from different backgrounds, bonded together in flights and battled valiantly. Apart from the AAF Squadrons, the squadron commanders and flight commanders were pre-war regular officers. It was a surprise and comfort to find that Volunteer Reserve pilots quickly proved their worth in the squadrons. In addition, we had volunteer pilots from 14 other countries, including 145 pilots from Poland and 88 from Czechoslovakia, who had battled their way across Europe and North

Africa, determined to fight back against the Nazis who had invaded and overrun their country. Surprisingly there were only 13 pilots from France in the Battle.

The Poles and the Czechs were retrained in England in time to form two Polish and two Czechoslovakian squadrons that made their own mark in the Battle.

The list on page 102 shows the countries represented, a record that not only Britain but the whole of Europe should treasure.

Although most of the fighting took place over 11 Group territory with 11 Group squadrons, 10 Group squadrons were involved in a great deal of the action, and their pilots made an important contribution to the victory. The pilots of 12 Group squadrons, who were for a while isolated from the real battle, fought with the same courage and tenacity as 10 and 11 Group pilots, as indeed had the pilots in 13 Group defending the north.

The average age of the pilots was the early twenties; both of my COs were 30 and we all thought they were much too old to be flying Spitfires. I think now we were wrong about age assessment. The first men chosen to fly into Outer Space some years later were in their forties! Perhaps being a successful fighter pilot was more a function of the spirit than of the numbers of years.

They were wonderful young men full of humour, waiting for the bell to ring to send them off to intercept German formations that outnumbered them, sometimes by as much as 10.1. Sadly 544 of them were killed in the Battle. The deaths of our friends were accepted and not discussed. Tomorrow it could be our turn. Funerals were rarely attended by pilots. We preferred our bereavement to be private.

In the mid-1930s Goering was bragging about the quality of the Luftwaffe aircraft to Marshal of the Royal Air Force Lord Trenchard, who replied to him, 'It's the men that matter Goering, it's the men'.

Knowing the background of the pilots, and the countries from which they came to fight the Germans, perhaps the real victory of the Battle of Britain was the triumph of a democratic Britain and her friends across the world, over the apparently invincible might of the military machine of the Nazi dictatorship.

The basic fighting units in Fighter Command were the squadron and the flights. They were very tight knit, in the air and on the ground. And so to hold them in my memory I quote from Shakespeare, Henry V:

'We few, we happy few, we band of brothers.'

I think we shall not see their like again.

Some fifty years after the Battle, a statue of Lord Dowding was erected outside the RAF Church of St Clement Danes in London, subscribed

NATIONALITY OF FIGHTER COMMAND PILOTS
IN THE BATTLE OF BRITAIN

COUNTRY	FLEW ON OPERATIONS
UK	2341
POLAND	145
NEW ZEALAND	127
CANADA	112
CZECHOSLOVAKIA	88
BELGIUM	28
SOUTH AFRICA	25
AUSTRALIA	32
FRANCE	13
EIRE	10
USA	9
SOUTHERN RHODESIA	3
BARBADOS	1
JAMAICA	1
NEWFOUNDLAND	1
TOTAL	2936

544 PILOTS AND AIRCREW MADE THE GREAT SACRIFICE

to by his pilots and others who appreciated his great achievement. Queen Elizabeth the Queen Mother unveiled the statue, but there was no contribution or presence from the British Government and no official appreciation from the many countries in Europe who owed their freedom to his victory over Nazi Germany.

The Battle of Britain Was Well Won

There can be no doubt that the Battle was won. There was no invasion in 1940 or in 1941. Although officially the Battle ended on 31st October 1940, the Luftwaffe continued to fly in small numbers by day over British territory in November and for some months after that. If we accept that the Battle was fought to prevent invasion, then it was certainly won by 30th September, the last day of major attacks on London. It was by then too late for an invasion. However, earlier in the month the invasion barges had started to move away from the French ports. With the change of tactics and the adverse weather expected in October, the Air Ministry must have known that the 1940 defensive battle was over. In fact Hitler had already cancelled the invasion on 17th September, but made no public announcement of this defeat of his great Luftwaffe.

We had won the Battle but had the Battle been won well? I should have thought that having prevented the invasion of Britain and thereby saving us from the awful horrors of Nazi occupation, our people and history would say it was indeed well won. But the air marshals at the Air Ministry were intent on removing Dowding without acclaim for his great achievement. I trust my work has given convincing evidence to prove that from a strategic and tactical aspect the charge invested in Dowding in July had been well met. The evidence shows Dowding's and Park's tactics of using single and pairs of squadrons throughout the Battle to have been totally correct. Leigh-Mallory, a disloyal subordinate, challenged his Commander-in-Chief using a five-squadron wing over 11 Group without prior consultation. History has now shown his wing to have been unprepared, badly led and ineffective, except for a few good weather days in September with major raids on London. It could also have been disruptive in the control of finely tuned interceptions over 11 Group.

Air Chief Marshal Dowding's contribution to the victory was outstanding. He was the Architect and Victor of the Battle of Britain.

It is difficult to assess what could be considered as acceptable casualties. All casualties are too many. Could we use the 80% casualties in the 1st Airborne Division at Arnhem in 1944 as a yardstick? How can anyone attempt to make a finite judgement on the deaths of over 500 of our pilots and aircrew with many others wounded, battling against overwhelming odds at 20,000 feet?

And what about the many thousands of civilian casualties caused by the German bombing. Dowding had a moral responsibility for these too. His decision to attack the enemy immediately they were in range must have significantly reduced civilian casualties, compared with allowing the enemy to drop their bombs before attacking, as favoured by Douglas and Leigh-Mallory. Undoubtedly this policy increased the hazards to our pilots, but who would be prepared to weigh the balance?

Although heavily outnumbered, our fighter squadrons beat back the Luftwaffe bombers and fighters, and the Germans abandoned their plans to invade and occupy Britain, which remained a free and democratic country. Four years later we became the springboard for the Allied forces to invade Europe and free the many occupied countries.

In 1940 the ordinary people of Britain saved democracy – in the air, at sea and in the cities of our beloved Country. We all believed then that in winning the Battle of Britain we had retained British sovereignty, freedom and independence for centuries. I pray that 65 years later we ordinary people will once again stand firm and save Britain and its people from undemocratic domination by power-seeking European politicians with no regards for the rights to freedom of the British people.

A Great Nation

Britain's history of fighting for the people's freedom goes back many centuries, but we have failed to teach our children pride in Britain's never ending battle to be free – not only for ourselves, but for most of the countries of Europe. We stood defiant against Nazi Germany in 1940, and but for Britain's sacrifice we would all be speaking German. Religious and ethnic minority groups would not exist.

We must not allow the freedom we cherish and have fought for at great cost to be taken by default or stealth. We have survived as an independent nation, respected for our English traditions throughout the world. Sadly at the present time our national flag appears to have greater honour and standing in the world outside than it does at home.

If we give up our freedom and our currency, our English laws and Parliamentary democracy to be totally committed to membership of a United States of Europe as one of 25, or even more, miscellaneous nations, we shall lose sovereignty and freedom and we shall merge into anonymity with no pride in our country and ourselves. We will have no rights as citizens. Our great sacrifices of 1940 will have been for naught.

If we finally commit to the European Union without democratic consent, the Battle of Britain will not have been a Great Victory – it will merely have been a pointless sacrifice by our people. Our freedom and way of life are being stolen away from us by clandestine policies, and will soon have been lost forever. There will be no way back. The citizens of Britain will be irretrievably lost in the morass of Brussels bureaucracy.

In 1940 we fought and sacrificed for the right to be free people, able to decide our own future. What are the generations of today going to do? It is getting very late.

Our lives have become locked into undemocratic regulations and the blackmail of political correctness – not simply because of the machinations of power-seeking people, but because the voices of ordinary decent people are not heeded. We must not let it happen. When I was a young man in 1939 I was so proud to be English. Now after a thousand years of history I am told that there is no such nationality.

How could I explain to our pilots and our people of 1940, many still alive, that their great sacrifices were in vain and that 65 years later we could soon be a single state in a conglomerate of European countries, having lost our English birthright, our freedom and our right to elected self government? Our fight for our independence over the centuries will finally have been lost by stealth.

I now believe that our freedom as a nation, so nearly lost in 1940, has been insidiously taken from us, without the knowledge and democratic consent of the ordinary people. The British people and the English nation will soon be lost to history in a mass of at least 25 unrelated countries with no common cultures or language, or democratically agreed codes of law. Is this how it is all to end? We English people are proud people, as proud of our nationality as the Scottish and Welsh people are of theirs. We deserve better.

In this book I have tried to tell the truth about a part of Britain's heritage, but it should really have been set in stone, as the European Union has already set out to obliterate our history, and perhaps soon my book could be banned. They have already deleted England from their political structure. In 1940 Hitler and his Nazis found that the spirit of a great people could not be destroyed by air armadas. We must now ensure that England cannot be erased from our lives and great past, by the machinations of bureaucrats in Britain and across the Channel, and replaced by seven unelected quangos, subject to the authority of faceless men in Brussels.

Wake up England!

Part Two

Dowding A Man of History

1

The Big Wing Philosophy

Introduction

In July 1940 Britain was in mortal danger. The Germans had over-run Europe and had manned the French coastal regions across the Channel some 23 miles away at the nearest point. The Germans planned to invade and occupy England, and the rest of the world expected us to surrender or to be beaten if we fought on.

Back in England, even with our soldiers evacuated from Dunkirk, we had no defence on the ground adequate to defend our shores. The guns, armoured vehicles, and heavy equipment of our British Expeditionary Force had perforce been left behind. But the Germans could not invade across the Channel until they had destroyed or neutralised Fighter Command, and had achieved continuous air supremacy over the Channel and the south of England. Only our fighter squadrons could save Britain from destruction by the Luftwaffe bombers, followed by invasion. Winston Churchill's quote at the time, 'Our fate now depended upon victory in the air', set the scene simply and with alarming clarity.

It was in this environment of great danger to Britain's existence that strenuous efforts were made by a cabal of senior officers and members of Parliament to have Air Chief Marshal Sir Hugh Dowding removed from his vital position as Commander in Chief of Fighter Command.

There have always been a breed of 'men of ambition', for whom ambition dominates their lives. They will use events and people without hesitation to attain their goals. Wars are used as opportunities and people are numbers. Where total ambition exists, honour and loyalty have little place.

Part Two of this book is also about the Battle of Britain, but it is not just an exposition of battles in the sky, and tactics and pilots, it is also a study of commanders and leaders in time of war and great danger. To understand what happened in Fighter Command and the Air Ministry in 1940, it is necessary to understand the character and motivation of the personalities involved. War brings out the best in some people and the worst in others.

When I first started my research for my book about the restoration of honour to ACM Sir Hugh Dowding, it was planned as a self-contained volume. Events over the years have modified my intention, as I realised that his great achievement depended on many other people who should also be honoured and remembered by our present generations. Part One of the book can show to the British people of today that Fighter Command and the citizens of my generation won the Battle. A 'Great Victory' stands alone, but it is an essential component in the claim for the restoration of honour to Dowding.

Part Two is quite a different story, which tells of dishonour, a cabal and machinations by senior RAF officers to degrade the achievements of the Architect of Victory. They carried out their plotting to further their personal causes and ambitions during the time when Fighter Command was fighting for its very existence.

The following pages will show that their behaviour is to the shame of the Air Ministry of 1940. This however, can in no way harm the great reputation of the Royal Air Force, built up and honoured since its formation in 1918, by the courage and achievements of its young pilots and aircrews in all the Commands.

CHAPTER 1

The Commanders

Air Chief Marshal Sir Hugh Dowding

In World War One in 1916, Lieutenant Colonel Hugh Dowding commanded a Wing of fighter squadrons in France. After one of his squadrons had received very heavy casualties, he asked Major General Hugh Trenchard, his commander, for the squadron to be sent on rest. Trenchard refused at first but finally agreed. He considered Dowding as being soft because of his concern for his pilots, and soon relieved him of his appointment, returning him to Britain where he commanded a training brigade.

Dowding had also challenged Trenchard about the danger of fitting a new propeller to his squadrons' aircraft. At some risk to himself Dowding tested the propeller in the air and proved Trenchard to have been wrong. Trenchard realised that Dowding was his own man and would challenge him for a good cause. At this time, Dowding as a Lieutenant Colonel was not a threat to Trenchard, only an irritation, but he was still put safely away from the action

In his biography of Dowding, Robert Wright states that, at the end of the war, Dowding received a letter informing him that his services would not be required in the Royal Air Force, and that he was to return to the Royal Artillery, his original service. This must have been a serious blow to Dowding. Fortunately at that time Dowding was serving under the command of Vice-Admiral Sir Vyell Vyvyan, who was aware of his qualities. Vyvyan went out of his way to tackle Trenchard several times about the situation and finally Dowding was granted a permanent commission as a Group Captain in the RAF. This difficult relationship between the two men was to emerge again in the late thirties by which time Dowding was an Air Chief Marshal.

A prime difference between the two men is characterised by Trenchard's decision in WWI to refuse the use of parachutes for our pilots, as he felt that they might have been tempted to bale out too soon. Many of them were thus faced with the choice of jumping out to their death or staying with their aircraft, which was on fire or out of control. Balloon observers

112

were however equipped with parachutes. Fortunately for so many of our pilots, Trenchard had no influence on the use of parachutes by WWII. From personal experience I know that pilots only take to their parachutes when the alternative is almost certain death. Dowding however was most concerned about the welfare of his pilots and always fought to ensure that they had the best equipment, including bullet proof windscreens and armour plate protection in the cockpit.

Dowding with the help of his loyal officers and his pilots won the Battle and saved Britain. To the shame of the Air Council and the politicians, this was never publicly acknowledged, not even when the Victory Bells were rung in the churches, to celebrate that the German attempts to invade us in 1940 had been defeated.

As a contrast later in the war, Lieutenant General Sir Bernard Montgomery received instant acclaim after his victory at El Alamein, which was far less crucial to Britain's existence. To achieve this he had higher strength than the Germans, on the ground and in the air. He was certainly not outnumbered as Fighter Command had been. Within weeks of his victory, he had been promoted to General and awarded the KCB.

As Commander-in-Chief of Fighter Command, Dowding's responsibilities also included the Radar Defence System (RDF), the Observer Corps, the Balloon Command and close liaison with our anti-aircraft gun defences. He carried the burden of defeating the Nazi aerial armadas to ensure that we remained a free and democratic country. When the Luftwaffe attacks on Britain started in earnest in mid-August, Winston Churchill, for the only time in the war, was powerless to take action to fight for the destiny of Britain. He could only watch and wait with the rest of Britain and indeed with the whole world.

I wonder if Churchill, at the time of Fighter Command's greatest strain in early September, remembered Dowding's successful protest the previous June against him sending any more Spitfires to help France fighting a battle that was already lost. If so, he must surely have been grateful for the courage and integrity of this man who dared to challenge his decisions as Prime Minister.

The Charge Given to Dowding

After three years' service as Commander-in-Chief, Dowding's retirement from the RAF had been considered by the Air Ministry for the *fourth* time in July 1940. With his previous appointment as Director of Research and Development at the Air Ministry, he had been responsible for the development of our eight-gun high speed fighters, the RDF warning system so crucial for our fighter defence, and for later setting up the Group organisations and the system of sector control of our fighter squadrons, the most advanced in the world. There really was no one else who could have been entrusted with our defence against such a formidable and evil enemy, certainly the most powerful air force of any nation.

The Chief of Air Staff, ACM Newall, extended his date of retirement to 31st October 1940 – a date which Dowding had to accept. How odd to be setting a retirement date only three months away of the only man who could save Britain from invasion, when the battle for survival was just about to begin. This is an example of the strange behaviour of some Air Ministry senior officers, remote from the realities and perils of the impending battle. The need for Dowding's early removal from the Royal Air Force was still dominant in the minds of a powerful group of people even though we were now at war with Germany and faced with the threat of invasion. However, this October date was changed once again and delayed to an open one after intervention by Prime Minister Churchill.

The charge to Dowding as leader of the defence, either written, spoken or implied should have been quite clear and precise. There is I believe no written record of such a charge, crucial to a military leader with such heavy responsibilities.

It should have been simply: 'The Germans are planning to invade Britain within the next three months. They cannot do so until and unless Fighter Command is destroyed or rendered ineffective. You are to resist their attacks on this country at least until the end of September, but must at all costs remain a viable fighting force.'

Air Vice-Marshal Keith Park AOC 11 Group

Keith Park, a New Zealander, had been a very successful fighter pilot in World War I, and afterwards he continued to extend his fighter experience in the RAF. By 1938 he was a Group Captain commanding Tangmere Fighter Station. He was promoted to Air Commodore and transferred to HQ Fighter Command for the very important post of Senior Air Staff Officer, effectively Dowding's deputy. He worked well with Dowding who in early 1940 promoted him over the heads of air vice-marshals in Fighter Command, to take over the key command of 11 Group in the south-east of England with promotion to Air Vice-Marshal. This group would bear the brunt of the Battle with the Luftwaffe, just across the Channel and less than 100 miles from London.

He had a formidable task – to defend 11 Group and London with a maximum of 300 day-fighters available against a large proportion of the 2,000 Luftwaffe aircraft, that had been concentrating across the Channel. The German tactics changed weekly and then daily. Park controlled the defensive battle hour-by-hour, adapting to the changing tactics, composition and size of the German formations with the best information he could receive from the RDF stations and the Observer Corps. He believed that his prime purpose was to shoot down the bombers before they reached their targets, a policy expressed by Dowding, but which was surprisingly opposed by AVM Douglas the Deputy CAS and others at the Air Ministry.

His promotion to 11 Group had been a serious rebuff to AVM Leigh-Mallory who previously had been one rank senior to Park, and had already been the 12 Group Commander for two years. With the slight of Park's promotion, friendly co-operation between them was never likely. The relationship between Dowding and Leigh-Mallory had never been good, but this passing over in 1940 could only have exacerbated his feelings against his Commander-in-Chief.

Air Vice-Marshal Trafford Leigh-Mallory AOC 12 Group

Leigh-Mallory, 48 years old, commanded 12 Group, which had the responsibility for the defence of the Midlands with its industrial targets. He was very ambitious and had risen from the rank of Squadron Leader in WWI to the status of Group Commander in 1940 with the rank of Air Vice-Marshal. Although Leigh-Mallory was a very experienced specialist on army co-operation tactics, his lack of fighter experience was a disadvantage. He never seemed to achieve a real understanding of the operational handling of his fighter units in a defensive battle, or even offensive battles later in the war.

When the Germans attacked and blitzed through France in May 1940 and occupied the Channel coast, 12 Group responsibilities should have been changed. The main thrust of any bomber attack by day would come from northern France and Belgium. It was soon proved that German bomber formations could not operate by day without heavy fighter escort. This limited the bombing and therefore the fighting to the 11 Group Sector. No. 12 Group had no major enemy to fight, and so there were no victories and no glory for their commander. It had been relegated to the second division, although still with the responsibility of defending the Midlands against unlikely major day attacks.

Operating from Digby in 12 Group, my squadron saw no changes in previous routine operations apart from our action over Dunkirk. Through July and the first half of August, we waited day after day without engagement with the enemy. From newspaper and BBC reports we knew that our fellow squadrons were already engaged in heavy fighting over the Channel with the Luftwaffe fighters and bombers. At the end of August, when the 11 Group squadrons were under severe pressure from the Luftwaffe, we used to fly south into Duxford, adjacent to the 11 Group Sector, to join other squadrons there to patrol over 11 Group airfields. We were still not being directly vectored on to the enemy, and we resented this because we believed we had a right to be part of the action. At that time I personally felt that there was a brick wall between our groups preventing us from helping our hard-pressed comrades.

Leigh-Mallory needed a way to build up a reputation for 12 Group, and Squadron Leader Bader, already the national legless hero of No. 242 Squadron, seemed to be the key especially after his exceptional claims of victories on 30th August. To achieve success he needed a 12 Group persona. For a number of days 12 Group had 'loaned' single squadrons to patrol 11 Group sector airfields, but with little action and so there was no publicity.

His pilots were anxious for combat with the Luftwaffe. After the action of 30th August, Leigh-Mallory initiated the first ad hoc Wing of three squadrons led by his protégé Bader with No. 242 Squadron. The Duxford Wing was made available to 11 Group only as a three- or five-Squadron formation with the Duxford cachet or not at all. Leigh-Mallory had crossed swords with Dowding in the past, and his loyalty was to be put to the test. With his resentment of Park's rapid promotion he could have welcomed the chance to put forward his own defensive policies.

At the end of his biography of Leigh-Mallory, *Big Wing*, Bill Newton Dunn his great nephew writes:

> Leigh-Mallory, of course never had the 'right' job. Sidelined at 12 Group in 1940, in Fighter Command in 1943 when the short range of our Spitfires prevented any real offensive work, and in 1944 the wretched unwanted Allied Expeditionary Air Forces (of which he was Commander-in-Chief) for the invasion of France.

His 11 Group sweeps over Dieppe and France in 1941 and 1942 with heavy casualties can hardly be considered right jobs. Perhaps the simple answer was that he was never the 'right' man for operational posts. Perhaps he was just an administrator as assessed by German Intelligence staff.

When the battle cruisers *Scharnhorst* and *Gneisenau* made their startling dash from Brest through the Channel past Dover, his staff had difficulty in persuading him to leave a grand parade he was inspecting, so that he could take crucial decisions for action by Fighter Command aircraft against the enemy ships. Incredibly the battle cruisers won through to Germany although finally damaged by mines.

CHAPTER 2

Defence Structure

Structure and Responsibilities

By the time the Battle commenced in July, Fighter Command had been organised into Groups, 10, 11, 12 and 13. All the Groups had Hurricane and Spitfire squadrons for day fighting. Groups 12 and 13 each had a squadron of Defiant day-fighters which had been transferred to night fighting duties. There were six squadrons of twin engine Blenheims for use against the German night bombers.

No. 11 Group commanded by AVM Park with 19 day-fighter squadrons was responsible for the defence of the south coast and London. With the Luftwaffe across the Channel and bomber raids only possible with Me109 support, the fighting would be mainly confined to the 11 Group Sector. This is where most of the battle was fought with most of the casualties.

No. 12 Group commanded by AVM Leigh-Mallory with 11 squadrons had been crucial to the defence of the industrial Midlands in 1939. With the defeat of France and the move of the Luftwaffe to operate from airfields near the French coast, the role of 12 Group should have changed, and its function could sensibly have become that of an active operational reserve.

No. 10 Group commanded by AVM Sir Quinton Brand with 7 day-fighter squadrons, protected the West of England and Wales. Its task was to defend against Luftwaffe bombers flying in from the Cherbourg area, a long sea crossing for Me109s, but within range for Me110 fighter escorts. It was immediately to the west of 11 Group, facing the Channel and the enemy, and was strengthened by mutual support with 11 Group

No. 13 Group commanded by AVM John Saul with 10½ day-fighter squadrons protected the north of England and Scotland. On 15th August the Luftwaffe 5th Air Fleet made a major attack across the North Sea from Norway against the north of England. It was a disaster for the German bombers with unacceptable losses. For the rest of the Battle no major German formations attacked the north-east of England. However 13 Group maintained continuous convoy patrols and intercepted small coastal raids.

The Groups had between 4 and 7 Sectors, with up to 4 day-fighter squadrons each, normally operating from 2 airfields. The enemy raids were territorially allocated by Fighter Command to the Groups, who ordered their Sectors to come to readiness or to dispatch squadrons against specific raids. Dowding's instructions were quite clear from 1939, that Group Commanders dealt with raids over their own territories. The warning plots received at the RDF stations were passed to Fighter Command who used this information to plot the enemy activity – in numbers and in height. The Observer Corps continued the plotting inland, but the quality of this information depended on the cloud conditions and visibility.

In principle, Dowding's structure was quite rigid, but with the speed of flight and unexpected changes in direction, flexibility of control was essential. Fighter Command's prime responsibility was to stay in being; but its other responsibility was to attack the bombers before they reached their target whenever possible. At all times the squadrons had to be ready to fly to the beaches to repel the invasion when it came. AVM Park issued a directive warning to squadrons that in the event of invasion, squadrons could expect to carry out eight sorties a day, landing mainly only to re-arm. This 'hit, return, and re-arm' would need to be carried out by small formations. He was certainly not thinking in terms of Big Wings for defensive operations when the invasion started.

Fighter Command was fighting a defensive battle against an enemy with vastly superior numbers, 750 day-fighters versus 2,350 enemy bombers and fighters. Dowding had to protect the whole of the British coastline and had to divide his forces, so that only 19 of his squadrons faced the Germans across the Channel with reserve support from 10 Group and, it was hoped, from 12 Group.

The Germans could pick the day and the time or times, the target or targets, the number of bombers, the number of fighters, and the raid formation. They could also send up large groups of Me109s, free of commitment to the bombers, to bounce our squadrons. Park soon recognised the traps and avoided the one-sided combat. To defend against these enemy advantages, two factors were paramount.

1. The quality of the RDF and Observer Corps plots received and their assessment.
2. Highly competent interception by an effective number of squadrons with adequate height.

Concentration of Strength

Leigh-Mallory, Douglas and other senior officers at the Air Ministry with WWI experience were supporters of one of the basic rules of war – that of the benefits of concentration of force. Obviously this is only effective if it is applied at the right place and at the right time. It requires that the force is collected together and held until a precise moment. It also requires accurate information as to the strength, composition, position and movement of the enemy. This philosophy can be carried out successfully by an army on the battlefield, in sea battles, and also in the air with a bombing attack on a stationary ground target used as a means of overwhelming the defences. This was exemplified by the 1,000 bomber raid on Cologne in 1942. It is, however, extremely difficult to use against an enemy, in formations 10 miles long, several thousand feet in depth, and moving at up to 180 miles per hour. The strength and composition and ultimate direction would not be known with any certainty until the last moment.

For a concentrated force to attack a much larger force at only one point could be counter-productive. After the first attack the Wing would be broken up, and could not be used again as a Wing formation until it had straggled back to its bases at Duxford and Fowlmere and refuelled and re-armed.

Concentration of strength is not effective with 5 squadrons attacking at one point against a formation spread out over several miles. German pilots were highly professional and battle-trained. With rigid discipline their formations did not break up, except perhaps from head-on attacks, which were rarely possible. Dowding was right in 1939, when he expressed the view that the basic fighting unit should be the squadron. Two squadrons flying as a pair from the same airfield is a natural increase in strength with no loss of mobility, although when the action started they would fight as two separate squadrons. When based with No. 603 squadron at Hornchurch in October we welcomed flying in a pair with them.

When a number of squadrons are required to attack a large formation together, this can only be effectively and economically achieved by the Group and Sector Controllers who are in touch with the enemy movements and our own aircraft. With time to spare for the long run in to London, it was possible to scramble pairs of squadrons along the route and then to concentrate strength over the Capital as happened on September 15th 1940.

Controllers

In an aerial war, taking place at high speed and with changing altitudes, interceptions were nearly always with an ill-defined force with the potential at any time for a significant variation in its presumed substance. It is important to realise the problems of the Controllers in managing the battle – and to understand why, in all Groups and with all squadrons, it seemed that so often they were sent off late and arrived too low. In Dr Alfred Price's *Battle of Britain Day*, Wing Commander Lord Willoughby de Broke, Park's senior fighter controller at 11 Group, is quoted:

The Group Controller's job was like a glorified game of chess, only infinitely more exciting and responsible as so much was at stake.

When talking to Price in a taped interview many years after the Battle, Squadron Leader Bader said: 'You couldn't blame the Controllers as none of them had been doing it for very long.' This was an unfounded comment as some of the Controllers had been doing the job before Bader had become an operational flying officer and were at least as qualified for their work as he was for his.

Many of the Controllers were or had been RAF pilots, some of them in WWI. This created a special relationship between us with an understanding of our difficulties with the weather, poor visibility, and above all the realisation that the sky is a very big place needing a continuous search in all directions and at all heights, from an enclosed cockpit with a Perspex hood. The basic principle of control was that the controllers were responsible for directing the squadron on to the enemy giving vectors, height and speed. Once, however, the enemy had been sighted and confirmed, total control passed to the formation leader. Disciplined radio communication between the controller and pilots was essential, as without it the whole system of controlled interception would be jeopardised.

At the end of August and the beginning of September when the Luftwaffe attacks were pressing heavily, our formations were often being vectored on to the enemy too low, and were being bounced by Me109s and even Me110s with very heavy casualties. Eventually the flight leaders took matters into their own hands, ignored the Controller's vectors and initially flew north to gain height before making the interception. Even in October we generally took this action to be able to meet the Me109s with a fighting chance. Park realised what was happening but, although he disapproved, our flight commanders still continued to do this with our total support.

The last thing Park needed in his control of this rapidly changing Battle was the presence of a 12 Group maverick wing of fighters anywhere in 11 Group's skies, without discipline and R/T control. Either Bader was totally ignorant of the Fighter Command principles of defence in the use of his squadrons, or he was wilfully defiant of the principles and disciplines to further his own ambitions.

CHAPTER 3

Fighting the Fight

The Battle until 30th August

The German attacks had varied in scale and direction during the Battle. The major coastal attacks had been fought off and now they were attacking the airfields with doubled numbers of Me109s to defend the bombers. From 24th August there was almost continuous sunshine with a great increase in enemy air activity putting a serious strain on 11 Group. Park requested squadron help from 12 Group to protect his northern airfields and particularly his Sector Stations, while his squadrons were away fighting or on the ground refuelling. 12 Group gave single squadron back up, but our pilots were unhappy at this failure to give them a real chance to share in the action. These widespread attacks by the Luftwaffe were difficult to master, and squadrons and even flights were being despatched with only the minimum time to intercept. The increased numbers of Me109s led to the squadrons being bounced on their way up to the bombers and severe casualties resulted.

On 29th August the Luftwaffe despatched more than 650 fighters on provocative sweeps, to which Park wisely made no response, leading the Germans to believe that Fighter Command was at last beginning to weaken. With several raids to fight against in a day, 11 Group needed all the squadrons and flexibility it could obtain. Big Wings would have been useless to defend against these widespread attacks, which continued with the good weather into September. Single squadrons or pairs, readily available from 12 Group were needed. I believe that for a while 11 Group squadrons were scrambled and vectored into the attack with a serious disadvantage of time and in height because of Park's determination to attack the bombers before they had dropped their bombs, laudable with regard to the ground targets but resulting in higher losses for the squadrons. Already under great pressure the squadrons and flights would be sent off, sometimes short of their complement, to arrive at the interception too low. With a preponderance of Me109 fighters in the enemy formations this was a guarantee of disaster.

One of the problems was that the plotting tables were two-dimensional whereas of course the sky is three-dimensional. To the plotters it could appear that an interception had been made but, although the heights were tagged, the crucial importance of accurate height information was not always appreciated in the Ops Room. Plots were not always reliable as to height, as I know to my cost when later, after the Battle, I was bounced at 25,000 feet. I feel that for a while AVM Park may have lost sight of his prime responsibility of the need to preserve Fighter Command, even at the cost of civilian casualties and damage on the ground. Our pilots would always attack the bombers whatever the odds, and Park should have given clearer instructions to the Controllers to make certain that the squadrons were not put into action until they had adequate height, even if the interception was delayed by two or three minutes. Of course the precise height of the enemy aircraft would only be known when they were intercepted – sometimes too late. This is a rare instance in which Park's tactics could be criticised.

Comparison between 11 Group and 12 Group

There were basically two battles taking place with the later addition of a third by the introduction of the Duxford Big Wing. The real battle to the death was fought by 11 Group aided by 10 Group, which normally met the Me110 long-range fighters as well as the bombers. The fighting was continuous with airfields, sector stations and living quarters being bombed. Pilots were exhausted, casualties were high and squadrons had to be drawn out of the line and sent north to be rested. A squadron could despatch the first flight of the day with the full 12 pilots and aircraft and the last sortie could be made with 8 or 9 aircraft or even fewer. Squadrons lost their squadron and flight commanders as well as their pilot officers and sergeant pilots.

In 12 Group there was minimal action and pilots sat around waiting dispiritedly at dispersal, their main sorties being boring convoy patrols over the North Sea in sections of three, and chasing X-raids which were plots on the operations board, generally single aircraft, which had not yet been identified. Our pilots knew that the pilots in 11 Group were fighting to the death, and they wanted to share the action with them. There were no day bombing raids inland in 12 Group to threaten the industrial Midlands during the battle. The pilots were never exhausted and there were few casualties, and our squadrons never needed to be rested. It just didn't make sense.

When the Duxford Wing was set up, Duxford squadrons and associated 12 Group Squadrons suddenly got into the action on 7th September, and on the 9th, 11th, 15th and 18th. At last they were real fighter pilots. Bader's Wing had given them the opportunity to fight the Luftwaffe and they were very grateful. After the first three sorties the three Hurricane squadrons

1. Britain's great wartime leader Winston Spencer Churchill, who became Prime Minister and led the country to fight the Nazi menace and preserve our sovereignty and freedom. Courtesy of the Imperial War Museum HU55521

2. King George VI visiting Fighter Command pilots of No. 611 Squadron at readiness at Digby, Lincolnshire in late 1939. The author is pictured in the squadron line up 2nd from left. Peter Brown Collection

3. Germany's Führer, Adolf Hitler, who brought devastation and terror to most of Europe with his plans to conquer the democratic countries and establish a German master race. Here he is seen in Paris in June 1940. Courtesy of the Imperial War Museum HU3266

4. Reichsmarchall Hermann Goering, Commander-in-Chief of the Luftwaffe. A veteran ace of World War One, he promised Hitler he could destroy Fighter Command within eight days and open the way for an invasion of Britain in the summer of 1940. Courtesy of the Imperial War Museum MH6041

5. Dunkirk, May 1940. The desperate plight of soldiers of the British Expeditionary Force waiting to be rescued off the beaches, after they had been driven back by the German Blitzkrieg. While waiting to embark, the troops were under constant enemy aerial attack in spite of a Fighter Command umbrella at 15,000 feet. Courtesy of the Imperial War Museum NYP68075

6. The miracle of Dunkirk. More than 300,000 Allied troops were brought safely to English shores by the many varied ships and small vessels that took part in the evacuation, some of which were crewed by civilians, who came under heavy fire. Courtesy of the Imperial War Museum HU2108

7. Fighter Command's secret weapon – RDF (Radio Direction Finding) later known as Radar. Developed by scientists under the leadership of Robert Watson-Watt during the mid 1930s. Fortunately Air Chief Marshal Hugh Dowding could envisage the incorporation of this new technology to give early warning of aerial attack within the Fighter Command structure. The photograph shows aerial masts of a Chain 'Home' RDF Station. Courtesy of the Imperial War Museum CH15173

8. Women of the Women's Auxiliary Air Force working in a Group Operations Room undertake the job of plotting RAF and enemy aircraft movements from information gathered by RDF and Observer Corps sites. This information helped to direct RAF squadrons for interception and attack against the Luftwaffe. Richard Smith Collection

9. A formation of Heinkel He111 twin-engine bombers, used extensively for the bombing of Britain by day and by night. By day they had to be protected by large numbers of Me109 fighters, which limited their activities to the south-east of England, within the confines of 11 Group. Courtesy of the Imperial War Museum MH6547

10. This photograph shows typical damage inflicted by our Hurricanes and Spitfires, on the rudder of a Heinkel bomber, which successfully returned to its base in France. Richard Smith Collection

Opposite page

11. *Above left:* Air Chief Marshal Sir Hugh Dowding, Commander-in-Chief of Fighter Command during the Battle of Britain. It was Dowding's foresight and tactics that preserved Fighter Command during the Battle of France that gave Britain a fighting chance in the summer of 1940. Courtesy of the Imperial War Museum DI417

12. *Above right:* Air Vice-Marshal Keith Park, Commander of No. 11 Group Sector, which bore the brunt of the fighting during the Battle, and successfully beat back the Luftwaffe formations. Courtesy of the Imperial War Museum CM4986

13. *Below left:* Air Vice-Marshal Trafford Leigh-Mallory commanded 12 Group, which was responsible for the defence of the industrial Midlands. He was also responsible for the introduction of the controversial Big Wing tactics. Courtesy of the Imperial War Museum PL14388

14. *Below Right:* Squadron Leader Adolph 'Sailor' Malan, a South African, was an outstanding fighter leader during the Battle of Britain and achieved one of the highest personal scores. This photograph was taken later during the war. Courtesy of the Imperial War Museum CH13613

This page

15. *Above:* Squadron Leader Douglas Bader, well known as the legless fighter pilot. In spite of this incapacity, he first led a squadron of Hurricanes and then the 12 Group Big Wing in September 1940. Courtesy of the Imperial War Museum CH1342

16. The Supermarine Spitfire, famous for its elegance, its performance and its ability to master the German Messerschmitt 109. Courtesy of the Imperial War Museum CH1453

17. The Hawker Hurricane, renowned for its ruggedness and its aptitude for destroying German bombers. This aircraft accounted for two thirds of the enemy destroyed in the Battle. Courtesy of the Imperial War Museum HU54417

18. The Boulton Paul-Defiant was a single-engine fighter, whose only armament was a Frasier-Nash turret with four 0.0303 Browning machine guns fired by an air gunner. Early in the Battle, it was found that the aircraft was no match for the Me109s and after courageous fighting and heavy casualties it was withdrawn from day service. Courtesy of the Imperial War Museum CH871

19. The Bristol Blenheim was a twin-engine aircraft used by Fighter Command mainly for night fighting. The aircraft was underpowered and the Air-Interception equipment carried was unreliable. Courage and persistence was not enough to give defence against the German night bombing. Courtesy of the Imperial War Museum MH165

20. The Messerschmitt Bf 109-E, named by most Allied aircrew as the Me109, was the outstanding German aircraft during the Battle. It was a high performance aircraft equipped with cannon and machine-guns which inflicted high casualties on our squadrons. Fortunately the Spitfire was able to meet the threat. Courtesy of the Imperial War Museum HU54649

21. During late August and early September, the Luftwaffe set out to put RAF airfields out of action. This photograph shows a German bomb exploding at an RAF Station on 27th August 1940. Courtesy of the Imperial War Museum CH1300

22. The outstanding work of the RAF Ground Crews cannot be praised highly enough. Armourers service the machine-guns of a Hawker Hurricane of No. 85 Squadron, while a third unpacks belts of 0.303 ammunition. Courtesy of the Imperial War Museum HU54510

23. Pilots are scrambled to their aircraft, as another German raid is picked up by RDF. The pilots were expected to be airborne within two to three minutes. Author via Press Association

24. *Above left:* The author at readiness with No.41 Squadron at Hornchurch. The German *Schwimmvest* was acquired from a captured pilot he had shot down and worn in preference to the RAF Mae-West. Peter Brown Collection

25. *Above right:* Lord William Beaverbrook, Minister of Aircraft Production and a great friend to Fighter Command. Beaverbrook Insured that we were never short of Hurricanes and Spitfires during the Battle. Like Dowding, he had a son serving as a pilot in Fighter Command. Courtesy of the Imperial War Museum HU88391

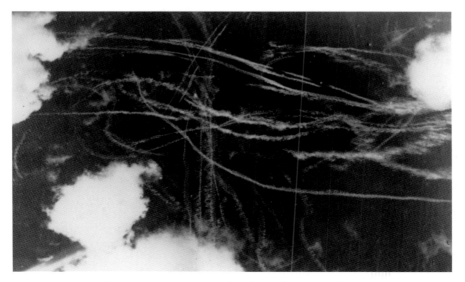

26. Markers in the Sky. Aircraft contrails show that battle has been met as Luftwaffe and RAF fighters twist and turn in combat. Courtesy of the Imperial War Museum H4219

27. Sir Hugh Dowding, Commander-in-Chief, Fighter Command, welcomes King George and Queen Elizabeth to Bentley Priory on 6th September 1940. Bentley Priory was the headquarters of Fighter Command from where Dowding planned his operations through to victory. Courtesy of the Imperial War Museum CH1233

28. Bentley Priory as it stands today. The building is no longer used as a Group Headquarters and is now the parent unit for various lodger units within the Royal Air Force. Richard Smith Collection

29. The effect of the bombing. A dusty civilian and policeman with clothing salvaged from homes destroyed by German night bombing during October 1940. Courtesy of the Imperial War Museum HU66203

30. The author pictured in his Spitfire preparing to take-off from Hornchurch on another sortie during October 1940. Peter Brown Collection

31. *Above left:* Seek and Destroy. The author has always been proud to have served with No.41 Squadron. Seen here dressed for 30,000 feet. Peter Brown Collection

32. *Above right:* Pilot Officer Eric Lock of 41 Squadron, top scorer in the Battle with 20 enemy aircraft destroyed and 7 probably destroyed. Peter Brown Collection

33. 41 Squadron pilots at Hornchurch, which could be representative of all pilots who served during the Battle. Peter Brown Collection

34. *Far left:* Marshal of the Royal Air Force Sir John Salmond. He was very active behind the scenes of air force policy making, even up to 1940. The RAF Museum, Hendon

35. *Left:* Marshal of the Royal Air Force, Lord Hugh Trenchard, was a powerful factor in the formation of the RAF and still held considerable influence in the critical years of 1938–40. He had clashed with Dowding as early as 1916. Courtesy of the Imperial War Museum CH10979

36. *Above left:* Air Chief Marshal Sir Cyril Newell. He was Chief of Air Staff during the critical years of 1937–1940. In his appointment as CAS, he finally became senior to Dowding. Courtesy of the Imperial War Museum CH652

37. *Above right:* Air Marshal Sir Charles Portal, Air Officer Commander-in-Chief of Bomber Command. In October 1940, he was promoted early to be Chief of Air Staff. Courtesy of the Imperial War Museum CH12267

38. *Above left:* Sir Archibald Sinclair was appointed Secretary of State for Air in May 1940 by his old friend Winston Churchill. He was closely involved with the resignation dates for Dowding and specifically with Dowding's removal from office. Courtesy of the Imperial War Museum CH10270

39. *Above right:* Air Vice-Marshal William Sholto Douglas held the position of Deputy CAS during the Battle. He was the Chairman at the high-powered meeting on 17th October 1940, when he sought with others to belittle Dowding's competence as the victor of the Battle and upheld the performance of 12 Group's Big Wing. Courtesy of the Imperial War Museum CH11834

40. *Above:* Air Vice-Marshal Douglas Evill. He was SASO to Dowding and effectively his second in command. Evill was fully aware of the discord between Park and Leigh-Mallory with harmful effects, and failed to take action or persuade Dowding to tke action to deal with it. He appeared to sit safely on the fence. Courtesy of the Imperial War Museum CH162745 were protected by two squadrons of Spitfires, a measure of safety beyond the dreams of 11 Group Squadrons, and so their casualties were very low. The Wing made a number of sorties without interception and finally engaged the enemy again on 27th September.

However by the end of October, the Duxford Wing had only gone into action once after 18th September 1940. No. 12 Group had been sidelined for the second time.

Squadron Leader Bader and 242 Squadron

It would of course be possible to write a treatise on Bader alone, but many books and essays have already been written about him. Bader was an extraordinary person with tremendous force of character, and was able to exert his influence over so many people – not only those junior to him, but also over senior RAF Officers as well. His operational career flying fighter aircraft in a war against the Luftwaffe, in spite of his self-inflicted handicap of the loss of two legs, rightly made him an RAF legend. Only his indomitable spirit enabled him to survive his crash and injuries, and seven years later build up and lead a Hurricane squadron in action.

But my concern is to review his activities in the Battle of Britain and to present the truth, or my truth, about this part of his career. Throughout his life, Bader had been seen as aggressive, with an overwhelming need to be in the front of the action and to be the top man, whether it was in sport or in battle. Helped by the Cranwell Brotherhood, he had been selected to lead a squadron in 12 Group into action less than 12 months after having been a civilian for the previous seven years. He was given command of No. 242 Squadron, which had fought in France with heavy casualties. The morale of the pilots was low, but Bader, with his combative style, was exactly the right man to rebuild the squadron with new additional pilots, into a fighting unit, ready for action.

However, he had little experience of leading a formation in battle and had no real understanding, or perhaps acceptance, of Fighter Command defensive strategy, and with no intention of following it unless it put him and his squadron in the front of the action. His continued logbook assessment as an exceptional fighter pilot, which was hardly supported by his poor airmanship and limited flying on modern fighters, confirmed his belief in his own ability. He has for so many years been described as a great fighter leader in the Battle. I take issue with this; he was not. He was a great morale raiser for inexperienced or dispirited pilots. This is quite separate from the professional leadership of 12, 36 or 60 aircraft in a defensive role fighting to protect the Country from invasion. I doubt if his arrogant and bombastic style would have impressed many of the veteran pilots of 11 Group who were already battle honed.

Bader saw the war primarily as a means of achieving his ambition of emulating WWI 'aces' in being a great fighter pilot with the highest score of victories. He always led his squadron and wings so that he could be the first to fire his guns. Air Vice-Marshal Johnnie Johnson, Britain's top scoring fighter pilot and with great experience in leading wings in action, wrote in his book *Wing Leader*:

Tactics must be simple, and the leader's task is to bring all the guns of his fighters to bear against the enemy in the shortest time... Leadership in the air consists not in scoring a personal kill, but in the achievement of a decisive success with the whole force.

Bader's philosophy of 'follow me chaps' confirms his failure to place his squadrons in a tactical position. His obsession with increasing his own personal score finally resulted in him becoming a prisoner of war in August 1941. Often the best squadron and flight leaders in 11 Group did not achieve high personal scores.

Bader had an unacceptable disregard of rules and procedures and often ignored the Controller's instructions. He had no intention of fitting into the Command control strategy essential for a defensive battle. His ambition was to fight his own war, flying over 11 Group territories – free of control and tying up three or, better still, five first class squadrons. Within a few months of becoming a fighter pilot he had crashed two Spitfires and damaged two others. Any other squadron pilot would have been grounded and returned to an Operational Training Unit for further training. Instead he was rewarded with promotion to squadron leader and given his own squadron. His RT behaviour was typical Bader. His chitchat with the Controllers was totally at variance with the need for his squadrons to keep radio silence except in emergencies. His independent attitude, his lack of fighting experience, and his disregard of proven procedures made him unsuitable to lead major defensive formations in the Battle of Britain. This lack of control over one squadron could have been a problem, but the lack of control over a squadron leader leading five squadrons could have been disastrous. The relationship between Bader and Air Vice-Marshal Leigh-Mallory is fascinating, and was based on the fact that each provided what the other needed. Bader was by then a national figure whose exploits would receive national coverage. Leigh-Mallory had inactive squadrons to give to Bader, who could then provide 12 Group and Leigh-Mallory with a national reputation. Bader led the Wing at every opportunity and never delegated leadership when he was flying.

There is evidence to show that Bader was 'casual with numbers'. Leigh-Mallory never seriously investigated his exaggerated claims and the real effectiveness and efficiency of the Big Wing actions. Both he and Bader were locked into the numbers game. Leigh-Mallory readily accepted Bader's astonishing claims, which were used by him as a stick with which to beat Dowding and Park. His high award of decorations to the pilots of 242 Squadron for squadron service with the protection of a Wing, exceeds the recognition given to 11 Group squadrons fighting daily on their own in the real war. Bader's personal claim of 12 aircraft shot down throughout the Battle is now generally accepted as 4 confirmed.

Despite Bader's lack of respect for the policies of the Commander in Chief, no one would accuse him of any deliberate involvement in the plot to remove Dowding from office. However, his ambitions and attitudes were used as part of the attacks against the C-in-C. Bader's aims were personal and quite clear. He wanted to be the top ace in Fighter Command with the freedom to roam the battlefield without control. Everything he did was self centred and planned for him to shoot down the maximum number of enemy aircraft. He was possibly born in the wrong century and with his temperament could well have led the Charge of the Light Brigade in the Crimean War.

I am sure that Bader believed that his destiny in life was to be the greatest fighter ace and leader. Events have shown this not to be. His real destiny lay in the outstanding humanitarian work he carried out after the war, when flying all over the world for many years, bringing comfort, encouragement and support to thousands of people of all ages and all nations, who were battling with difficulties and disabilities due to the loss of limbs. He was living proof that serious disability could be overcome and he showed so many others the way. He was awarded the CBE for his services and was later Knighted, an honour he richly deserved. The Douglas Bader Foundation in London SW15, which carries on his much needed work, is his true Memorial.

30th August 1940

On this day, to become of unexpected significance, 12 Group had assembled four of its squadrons at Duxford and its Fowlmere satellite airfield three miles away. They included No. 242 and No. 310 Hurricane Squadrons and No. 19 and No. 611 Spitfire Squadrons. I had flown in to Fowlmere with my squadron from Digby in Lincolnshire. At about 16.30 hours, No. 242 with 13 pilots was scrambled to investigate a plot north of London of 50+ aircraft, which soon proved to be more than 100. Bader detailed a section of three to investigate three unidentified aircraft below. He then led the remaining ten Hurricanes to attack a formation of 60+ Heinkel bombers and 30 Messerschmitt 110 long-range fighter escorts, west of Enfield to the north of London. There were no Me109 fighters as escorts. In the battle that followed, Bader and the other nine pilots claimed 12 enemy aircraft of which 11 were reported to have been seen to crash or disintegrate. In the event the squadron is now credited with having been responsible for only 4 enemy aircraft destroyed – and Bader with none.

On landing, Bader reported to Leigh-Mallory that his 10 aircraft had on their own attacked a German formation of more than 100 aircraft and had destroyed 12 with a further 5 probable, adding that with more aircraft he could have shot down more of the enemy formation. In fact the 3 other squadrons waiting at readiness at Duxford and Fowlmere could have provided these extra fighters. It is clear that the 12 Group philosophy to attack with massed squadrons had not yet been considered. One might wonder why Bader was sent off on his own when No. 19 Squadron of Spitfires was left on the ground with 2 other squadrons in reserve. In fact the controller was knowingly sending the pilots off to be outnumbered by at least 4:1 or even 8:1 This was to be the first time Bader had led a squadron into action.

On this day Squadron Leader Tom Gleave of 253 Squadron was credited with the shooting down on his own of five Me109s, an incredibly courageous and skilful achievement. As a tongue in cheek alternative to Bader's claims of the benefits of bigger formations, I could equally well propose that our new battle tactics should have been to send off all our pilots to attack the enemy in pairs. It was found in the fighting over Dieppe in 1942 that Big Wings were ineffective against the Luftwaffe bomber attacks. Leigh-Mallory reluctantly changed tactics on advice from pilot Group Captain Broadhurst on a sortie over the beach-head, and sent our fighters to operate in pairs of aircraft instead with more effective results.

Too Late

During the Battle and after, Bader and Leigh-Mallory claimed that, first the Duxford squadrons and then the Big Wings were always called too late, so that either they missed the interception, or intercepted at too low a height at a serious disadvantage. Most of the squadrons in Fighter Command could frequently have made the same claim.

If Bader arrived late or low why should he have been surprised when he was leading a wing of mixed aircraft climbing at his chosen speed of 140 mph, the speed of the slowest aircraft? If he had led a pair of Spitfire squadrons he would have been more effective. Bader never understood or accepted that the Battle of Britain was fundamentally defensive and that our fighter resources had to be organised to shoot down the enemy in a co-ordinated way and to keep Fighter Command in being as an effective fighter force.

A detailed examination of the sorties by AVM Evill, the SASO of Fighter Command, showed that Bader and Leigh-Mallory were quite wrong and unfair in their claims. If the squadrons and the wings were airborne within the three to six-minute time allotted, there was adequate time to intercept. When interceptions did not take place it could simply be that the enemy formation had changed direction. Air formations moved at three miles a minute and approached or flew away at up to six miles a minute. All fighter pilots knew of the bewildering sensation of being in a melee of 100 aircraft, and then a minute or two later of being unable to see a single aircraft in the sky. Equally of course aircraft appeared with startling rapidity as when a squadron or flight was bounced.

The real problem was that of height and not time, although of course both were linked. RDF and Observer Corps heights were not always correct. A single German attack could stretch from 15,000 feet up to 25,000 feet. Sometimes an interception at 20,000 feet would be fine, but if Me109s were with the plot then it could be that such a height could be disastrous. Bomber attacks protected by Me109s and intercepted by the Duxford squadrons with mixed aircraft would usually have a height advantage. The Spitfires were tied to the Hurricanes and had to fly and climb at their lower speed. If the Spitfires had been detached as a 'free-swarm' above and in front of the wing, this height problem might have been alleviated. The Germans often put a 'frei-schwarm' of Me109s above and in front of their main raids.

There was no way in which a 12 Group mixed Wing could have achieved height superiority against such an independent formation of Me109s without more time for the interception. One way of being on time at the right place and height is by the maintenance of standing patrols. These are expensive in the use of aircraft and pilot flying time and in any case we didn't have spare squadrons to use in this manner. The other way of being on time would be to allow the enemy bombers to bomb their targets and get into position waiting to attack them on the way home, if you were certain of their return route and had the speed. Certainly the Wing at 140 miles an hour was not fast enough. However, fighters on fixed patrol lines would often have been an easy prey to marauding Me109s.

Dowding's policy on this was quite clear – the bombers would always be attacked *before* they dropped their bombs. Senior staff at Air Ministry did not hold to this policy and would have been prepared to wait and assemble large unwieldy formations if necessary to attack the bombers on their way home.

Although Bader criticised the Controllers, in fact by then of course they were very experienced, but were fully stretched trying to forecast enemy movements. If Bader arrived late with his five-squadron Wing it was likely to be his own fault. Why didn't he send the Spitfires up ahead – higher and faster – to protect the Hurricanes? I suggest that the real reason he led as he did, was that he always intended to be the first in the wing to fire his guns.

Over-claiming

Most pilots over-claim, the RAF by an average of 2:1, the German Luftwaffe over England 3:1 and Bader's 242 Squadron by 3:1. The Royal Navy and Coastal Command over-claimed the sinking of the German U-Boat fleet by a high figure. It should not be held as a criticism of the pilots who are fighting with high adrenaline in the confusion of battle. Does it really matter? That depends – if aircraft numbers matter then it is critical. For the Luftwaffe who had to destroy Fighter Command it was important to assess how many RAF fighters were left after each engagement, and how many new and repaired aircraft had come into the line. This was especially important as the battle had become a war of attrition with a specific dead-line to meet for the invasion to take place. The Luftwaffe over-claimed by 3:1; their figures were believed by their High Command and almost certainly by their fighter squadrons. The graph on page 129 shows how the Luftwaffe Intelligence Units could have been disastrously misled by pilot over-claims into believing that Fighter Command was near to the point of total defeat by the first week in September. How wrong they were.

For Fighter Command in general it was not so important. As long as the Germans kept attacking, then we kept on fighting, however many aircraft they had available and however few aircraft we could muster. It was only dangerous for Fighter Command in respect of the three times over-claims of Bader's 242 Squadron in their first action as a squadron, which misled Leigh-Mallory into giving Bader extra squadrons. The 12 Group wing was later used to challenge Dowding's handling of the battle. Did Leigh-Mallory really believe that on their first squadron action they could so easily surpass all of the 11 Group battle experienced squadrons? Yes, because it gave a special prestige to Bader and his 12 Group squadron and placed them centre stage.

To change major tactics in the middle of a defensive battle on the basis of exceptionally high claims by an inexperienced squadron commander, and on the whim of an inexperienced group commander without serious investigation, assessment and rehearsal would be to court disaster. No commander-in-chief could be expected to take such a major decision on the first battle reports of a junior squadron commander. At the time it was not known that 242 Squadron were over-claiming by 3 to 1, but the superior results obtained by such an inexperienced leader and squadron should have been queried by Leigh-Mallory and not blindly accepted. Certainly Dowding had his doubts about the accuracy of 12 Group's claims, which he minuted to Evill, his SASO.

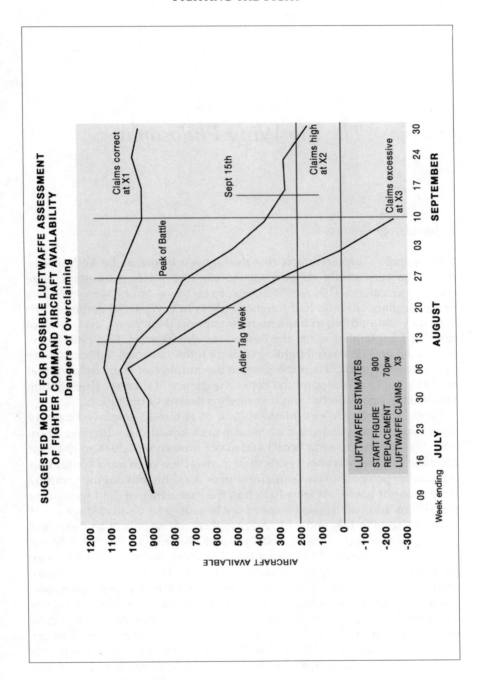

SUGGESTED MODEL FOR POSSIBLE LUFTWAFFE ASSESSMENT
OF FIGHTER COMMAND AIRCRAFT AVAILABILITY
Dangers of Overclaiming

129

CHAPTER 4

The Big Wing Philosophy

Prior Use of Wings

It is generally accepted that, within the higher echelons at the Air Ministry, there was very strong support for the use of big wings to attack large enemy formations. This would appear to be based on the views of some of the air marshals who had fought as pilots in WWI aerial battles. If this is so they did nothing to implement or support their views, certainly not until mid September when the Battle was almost won. This philosophy was based on WWI aerial fighting, mainly fighters versus fighters at very much lower speeds. Then the greater the number of their fighters that could be put in at one point the better the chance of success. This fighting was usually open combat and was rarely a defensive operation.

Over Dunkirk, Air Vice-Marshal Park of 11 Group employed pairs of squadrons, three squadrons and even up to six squadrons with mixed benefits. Was it better to send occasional major formations which might miss the main Luftwaffe bomber raids over the beaches, or to put a continuous but smaller presence of two squadrons over the ships and our men waiting to be brought home? At least Park had the experience of deploying large formations and had learned some of the benefits and disadvantages.

In 12 Group in July and early August, there are records of an occasional practice of two squadrons at Coltishall and Wittering in 12 Group, flying as pairs when training up 242 squadron, but there was no formal 12 Group policy of interception by two squadrons or more. 11 Group had sometimes used pairs of squadrons in their defensive operations. A pair of squadrons, generally from the same airfield, is a natural extension of squadron activity, although when going into action the squadrons act independently. I have found no evidence of any 12 Group policies to use formations larger than one squadron in action against the Luftwaffe until September 1940. This is clearly confirmed by the despatch of only one squadron from Duxford on 30th August, to intercept a raid of 50/100 enemy aircraft although four squadrons were available. Two squadrons should have been the minimum sent against a raid of this size unless other raids had been plotted in or close to the sector.

The type of activities that 12 Group were involved in at that time were coastal interceptions of small enemy formations, for which large defensive wings were quite useless. The setting up of a three-squadron wing by 12 Group on 7th September could only have been intended for action over the 11 Group sector, and one would have expected that the Commander of 11 Group would have been consulted or advised by Leigh-Mallory about the plans. I have found no evidence of such supportive action.

Big Wing Controversy

The Big Wing controversy was a dispute at the highest level of the Royal Air Force as to the most effective use of day fighter squadrons in the Battle of Britain, clearly a defensive battle of incalculable importance. The use of single squadrons, and occasionally pairs of squadrons, was the standard practice employed successfully by Park throughout the Battle. In this defensive battle, the Luftwaffe heavily outnumbered Fighter Command, so that flexibility of the disposition of squadrons and their readiness was essential. From 7th September, when the Luftwaffe had been given permission to attack London by day and night, the tactics of the battle would need to be reconsidered.

If there had been no Duxford Wing and these five squadrons had been made freely available to Park, the Battle could have been won with fewer casualties and with less strain on the 11 Group pilots. In August, 12 Group had as its primary responsibility to defend the Midlands from bomber formations from Germany, but found itself out of the action and taking no significant part in the Battle. With the Battle clearly concentrated over 11 Group, the function of 12 Group should obviously have been that of a tactical reserve. This role was not welcomed by Leigh-Mallory of 12 Group, who wanted a share of the battle and the accolades. Dowding had drawn up his final lines of command in early 1940 before the Germans had over-run northern France and were established on the Channel coast. No 12 Group were facing the North Sea. Dowding stuck to his original plan for the Group Commanders to handle their own enemy intrusions but had given no clear instructions as to working relationships between the Groups, particularly 11 and 12, to help balance the load. As there was personal animosity between the two commanders the required support became contentious. On the other hand, 10 Group and 11 Group faced the enemy side by side across the Channel, and then support for each other was standard practice.

For Bader, commanding 242 Squadron, a defensive role was totally alien to his character. He needed desperately to get into the action and to build up his own personal score of victories, having been left well behind in the race by pilots ten years younger. No. 12 Group squadrons had been sent over the 11 Group sector to protect sector airfields, but 12 Group were not receiving publicity for their role in the Battle. The media naturally gave their attention to the major actions in 11 Group with battles and casualties every day.

When the Duxford controller scrambled only one squadron, No. 242, out of the four at readiness, who decided that only Bader's squadron of Hurricanes should be sent off, when an additional squadron of the Spitfires available could have intercepted more quickly and increased the Luftwaffe losses? In fact there were several other squadrons from 11 Group involved and 242 only accounted for four of the aircraft shot down. But the numbers game had started and from then on Bader's three times over-claim figures were used by Leigh-Mallory as a weapon. Compared with the hard won results and high casualties of Park in 11 Group, these reported results were miraculous, even bearing in mind that it was one of the very few raids over southern England without any Me109 fighters to protect the German bombers.

When Bader claimed to Leigh-Mallory that if he had had more fighters he could have shot down more Germans, I suspect that he was simply hoping that he would be given another squadron to lead as a pair, particularly as he had practised leading a pair of squadrons before the Battle. This could have been a reasonable and practical response, but Leigh-Mallory saw the bigger picture.

Unbelievably Leigh-Mallory responded to Bader's statement of the obvious with a telephone call giving him two additional squadrons, Nos 19 and 310 stationed at Duxford and Fowlmere to fly as a wing under his command. This was to an acting Squadron Leader who had for the first time led a single squadron into action only days before. Following this instant decision the Big Wing was later claimed to be a well-conceived, highly trained tactical unit, later publicised as a planned and improved tactical alternative to deal with the large German raids, led by Bader acting largely on his own initiative. The truth was that the three- and five-squadron wings were never more than convoys used to obtain concentration of strength at one point. The squadrons took off one after the other and 'followed the leader'.

In this spontaneous manner the Myth of the Big Wing was born without a meeting, formal planning, or serious discussion. It could not have been more casual. The Wing was clearly to be led by Bader in 242 Squadron, which remained stationed at Coltishall, 68 miles away, and flew to Duxford every day returning every evening. Until he arrived and refuelled, the Wing could not be considered to be at readiness.

The over-optimistic claims of the action were received at the Air Ministry with high praise and special interest from the Chief of the Air Staff and the Secretary of State for Air. The latter and the Under-Secretary-of-State for

Air later paid private visits to Duxford to meet Bader and the Squadron. The Squadron Adjutant, F/Lt MacDonald, as a Member of Parliament, felt free to discuss the apparent achievements and later the complaints of the squadron directly with the Air Ministry. This 'backstairs approach' was of course against all service procedures and should not been permitted by AVM Leigh-Mallory. The campaign against Dowding was now coming into the open.

The claims of the first five sorties were later used by the Air Ministry to challenge Dowding's handling of the battle. Without the Bader/Leigh-Mallory relationship there would have been no Big Wings. This very unusual partnership was soon to cause dissention and disruption in Fighter Command over 11 Group skies.

Specification for Planning a Duxford Big Wing

In all the discussions, arguments and philosophies concerning Big Wings in the Battle of Britain, I can find no record of what a Duxford Big Wing in 1940 should have been or should have done. Almost all authors seem to have accepted that the Big Wing of 12 Group was a tried and tested concept intended for tactical use, as a serious alternative to the single wing or pairs philosophy used since the Battle started. This is simply not true. The setting up of the Duxford Wings was no more than the assembly of a number of squadrons led by Bader of 242 squadron, with no serious appraisal beforehand of its potential as a fighting force in the Battle.

As far as I know, no one had published a written specification for a *defensive* Big Wing before September, because other than the Duxford Wing, the use of Big Wings specifically for the defence of Britain was never seriously implemented by Fighter Command or 11 Group. In fact Park experimented with three-squadron wings in 11 Group for a while but apparently they were not effective enough to be used widely in the group. However, in view of the apparent numbers success of the Duxford Wing, Park must have felt under considerable pressure to investigate further the use of Big Wings. He certainly would not have readily agreed to have 12 Group's wing flying over his territory, unless under his direct control.

On 1st October Park wrote to his station commanders opposing the views of some people that the only way to beat the enemy was by the use of three-squadron wings. He makes an excellent case for the use of two-squadron wings for most fighting, and rightly explains that Big Wings are only effective with the right weather, major enemy formations and with time for a wing to form up.

He was obviously still under some pressure on 6th October because he wrote again to his station commanders this time supporting big wing formations. What had happened?

Within five days he had apparently become much more committed and positive about the use of three squadrons by all his stations. Perhaps he was getting worried about the widely publicised success of the Duxford Wing. However, he must have known then that weather conditions over Britain would not be suitable for defensive wings for many months.

In retrospect it seems so obvious now that the formation structure for a defensive Fighter Command should have been based on a squadron, then on a pair taking off at the same airfield. Then if needed, the controller could assemble two pairs in the air making a total of 48 fighters, a formidable defensive unit. When going into action, the pairs could separate and then the squadrons could attack individually, as they always did, except in Bader's Wing. It is easy to be wise after the event, but the reality was that all involved in the action, the controllers, the squadron commanders and the pilots had to take each day and each event as it came. Planned action was not an option, and flexibility and rapid response were the keys.

The Duxford Wing was different in that it was intended and used as a full-time unit standing at readiness every day, with its squadrons committed to the Wing except in the case of dire emergency in 12 Group. They waited at dispersal for many hours without action.

I have always claimed that the Duxford Wing was strictly ad hoc and that no formal time was spent in its planning and that no specification for its setting up was prepared. I have prepared my own specification for setting up a committed Duxford three- or five-squadron wing, for defensive operations, which is detailed in Table 1 for consideration. If it is accepted that it is realistic and functional, then we can use it to assess the philosophy and performance of what has been called the 12 Group Big Wing. Perhaps the most crucial feature of the Bader Wing assessment is that nothing was planned. When making my early research in 1996, I realised that, despite the claims by eminent authors that before going into action the Wing had practised for several days, the truth was that the Wing had *never* practised once, not even a simple take off, forming up, and landing. The authors had accepted what others had written because no one would dream of forming and sending a new three-squadron wing into action over another Group without planned rehearsal. I knew that my squadron, No. 611, had never rehearsed. I examined my copy of Bader's logbook and there was not a single reference to a Duxford Wing practice flight. I checked with Wing Commander George Unwin who had flown with 19 Squadron in the Wing, who confirmed that his squadron had never rehearsed. I had then confirmed that two out of three squadrons and three out of five squadrons had never rehearsed. We can be very certain that if Bader didn't lead the wing in practice flights then there weren't any. An examination of PRO squadron records has confirmed that none of the Wing squadrons had taken part in rehearsals.

This was to me the key factor that showed that Leigh-Mallory's vaunted

Big Wing Philosophy was a myth and that the Wing was never more than a convoy. There had been no master plans, or if there were, none have ever been produced. There were no briefings, no plans for change of leadership, no practised take offs, no rehearsals for fast re-arming and refuelling after battle. Bader and 242 flew home to Coltishall every night, sometimes direct from patrol. Obviously there was no substance to the Big Wing philosophy.

This realisation was for me the first step in proving that Dowding had been dishonourably dismissed.

Table 1 – Planning a Duxford Defensive Big Wing

1. It needs to be envisaged and to have a defined purpose.
2. Ideally it should be planned with experienced leaders of squadrons.
3. The same squadrons and aircraft mix should be retained if found to be effective.
4. Briefings should be held with the leaders of the squadrons.
5. There should be practices of wing scrambles, manoeuvres, weather problems, and change of leaders. Also of fast refuelling and rearming.
6. Logistics for full time readiness of all squadrons needs to be considered.
7. The siting and servicing of squadrons will need to be organised.
8. Review relationship between Sector Controllers and Wing Leaders.
9. Define R/T communication and discipline. Select frequencies.
10. Leader and Deputy Leaders to be appointed and trained.
11. Review aircraft climbing and cruising speeds and range of operations.
12. Liaison channel with 11 Group and Fighter Command for tactical operations.
13. Consider tactics to be employed in varied weather conditions.
14. Ideally the most experienced wing leader available should be selected to lead it. He should be aware of the need to operate and co-operate within the Fighter Command defensive structure and to accept its discipline.

The purpose of such a wing or wings could be envisaged as a trained and disciplined group of squadrons, held on the boundary of 12 Group ready to be sent into 11 Group at the request of the 11 Group Commander or Fighter Command, to give assistance in the interception of major formations of the enemy. The squadrons would still be at readiness to defend the Midlands from attacks on 12 Group, which would be without Me109 escorts.

Table 2 – Duxford Wing Assessment

1. The Duxford Wing was not envisaged before September 1940 and did not have a clearly defined purpose except to give Bader more aircraft to fight his own individual war, and provide status for 12 Group.
2. The Wing was never planned. It was first set up by a phone call between Bader and Leigh-Mallory, although later on 10th September Bader flew up to Hucknall to meet with Leigh-Mallory, almost certainly to discuss a five-squadron wing.
3. The squadrons, numbers and aircraft varied.
4. There were few if any tactical discussions with the squadron commanders. Bader was based at Coltishall and led his squadron back there every day.
5. The Wing never practised any aspect of the proposed operation – take-off, manoeuvres in the air, or refuelling. There were no rehearsals.
6. There could be no full-time readiness for five-squadron wings until the additional squadrons had flown into Duxford or Fowlmere. Bader's squadron was 65 miles away.
7. Two additional squadrons in a five-squadron wing were based 70 and 130 miles away from Duxford.
8. Bader rejected sector control discipline.
9. Bader's RT discipline was reprehensible.
10. Bader only considered his own leadership. I know of no specific plan or opportunity for another squadron or squadron commander to take over and lead the Wing to practise leadership.
11. Bader set the Wing climbing speed at 140mph. This was slow for interception and manoeuvre and quite unrealistically slow for the Spitfire Squadrons.
12. I am unaware of any pre-planned liaison with 11 Group or Fighter Command or indeed if they had any pre-knowledge.
13. I am unaware of any serious consideration of the problems to be expected with cloud formations and poor visibility. This would have shown to Leigh-Mallory the limitations that could have been imposed on the use of five-squadron wings in the autumn and winter and even in an English summer.
14. Bader had only led a squadron into action on one occasion and was one of the least experienced squadron commanders in Fighter Command. His lack of discipline and his refusal to accept the Controller's authority made him unsuitable for command of a defensive wing.

When Leigh-Mallory introduced the Wing in early September, 11 Group was fighting a desperate battle. What they needed was support from Leigh-Mallory. If he was to introduce a new tactical unit at this critical stage, thereby tying up three or five 12 Group squadrons, they would have expected it to have been planned, tested and led by an experienced leader. Two such men were available, either of whom could have been the obvious choice. These were Squadron Leader 'Sailor' Malan who was regarded by his contemporaries as the outstanding leader and fighter pilot of the Battle, and Wing Commander Broadhurst who had had battle experience and had commanded a squadron of fighters before promotion to station commander. Both of the pilots were immediately available in 12 Group. This was no time to be learning on the job. Bader's appointment would seem to have been patronage. The assessment above shows that the Duxford Wing failed totally to meet the needs of 11 Group. Dowding was well advised to resist five-squadron wings until after the danger was past.

Why hadn't the Air Ministry air marshals seriously investigated the potential for Big Wings instead of merely talking about it as a form of opposition to Dowding's established procedures, and finally calling a meeting of air rank officers to discuss tactics? Perhaps because, under the Trenchard Doctrine, a powerful Bomber Command had been considered an adequate safeguard for the security and protection of Great Britain against enemy air attacks.

CHAPTER 5

The Big Wing in Action

The Bombing of London

During the last week in August and the first week in September, the Germans continued their policy of bombing airfields, ports and aircraft factories and 11 Group was stretched to the limit. By the first week in September the Luftwaffe and their Intelligence Staffs were convinced by the gross over-claiming of their pilots that Fighter Command had almost been destroyed.

On 4th September Hitler gave his historic speech when he announced that as a result of the British bombing of Berlin a few nights earlier, he would unleash German bombers to bomb London *by night*. For every kilo of bombs the RAF dropped on Germany by night he would drop 1,000 kilos of bombs. This terror bombing of London by night started on 7th September and continued relentlessly. Its purpose was political and strategic. It could have no significant effect on Fighter Command and its defence against the planned invasion. But by this action Hitler gave the Luftwaffe permission to bomb London by day – which until then had been forbidden. The Luftwaffe realised that the best way to destroy the remnants of Fighter Command aircraft was to force them into the air where overwhelming numbers of German fighters would wipe them out.

The first daylight raid on the London area took place on 7th September, followed later in the day by the first night terror raid threatened by Hitler. On that day the first Duxford Wing of three squadrons was assembled in time to be scrambled to intercept this massed raid against London. The Wing was used again with effect on the 9th, 11th, twice on the 15th by when it had been increased to five squadrons, on 18th and then 27th September. But that was all.

After the raids from 7th to 18th September, the Germans didn't bomb London again in strength until the 27th, 28th and finally 30th September. The Duxford Wing had no anti-invasion value after 18th September and, although it sortied 15 times in October, there were no interceptions. The lack of suitable targets and the bad weather left it as an expensive RAF white elephant kept for Leigh-Mallory's prestige. Why was this crucial information not reported at the meeting of 17th October?

Duxford Three-Squadron Wings

This first time the Duxford Wing squadrons flew together No. 242, and 310 (Czech) Hurricane squadrons took off from Duxford already formed up in line astern. No. 19 Squadron with Spitfires took off from Fowlmere, three miles away and flew a few thousand feet above them.

When I flew with the Wing from Fowlmere in a later sortie, we could see the Hurricane squadrons taking off from Duxford, and we took off immediately behind 19 Squadron parallel to the Hurricanes into the prevailing south-west wind. There was no orbiting, as Bader simply turned 45 degrees left to the south on a course for London. As we climbed south the squadrons were already in the correct order and they adjusted to final position en route. There was no time wasted in forming up and orbiting as many experienced 11 Group leaders have claimed in their defence of single squadron philosophy. As mentioned previously, the Wing was slow because Bader climbed his Hurricanes at 140mph, his chosen speed, and the Spitfires stayed with the formation at that speed.

This first sortie climbed up above North Weald, an 11 Group sector station to the north-east of London, and Bader saw enemy aircraft at a higher level with an escort of Me109s. He immediately opened his throttle to full boost and climbed up to engage the Me109s with his number two, on their own, leaving the Wing strung out behind – a cardinal sin for the leader of a squadron, and even more so for the leader of a wing. The rest of the Wing fought back as best they could, but some were bounced and attacked by Me109s; four aircraft of the Wing were destroyed. The Wing claimed 20 enemy shot down – more fighters than bombers. These figures had been grossly over-claimed and the correct figure was probably nearer seven. The Wing had failed in its task to attack the bombers and Bader, who had deserted his Wing, had failed as a leader. Leigh-Mallory welcomed the over-claimed figures.

The second Wing of the same squadrons was scrambled on 9th September and attacked a formation of Dornier bombers protected by Me109s. Bader had been told to protect North Weald and Hornchurch airfields – but ignored his instructions and climbed up over Staines in Middlesex, more than 30 miles away to the west. Although he made an interception, apparently without control direction, he had again failed as a responsible leader and left two major airfields defenceless. The Wing claimed 21 enemy aircraft destroyed although the real figure was again nearer seven, with a loss of four of its own aircraft and two pilots. Once again, Leigh-Mallory accepted the Wing's claims. Bader claimed that in his opinion a further 20 bombers could have been shot down if additional fighters had been available. With three squadrons already to hand, after only the second sortie he is already making a play for an increase in squadrons. This loose talk only confirms Bader's failure to appreciate the reality and the seriousness of fighting to the death in 11 Group.

No. 74 Squadron of Spitfires was stationed at Coltishall, the same airfield as Bader's squadron. It was commanded by Squadron Leader 'Sailor' Malan, an outstanding fighter pilot and leader on rest from 11 Group. He had far greater battle experience than Bader and would normally have been an obvious choice to lead a new wing.

On 9th September he flew up to 12 Group with his flight commander Flight Lieutenant H. M. Stephen to meet Leigh-Mallory, and to discuss participation of his squadron in the Duxford Wing. It is reported that he agreed provided that he flew with his squadron at the rear of the formation. I imagine that he felt that this would give him freedom to operate on his own in the event of problems in the air.

The third Wing patrol on 11th September was quite different from the previous Wing patrols. Bader and 242 Squadron were absent, as was 310 Squadron. It comprised three Spitfire squadrons led by Squadron Leader Brian Lane with one flight of No. 19 Squadron and one flight of No. 266 Squadron, Squadron Leader James McComb leading 611 Squadron in line astern, followed by 74 Squadron led by Squadron Leader Malan. On patrol over London they were guided by AA fire to enemy formations near Gravesend. They intercepted and attacked some 150 enemy aircraft consisting of Heinkel 111s, JU88s, and Me110s. Unusually, the first two squadrons planned to attack the fighter escort while 74 Squadron was to attack the bombers. The Germans refused to co-operate however and a general melee ensued from which the Wing claimed 12 destroyed, but which was probably only four. The Wing lost three aircraft and one pilot. Once again, Leigh-Mallory welcomed the Wing's claims.

These three Spitfire squadrons with their greater speed and rate of climb led by experienced men were a formidable force. It is interesting that the rate of over-claim of these squadrons, with these leaders, was at the same high level of 3:1 as with the previous Wing sorties. I draw the conclusion that this high claiming was due partly to the confusion of battle with greater numbers of aircraft engaged, and the opportunities for more than one pilot to attack the same aircraft. In his report Leigh-Mallory refers to a general, mixed up battle. Hardly the planned and controlled action expected.

The third Wing patrol was different in composition, leadership and tactics and confirmed the ad hoc nature of the formation and operation of the Wing. It is essential however to understand that, whatever the formation or its leadership, until the enemy formation is actually sighted and assessed in size, content and direction, planned attack is not possible. So that in the event the squadrons have to deal with what faces them when they intercept, rather than what they would have wished. As a basic philosophy Me109s could be expected to arrive, seen or unseen, from forward, above, from either side or even behind the main bomber formation. Man's plans 'aft ganged a-gley'. Bader's leadership for the first two actions had been self-seeking and unprofessional.

Three interceptions with major enemy formations out of three sorties was certainly a powerful introduction for the Big Wing Philosophy – whatever that was at the time. Leigh-Mallory was so pleased with the results that the next day he gave Bader two more squadrons. Christmas had come early in 1940 for Bader.

Duxford Five-Squadron Wings

On 10th September Bader flew to Hucknall to meet with Leigh-Mallory presumably to discuss Wing philosophy. As a result of this, Leigh-Mallory increased the size of the Wing with 611 Squadron with Spitfires based at Digby 68 miles away, and 302 Polish Squadron with Hurricanes at Church Fenton 134 miles away.

Like 242 squadron, these additional squadrons flew into Duxford and Fowlmere to refuel and then come to readiness. Weather problems could restrict the readiness characteristics of the five-squadron Wing, as 242 Squadron had with the 3-squadron Wing. The visiting squadrons flew back to their bases at the end of the day landing at dusk or on the flare-path by night. Our flare-path at Digby consisted of a row of Glim Lamps, battery operated, and with a shield on the glass dome to prevent these rather small lights from being seen by marauding Luftwaffe bombers. As each Spitfire approached the boundary, at the last moment the Chance light, an enormous searchlight powered by a petrol driven generator, was switched on and illuminated the grass airfield. Unfortunately it overwhelmed the Glim Lamps and our flare-path disappeared from view. As soon as each aircraft had landed the Chance light was switched off again in case there was a German bomber in the vicinity. Landing at night in a Spitfire on a grass airfield could be very testing.

On 14th September a four-squadron Wing led by Bader was scrambled, but made no interception. The Wing then increased to five squadrons and again led by Bader took off again, but no interception was made. It is interesting that 242 Squadron did not make a full functional and administrative move to Duxford until 20th October, three days after the 'Meeting of Shame' and well after the Wing had ceased to have an operational value.

15th September 1940 – Battle of Britain Day

On the 15th September the Wing was scrambled late in the morning
when the Germans made a major attack on London. 611 Squadron was
scrambled from Digby and we were vectored on to the other four squadrons on their way to London in time for the action. The Wing comprised
3 Hurricane squadrons led by Bader in 242 Squadron followed by Lane
leading 19 Squadron and finally McComb with 611 Squadron, both with
Spitfires.

It has been recorded that, on this day with Prime Minister Churchill in
the 11 Group Operations Room, Park had requested three squadrons from
12 Group. He was probably unaware of the existence of the five-squadron
Wing, which had only flown for the first time the previous night. He only
needed three squadrons over London, which was being well defended.
In spite of this, 12 Group sent five squadrons, but only just, as we were
diverted from our flight to Duxford to join up with the Wing. This was
confirmation of Leigh-Mallory's philosophy 'five squadrons or nothing',
which could be considered a serious failure to co-operate, or even as a
dishonourable policy in time of war. Bader confirmed this philosophy in a
taped interview with Dr Alfred Price, which is discussed later.

We arrived over London to see the German formations being heavily
attacked. The Luftwaffe squadrons must have been totally astonished
and very frightened to see a wing of 3 Hurricane squadrons and 2 Spitfire
squadrons – 60 RAF fighters leisurely circling around their formations
before going in to attack. They had been promised by their Intelligence
staff that Fighter Command was almost destroyed.

Bader waited for the best opportunity to lead the Wing into the attack.
There were however more enemy fighters than bombers and Bader gave
an instruction for the two Spitfire squadrons to stay up and hold off the
Me 109s. He instructed the Hurricane squadrons to follow him in his dive
to attack the bombers. I felt that having to queue up to attack probably
meant we had too many British fighters at this particular point, although
it was a wonderful feeling for all our pilots, probably the first time that this
had happened.

The two Spitfire squadrons could have been sent to another part of the
formation or another responsibility. Perhaps 12 Group should have sent
the three squadrons requested by Park and kept the other two squadrons
in reserve at Duxford to cover the other airfields while the action squadrons were refuelling and re-arming. They could have requested an assign-
ment to chase up German stragglers on the way home, or could have been
ready to take off for the second raid. We went into the attack some minutes
later as the fifth and last squadron of the Wing, which reduced our potential contribution, as by then the sky was full of milling aircraft, quickly to
disappear.

The Wing claimed 26 victories for the loss of 3 aircraft and 2 pilots, an astonishing achievement welcomed by the 12 Group Commander.

After refuelling and re-arming at Duxford and Fowlmere, the Wing with reduced numbers was scrambled again, and once again we intercepted this second enemy attack of the day. Some of the pilots had missed the scramble because they were casualties, had landed at other airfields to be refuelled or were late returning. This regrouping was always likely to be a problem with a big wing.

The leading squadrons of the Wing, the Hurricanes, were attacked by Me109s and Bader ordered the Spitfires to attack the bombers. This was on the spot reversal of roles; so much for Leigh-Mallory's claim that his Hurricanes needed two Spitfire squadrons to protect them.

The Wing again claimed 26 victories for the loss of 2 pilots and 3 aircraft. I attacked a Dornier 17, finally breaking off blinded by oil from the bomber's damaged engine. I followed this by attacking a Heinkel 111 bomber, which I left when it was in a vertical dive with the pilot's escape hatch open.

The Wing claimed a total of 52 victories for the day and Fighter Command claimed 185 victories. This was wonderful news for Leigh-Mallory as it was indeed for Fighter Command and the Nation. As we now know, the total German losses on the day probably totalled 56 aircraft; still a nasty shock for the Luftwaffe pilots and their leaders. The Wing's over-claiming is once again confirmed, although Leigh-Mallory continued to use the claims as realistic in his report. In fact on this day of melee battles other Fighter Command pilots also over-claimed by 3:1. Dowding was however still suspicious of these extravagant numbers of enemy aircraft claimed.

I have always held the view, and it is generally accepted by both sides, that the sight of a Wing of some 60 British fighters appearing in both of the battles on the 15th had a traumatic effect on the morale of the German pilots; it certainly helped the morale of the British pilots. To take a realistic view, this was the only positive value that could be ascribed to it for its restricted operational life.

Leigh-Mallory's report on these five actions over a period of 9 days, with major attacks over London in good weather, was used as the basis of discussion at the Air Ministry meeting on 17th October. This took place more than a month later during which period the Wing had only been engaged on 2 more occasions. He had however made no published conclusions or recommendations after the third patrol of the three-squadron wing. Although a total of 56 aircraft destroyed by Fighter Command is the accepted figure, it is certain that a large number of bombers and fighters managed to reach their base in a badly damaged condition so that the real loss to the German squadrons was higher than this figure. These aircraft would undoubtedly have suffered crew casualties, and some of the aircraft would have been out of action awaiting repair. The high number of aircraft that failed to return, and the large number of damaged aircraft that did, together with the injured aircrew that had to be helped from their aircraft, must have been a traumatic experience for the Luftwaffe ground crews at this crucial stage of the Battle.

We must surely acknowledge that the 15th day of September 1940 was, and indeed still should be, our Battle of Britain day of victory. It should be a national day of great pride and thanksgiving for Britain and for Europe as well.

It was not the day with the highest number of victories in the Battle, but it was the day when the Luftwaffe pilots knew that they had met their match and could not win. After two weeks of fighting desperate battles in fine weather against high odds, our pilots had time to pick their targets to attack, and even had to queue sometimes to do so. The German decision to fly a long straight course over the 11 Group fighter stations to London, gave Park the time to alert, scramble in pairs, and place in position nearly every one of his 19 squadrons, and to call in significant squadron help from the adjoining groups. The afternoon raid having been dealt the same blow, the German pilots and Hitler now knew with cold certainty that this was not a coincidence but the reality. Although we did not know it at the time the invasion was cancelled two days later.

The high proportion of fighters to bombers in these two major raids illustrates not only their need for maximum fighter protection, but indicates that they were 'coat trailing' raids planned, as they believed, to force up and destroy the last remnants of Fighter Command. 'Some remnants!' as Churchill might have said.

CHAPTER 6

Effectiveness of Wings

Post 15th September

On 18th September the five-squadron Wing was sent off on three occasions with no interceptions on the first two. On the third patrol however, from London to Thameshaven at 24,000 feet, the Wing saw two groups of apparently unescorted bombers. The Hurricane squadrons went into the attack while the Spitfire squadrons remained in position above. After a while 19 Squadron dived through the cloud to attack and 611 Squadron remained above cloud to give continued protection. The Wing claimed a miscellaneous bag of 29 enemy aircraft, including Junkers 88s, Heinkels and Dorniers, without loss to themselves. In fact they are now assessed as having shot down only four Junker 88s – two credited to No. 19 Squadron and two to No.302 Squadron. Once again Leigh-Mallory accepted these imaginative claims as very welcome to his numbers game.

The Wing was scrambled on a further eight occasions without interception. Then on 27th September, a four-squadron Wing was sent off to patrol over the London area. When Bader could not find 'bandits' over the Thames estuary, he refused instructions from Control to return and flew south to the Dover–Canterbury area. Here the maverick wing sighted a formation of Me109s and dived down into the attack. Bader claimed 13 destroyed by the Wing, but in fact, only 5 have been confirmed. The Wing themselves lost 4 aircraft and 3 pilots. Hardly an effective result for four squadrons. This sortie confirms Bader's disregard for the Controllers. During the rest of the month and during the whole of October, the Wing made 19 sorties with no interceptions.

It is fair to say that the three- and five-squadron Wings had some success on five days, meeting attacks over and near London; but for the next 43 days, the Wing only went into action once. However, if used as five individual squadrons with 11 Group instead, they could have taken a very supportive part in the heavy fighting against Me 109s, achieving a number of victories and reducing the strain on the hard pressed 11 Group squadrons.

Leigh-Mallory's Report on his Big Wings

On 17th September 1940 Leigh-Mallory submitted a report on the five Wing engagements during the period 7th to 15th September. He gave details of the battles in which he pointed out the successes, but glossed over the failures, such as Bader deserting the Wing on the first sortie and leaving his post on the second. He listed the success of this nine-day period as 105 enemy aircraft destroyed and a further 40 as probably destroyed; for the loss of 6 pilots and 14 aircraft. A formidable achievement for his new tactics – if true. In fact the Wing probably only destroyed 36 during this period – a significantly different result.

This report by Leigh-Mallory was used by AVM Douglas, the deputy CAS, as the cornerstone of his attack on the professional competence of the Commander-in-Chief. After the results of the three three-squadron Wing actions, Leigh-Mallory made some fundamental tactical statements, listed below, which were not revised or added to after the other actions.

Tactical Conclusions – by AVM Leigh-Mallory 17/9/40
For an operation of this type to be really successful, three objects have first to be achieved.

(a) 1. To neutralise the enemy fighters while the attack on the bombers is being made.
2. To break up the bomber formations.
3. To shoot down the bombers after (2) is achieved.

(b) From the size of the formations we have met up to present, it was considered that at least two Spitfire squadrons are required to neutralise the enemy fighters.

(c) In addition to the two squadrons required to neutralise the enemy fighters, at least three squadrons are required to break up the enemy bomber formations and carry out the main attack on them.

(d) It is hoped that when the bomber formations had been disintegrated, one or two squadrons neutralising the fighters might be able to detach themselves and shoot down isolated bombers.

These 'tactical conclusions' by Leigh-Mallory can only be considered as theoretical fantasy with no substance.

In brief, a Duxford Wing is to consist of 5 squadrons, 3 to attack the bombers and 2 Spitfire Squadrons to defend the Hurricanes. He is not prepared to send in his fighters unless they have 2 Spitfire squadrons to protect them. What would they think in 11 Group – five squadrons – some 50% of 12 Group strength all tied up at readiness awaiting a special scramble? There could only be one wing of this kind in 12 Group. As all large German bomber formations were frequently escorted by 100 to 250 Me109s, how could 2 Spitfire squadrons with 24 aircraft neutralise them?

Leigh-Mallory's inexperience and lack of understanding of the battle parameters is once again exposed by his report. It presupposes that the Germans would arrive at his point of interception with the bombers in front and the fighters above. The combat reports from these actions show that this was rarely true. German bomber formations did not break up but his 12 Group Wings did, immediately after the first 'follow-my-leader attacks'. The discipline and safety of the German bombers ensured that they stayed close together at all costs. Their lives depended on it.

When sending the report to the Commander-in-Chief, he wrote: 'I hope that as the squadrons gain more experience in working together and in the tactics to be adopted, the results will improve.' We didn't have time to spare to gain experience; our 11 Group squadrons were fighting to the death every day.

Dowding, with keen perception on receipt of this report, wrote to Evill his SASO on 23rd September, commenting on the 'general exuberance in their claims' and 'some of which are mere thoughtful wishing'. One of the difficulties Dowding had with combat reports was the drawing of conclusions from the varied reports he was receiving. Dowding was not dazzled by the numbers game but Leigh-Mallory needed numbers to make his mark. Dowding also noted that the three-squadron wings gave better results than the bigger wings.

Review of Big Wing Effectiveness

Leigh-Mallory's report on the five actions over a period of nine days in September, with major attacks over London in good weather, formed the basis for discussion of the Big Wing effectiveness at the Air Ministry on 17th October, more than a month later, during which period the Wing, although at readiness, had only been further engaged on two occasions. This was building on shifting sands indeed. No one had analysed the work of the Wing for the whole period of 7th September to 15th October, or even to the end of September. If they had the results were not published – not surprisingly.

Although the controversy of the Big Wings has continued for many years, and in 1940 was a major excuse for the dismissal of Dowding, I had not seen a day-by-day analysis of its performance in the Battle of Britain when I carried out my research.

I have set out an analysis in a simple form with some startling results revealing the severe limitation of Big Wings as a defence force. The apparent failure of Leigh-Mallory and the Air Ministry to be aware of this, or their decision not to present it on 17th October, reflects either their incompetence or their devious behaviour.

The chart on page 149 details the Wing patrols and identifies those in which the Wing attacked the enemy formations. Many of the Wings were of five squadrons as required by Leigh-Mallory's policy. The sorties break down into three groups.

Period	Date	Sorties	Actions	Claims
9 days	7th–15th Sept *	7	5	105
15 days	16th–30th Sept	18	2	42
31 days	1st–31st Oct **	15	0	0
TOTAL:				
55 days	7th Sept–31st Oct	40	7	147
30 days	16th Sept–15th Oct	24	2	42
46 days	16th Sept–31st Oct ***	33	2	42

* The Air Ministry used only the Leigh-Mallory report on this period at the meeting on 17th October. It is mainly concerned with Luftwaffe raids on London.

** This was a period of poor weather and high-flying Me109s and Me109 fighter/bombers.

*** Activity after Leigh-Mallory report to the end of the Battle.

After Leigh-Mallory's report up to 15th September, during the next 30 days to 15th October and two days before the Meeting on 17th October, there were 24 sorties with only 2 engagements. The claimed results were 42 victories. How could a commander justify maintaining four or five squadrons at readiness for 30 days merely for the shooting down of a total of 42 claimed aircraft, and now believed to be only 14. Leigh-Mallory knew of this disastrous change in the results and did not disclose it. Of course Air Commodore Stevenson should have been aware of this and, with honesty, presented a fuller report re-assessing the value of the Wing squadrons over a much longer period of time with changes in weather and enemy tactics.

Political intentions are clearly disclosed in this corrupt use of a nine-day report by Leigh-Mallory out of 40 days of wing readiness. If a full report showing the ineffectiveness of the Wings for most of the period had been publicised, then the meeting of 17th October recommending six-squadron Balbos would have been nullified before it had commenced, and the main charge against Dowding would have collapsed. The claimed status of the Big Wings as superior to the use of single or pairs of squadrons for a defensive battle would have been destroyed together with its supporters. Chairman Douglas must or should have known from Leigh-Mallory, in broad terms at least, of the Wing results in the four weeks before the Meeting. His decision not to report these to those present suggests that he was prepared to be less than honest to pursue the path of infamy. Did the Secretary of State know? It hardly matters whether the retiring Newall knew, but did Portal the next CAS know? Did the 242 Squadron Adjutant McDonald know? He must have done, and if so did he pass the bad news on to the Air Ministry?

ANALYSIS OF BIG WING PERFORMANCE - 1940

O Sortie   ● Sortie with Action   ( ) Squadrons in Wing

SEPTEMBER				OCTOBER		
1				1	O	
2				2		
3				3		
4				4		
5				5	O	O
6				6		
7	● (3) Formation of Big Wing			7		
8				8		
9	● (3)			9		
10				10	O	
11	● (3)			11	O	
12				12	O	
13				13		
14	O	O		14		
15	● (5)	● (5)	105	15		
16	O			16		
17	O	LM Report		17	Air Ministry Meeting	
18	O	O	● (5)	18		
19				19		
20	O			20	O	
21	O			21		
22	O			22		
23	O			23		
24	O	O		24		
25	O			25	O	
26				26	O	O
27	O	● (4)	O	27	O	O
28	O	O		28	O	
29				29	O	O
30	O		42	30		
				31		0

September Total Claims **147**
Sorties **25**   Sorties with Action **7**

October Total Claims **0**
Sorties **15**   Sorties with Action **0**

Total claimed Sept/Oct **147** (now reassessed as 49)

In October at Readiness, Fighter Command destroyed 293 Enemy Aircraft - The Big Wing destroyed NIL

The conspiracy held firm and presumably no one sought to update Churchill on the failure of the Wing to maintain its early outstanding claims.

The analysis shows a defined period of success from 7th to 15th September with 3 sorties conducted by three-squadron wings and 2 sorties by five-squadron wings. These actions were against major raids on London with plenty of warning, which started on 7th September. The second period to the end of September gave 2 interceptions for 18 sorties. There were only a few major attacks on London and the five-squadron wings were of no value against widespread raids. The third period – the whole of October – resulted in only 15 sorties with no interceptions. The weather was often poor and unsuitable for large formations. Most importantly, however, the Luftwaffe raids in October were mainly high-flying 109 and 109 fighter/bomber formations – too high and too fast for the 140mph Big Wing.

It is clear that Big Wings could have served no purpose before 7th September and little after 15th September. It was quite useless in October and left 4 or 5 established squadrons locked up at Duxford and Fowlmere from where they could have fought alongside the hard-pressed pilots of 11 Group. Fighter Command destroyed nearly 300 enemy aircraft for their own losses of 149 during this period. Why did Leigh-Mallory not offer a Spitfire squadron pair to help Park in 11 Group against the fast high-flying Me109s? Presumably it was still five squadrons or nothing.

An investigation into the work of the wings shows that the squadrons employed would have been more effective as individual squadrons or pairs throughout September and October and even in the period the 7th–15th September. Dowding was absolutely right in refusing to be misled by vastly exaggerated numbers over a period of nine days. Unfortunately, the Air Ministry and politicians welcomed the suspect figures to support their political assertions. Although it is now accepted that the Wing claimed up to three times as many enemy aircraft as the real figures, judgement must be made largely on what was believed at the time. Whatever the accuracy of their claims, it is clear that the operation of the Big Wing as a defensive unit over England over a period of months had limited effectiveness. Throughout a battle of 114 days there were only 6 days when it could have earned its keep. This was too high a price for Fighter Command to pay merely to boost Leigh-Mallory's 12 Group ambitions.

Comparison of Big Wing Results with Other Squadrons

In *Aeroplane Monthly* in September 1996, historian John Alcorn first published 'Top Guns' an analysis of squadrons serving in the Battle with their claims, victories credited and casualties. This article made an important contribution to the literature on the Battle of Britain. His results for credited victories were lower than previous findings, but he has based his figures on proven *combat* results, whereas some authors have included *operational* losses and others have included non-combat losses and accidents to give a *total* loss. If we are to compare fighting performances then the Alcorn figures pertain. If we wish to evaluate attrition performance then total losses must be the standard.

My figures are generally based on operational casualties; which includes all squadron losses on sorties against the enemy. Variations of this are noted in the text or in the drawings. John Alcorn has since published in the July 2000 issue of *Aeroplane Monthly* revised figures based on a further in-depth review. I am grateful to be able to refer to his work to compare the Wing results with 11 Group single squadrons.

Analysis of Squadron Combat Claims

H – Hurricane, S – Spitfire

SQUADRON	E/A CLAIMED	GIVEN	OVER-CLAIM RATIO
Wing Squadrons			
242 H	71	22.5	3.2
302 H	18	5	3.6
310 H	35	13.75	2.5
19 S	53.25	26.5	2.0
611* S	16	10.25	1.6
Wing 5 Squadrons	193.25	78	2.5
Fighter Command Squadrons			
41 S**	91.33	44.75	2.0
43 H	75	35.2	2.1
74 S	55	26.5	2.1
92 S	66.8	40.2	1.7
111 H	46.5	31.5	1.5
603 S	85.8	57.5	1.5
609 S	86	51.5	1.7
F/C Total	2480	1194	2.1

Average per Squadron in Fighter Command   24 E/A Given.

* Author's 12 Group Squadron
** Author's 11 Group Squadron

The Squadron Analysis lists the results for firstly the three Hurricane Squadrons, then the two Spitfire Squadrons, then the total of the five squadrons – all for the whole of the Battle. Two thirds of the claims and credits of the squadrons in the Battle were made during their sorties in the Wings. The three Hurricane Squadrons over-claimed by 3.2:1, 3.6:1 and 2.5:1. The two Spitfire Squadrons over-claimed by 2.0:1 and 1.6:1. The Wing over-claimed by an average 2.5:1 against the total Fighter Command average of 2:1, which included the Wing's high average figure.

No. 19 Spitfire Squadron performed best of all of the Wing squadrons in 12 Group with 26.5 credited victories, but only achieved 20th place in the top scoring list of Fighter Command squadrons. I believe that this was a first class squadron that was denied its potential. No. 242 Squadron was half way up the list with 22.5 credited victories compared with some 11 Group squadrons with more than 40. The Fighter Command average was 24, and the average of the five-squadron Wing was 16. Although spending half of the Battle in Big Wings, the contribution of the Duxford Squadrons was below average, and Bader with 242 Squadron had a rare below average assessment.

These figures cannot be seen in isolation but must be compared with the alternative of what five squadrons could have achieved from 7th September to 31st October operating as single squadrons or pairs controlled by 11 Group. It is safe to say that on this basis the alternative use of operating the Duxford Squadrons as Wings had no significant effect on the course of the Battle. If the squadrons had been used individually with 11 Group squadrons, then the outcome would have been better with the load reduced on the hard-pressed southern squadrons.

In October Fighter Command, mainly 11 Group, lost 149 aircraft compared with the German losses of 293. The Wing destroyed nothing. For the second time in the Battle Leigh-Mallory's 12 Group squadrons had been kept out of combat. Operating as single squadrons or pairs, the Wing squadrons could have been expected to shoot down at least some 30 additional enemy aircraft in October.

Fighting as smaller units the casualties among the Wing pilots would have been increased, as would the casualties among the Luftwaffe squadrons, but the level of casualties among the 11 Group squadrons would have been reduced.

A feature of the Duxford Wing was the lower number of casualties. This can be related to the larger number of aircraft that they could put into one interception with a better combat ratio, and that they had enough aircraft to detach for protection against the escorting fighters.

Why the Wing in 12 Group?

Without Bader there would have been no Big Wings in 12 Group. He was aggressive, self-seeking, and ready to challenge existing structures within Fighter Command. If Big Wings had already existed when he was given command of a squadron, I am sure he would then have argued for a personal policy for him to lead a single squadron of Spitfires, taking off at dawn every morning, and roaming free over 11 Group and the Channel near the Pas de Calais. It can equally be said that without Leigh-Mallory, there would have been no Big Wings. The introduction of a Big Wing, led by an accepted national hero was Leigh-Mallory's chance of getting into the Battle and becoming known as a war leader. It can also be said that if the commander of 12 Group had been a colleague and close friend of Air Vice-Marshal Park, there would have been no five-squadron Wings. There would almost certainly have been two pairs of squadrons at readiness at Duxford and Fowlmere awaiting Park's call. These two pairs of squadrons would have been more effective than one Wing of five squadrons.

The Big Wing controversy was significantly influenced by the questionable actions of F/Lt McDonald MP, the adjutant to 242 Squadron. He gave great support to the Duxford Wing activities ensuring that Bader's claimed successes were passed to the Air Ministry. He also reported Bader's vociferous claims that the 12 Group squadrons were being kept out of the action by Park. As the Squadron Adjutant he certainly had no responsibilities for the operational performance of the squadron. Bader's route for complaint was through his Station Commander, Wing Commander AB Woodhall who was also his Controller and was most certainly aware of his criticisms.

For McDonald, an RAF administration officer, to report direct to Parliament his tactical criticisms of a Group Commander in battle, based on Bader's views, was behaviour that was not only unacceptable, but was insulting to Dowding and Park. That neither of these officers was aware of the support given by the Air Ministry to McDonald in this behaviour, indicates that he was being used in the plan to attack Dowding. The fact that Dowding and Park have since been proved to be right in their tactical policies, and the Big Wing to have been a failure, makes McDonald's behaviour even more disturbing.

Fighter Command was a shield in the Battle. Its committed leaders understood that the performance of a shield is dependent on its strength, its uniformity, its cohesion and its positioning with care. 12 Group did not seem to have understood this.

There were no serious plans elsewhere in Fighter Command for the immediate incorporation of three- and five-squadron wings at readiness.

CHAPTER 7

Canterbury Tales

Should Reserves Go In First?

Bader's friends and supporters have loyally claimed that he was a great tactician, but I can find no evidence to support this.

As far as I can ascertain Bader did not publicise his considered views on the use of Big Wings during the Battle of Britain in 1940, and there is no reason to believe that his Canterbury theories related in any way to his actual fighting in the Battle. The activities of the Big Wings in the Battle were very much off the cuff. There is a paucity or even absence of written evidence of any studied or prepared plans in 12 Group for the introduction and use of a wing. If there had been, with so many researchers of the subject, something would have been found. Could it be that his years as a prisoner of war gave Bader time to develop his Big Wing Philosophies for later publication? However, his simple plan of 'follow me chaps' sufficed for the Wings in 1940 with an intended final line astern attack by his three Hurricane squadrons.

On 2nd September, following his first action leading a squadron on 30th August, Bader wrote a guide to tactics when fighting the Luftwaffe formations for circulation. He was advised to do this by his squadron intelligence officer. There was little in it that wasn't common knowledge for 11 Group squadrons, who had been fighting the Germans with great intensity for several weeks. There was no reference in this guide to the benefit of operating with more than one squadron. The Big Wing Philosophy had not yet been conceived.

His master 'Canterbury' plan, presented after the war by him and his supporters, was that his five-squadron Wing should be sent into action as soon as significant enemy plots appeared across the Channel, and before any 11 Group squadrons were sent in. This would almost certainly have been the first time in history that a powerful group reserve – 20% of the total strength – had been sent into action against enemy formations before the main force. The plan was that they should intercept the enemy force over Canterbury, if they should happen to come that way, and break up the bombers and presumably Me109 units. This would then enable the waiting 11 Group squadrons to attack the fragmented bomber formations, which would, in theory, be very easy targets for them. Why shouldn't 11 Group do their own fragmentation? They could get there quicker.

Bader's lack of experience of fighting the Luftwaffe, and his lack of understanding of the control aspects of fighting a defensive battle, are clearly shown by this plan, which fortunately for Bader and his Wing was never put into action. The following points illustrate the defects in this ill-conceived tactical concept, which was intended simply to put Bader first into the action, with 60 fighters under his personal control.

1. At what stage of the plotting of a raid would the 11 Group controller be able to decide that it was a major raid to London over Canterbury, before he requested the committed despatch of a 5-squadron Wing?
2. While waiting to make this critical decision, the controller could have already despatched two Spitfire squadrons who could be at 20,000 feet within 18 minutes ready for action.
3. With his mixed 5-squadron Wing, with the best weather conditions and a straight course, Bader could not arrive at Canterbury in less than 35 minutes after the scramble call, assuming all his squadrons were refuelled and ready at their Duxford or Fowlmere dispersals. In rather less time 11 Group could have put up 10 squadrons at 20,000 feet with the Spitfires higher. Were 11 Group to wait at readiness or on patrol lines until Bader had finally arrived at Canterbury? How could he let 11 Group know? He had no radio link.
4. Any major cloud formation en route could have delayed or even broken up the Wing.
5. Soon after flying south over the Estuary, Bader would have been out of radio transmission range, and could not have received the latest information on size, types, height, speed direction or position of the enemy formation or formations.
6. Bader assumed, as did Leigh-Mallory and the Air Ministry, that the Luftwaffe would fly with the bombers leading low down, protected by their fighters above. This was far from the truth. There were 'Free Hunting Packs' of Me109s often positioned in front of the bombers.

If Bader had carried out his Canterbury plan on the morning of 15th September, he would have been 'bounced' by 30 or more 'free hunting' Me109s in advance of the main formation. This would have broken up the Duxford Wing with casualties. The Wing, which would have been seen miles away, had poor manoeuvrability. Those that survived would have been trying to attack a force of 25 twin-engine bombers and 21 fighter-bombers, who were protected by a further 150 Me109s. There would have been little chance of Bader's broken up Wing breaking up the bombers.

7. The successful defence in an aerial battle requires minute-by-minute control of the squadrons. The presence of a maverick formation roaming across the skies of south-east England would have seriously affected the work of the Sector Controllers and the Observer Corps.

8. It would be some time before the pilots of the Wing could be re-grouped, refuelled and re-armed back at Duxford some 80 miles away. Should the five broken up squadrons try to reform to continue combat or should they straggle back to base or to an alternative and nearer airfield?

9. If Bader had flown his Wing to Canterbury to meet a Luftwaffe raid on his own on 28th September, he would have been met by more than 200 Me109s escorting some 30 Ju88s. Hardly a battle of his own choosing! The Duxford Wing would have been bounced with heavy casualties.

10. As a permanent support for 11 Group, the five front line squadrons of the Wing would have to be kept at full readiness at Duxford and Fowlmere, all the hours of daylight, subject to weather, useless unless a major raid on or very close to London was anticipated. Leigh-Mallory's ready acceptance of one in ten interceptions as a worthwhile rate was hardly an intelligent appreciation of the effective use of his squadrons in the battle to save Britain. It confirms his isolation from the realities of the Battle.

11. Bader never considered himself or his squadrons as a reserve. He intended to be the point of the spear, the first to touch the enemy.

Dowding's Policy on Formation Size

In August 1939 Air Chief Marshal Sir Hugh Dowding had been questioned about the use of more than one squadron attacking large German formations. The concept at that time did not visualise the presence of Me109 fighters to defend the bombers. The enemy bombers were expected to take off from bases in Germany, and perhaps Holland and Norway, within the range of the cumbersome Me110 twin-engine fighters as escorts, but too far for the formidable Me109s. Dowding was quite clear that the squadron was to be considered as the basic fighting unit and that if two squadrons were sent off together they would still fight as individual squadrons.

This philosophy was correct in 1939 and Dowding had not changed his mind in the Battle. It is possible that Bader was never aware of this tenet of the C-in-C.

Park had operated large formations of fighters over Dunkirk in May and June with as many as six squadrons working together. Although useful experience, this did not correlate with the Battle as there was adequate time to take off and form up, and the squadrons were free flying without control from 11 Group. He had made some effort to evaluate a three-Squadron Wing in the Battle but with mixed results. Prior to 7th September Leigh-Mallory had had no experience of operating or controlling formations larger than one squadron.

The Bader/Price Recorded Interview

As part of his research work on the Battle, Dr Alfred Price, a leading Battle of Britain historian, had a special interview with Group Captain Sir Douglas Bader, which he recorded. It has become known as the Bader/ Price tape. Much of the conversation was concerned with Bader's involvement with Big Wings and specifically the Big Wing Controversy. I am indebted to Dr Price for his permission to quote from his exceptional tape. This interview is revealing about Bader even though it was made late in his life, when his recall may have been less than perfect.

Three times in the tape he refers to the 'so-called controversy' between Leigh-Mallory and Park and denies that such a controversy existed. Bearing in mind that he was present for the whole of the Meeting of Shame on 17th October 1940 to discuss Big Wings versus squadrons, and that he frequently complained that the Wing was requested too late by 11 Group, these comments are obviously untrue for whatever reason.

Bader confirmed his simplistic statement of 30th August to Leigh-Mallory that 'If we'd had more aeroplanes then we would have shot down a whole lot more'. He claims he flew to Hucknall to see Leigh-Mallory, and that then Leigh-Mallory created the Duxford Wing under Bader's leadership, with two extra squadrons to lead. Bader's logbook shows that he did not fly to Hucknall until 10th September; this was almost certainly to discuss the possibility of adding two more squadrons to form a five-squadron Wing. If his logbook is correct then the first two squadrons were presumably transferred to Bader via the telephone. Hardly the setting up of a thoroughly planned wing philosophy.

Bader claims that he was constantly arguing to be sent up at the first plots. He still didn't realise that this would have been disastrous for his Wing and 11 Group, and was utterly impractical. He criticised the controllers as inexperienced.

Extracts from the tape follow, together with my comments.

Bader: 'When we were above the enemy I would say "Diving, diving now, attacking now" and my section of three would go down followed by everyone else. As soon as we had made one pass, the formation [Wing] was broken up'.

I have always understood that Bader's primary plan was, in fact, to break up the German bomber formations, not his own! The Wing soon became involved in an uncontrolled melee of individual aircraft.

Price: 'But once you engaged each man knew what he had to do?'
Bader: 'Yes.'

How could they know until they had intercepted and assessed the enemy formation, except simply follow Bader into the identical location.

Price: 'After an engagement, what happened?'
Bader: 'We landed back separately. It was actually very difficult. A lot of these chaps [pilots] were very young and actually had little experience.'

This is evidence of the Big Wing deficiency in regrouping in the air or on the ground after battle.

Bader: ' … but my only vision was confined to my Wing getting at the enemy, not what the rest of Fighter Command was doing.'

This crystallises Bader's self-centred and undisciplined behaviour and his intention to run his own war.

He refers to two 12 Group Wings, the other led by Wing Commander Broadhurst, the station commander at Wittering, 'and they also went down south into action'. Broadhurst's Wing consisted of the sector's two day-fighter squadrons but it never went into action against the Luftwaffe. Although Broadhurst's logbook shows two wing patrols in September and one in October, there is no record of any interception or engagement.

Price: 'But I have heard from a former controller that Leigh-Mallory was reluctant to provide squadrons to cover 11 Group airfields.'
Bader: 'No, … Leigh-Mallory would not release our squadrons to 11 Group but said that we would stay in 12 Group, as the Duxford and Wittering Wings.'

Bader had in fact refused to stay on patrol over the airfields.

Price: 'A case of either you have a Wing or nothing?'
Bader: 'Yes. In other words I am not sending these squadrons down to relieve 11 Group squadrons and therefore lose them completely from 12 Group.'

This confirms the unacceptable decision by Leigh-Mallory to give support to 11 Group only as a Duxford Wing. On 15th September Park had requested three squadrons from Duxford but in fact 12 Group despatched the Duxford Wing of five squadrons. This was repeated in the afternoon.

Price: 'But it has been said that 12 Group was reluctant to send squadrons as top cover for 11 Group airfields?'
Bader: 'No! The problem was that they always asked for us too late. The Germans always came in at 17,000 feet.'

This is misleading as the Germans came in at varied heights and the Me109s could be at any heights up to 25,000 feet or higher.

This analysis of parts of the tape confirms that Bader always flew with 'Bader tinted goggles' and was still wearing them. His single-minded aggression was no substitute for the balanced judgement and leadership needed to control a large formation in a defensive role demanding an understanding and acceptance of the battle scene.

Wing Leader J E (Johnnie) Johnson

Air Vice-Marshal Johnnie Johnson, who flew as a young and initially inexperienced pilot in the Bader Wing over France after the Battle, has always spoken and written of Bader as a great fighter pilot. His praise and admiration for Bader has never been less than wholehearted. He flew with Bader when he was a VR pilot officer and felt very privileged to fly with the national hero in sweeps over France. After later service Johnson had become the top scorer in Fighter Command, and was probably the most experienced fighter wing commander in the RAF. In his book *Wing Leader* written in 1956, Johnson, with a few sentences based on his great experience, demolishes the calibre of Bader's leadership of Big Wings in the Battle and confirms the failure of wings larger in size than three squadrons. He also confirms unconditionally the correctness of Park's tactics in the Battle. I am grateful to be able to quote from his book to give professional and experienced support to substantiate the views I have presented.

Fighting Talk
There are other strong reasons for not committing fighters in too large formations. The vital element of surprise was often lost because the tight formations of Hurricanes and Spitfires could be seen from a great distance by the Luftwaffe's escort fighters. In addition, the leaders soon found that the larger the formation the more unwieldy it is in the air and the more difficult to control.

My own later experience on both offensive and defensive operations confirmed that two squadrons of fighters was the ideal number to lead in the air. Over France I led a Balbo of five squadrons, but we got in each other's way in a fight and only the leaders were able to bring their guns to bear.

A wing of two squadrons proved to be the ideal size for flexible operations of both offensive and defensive character. It is the task of the ground controller and not the wing leader to achieve concentration of fighters in time and space. Thus we can understand the reluctance of Keith Park to experiment with large formations during the heat and stress of battle; the passing years have undoubtedly proved the tactics of this distinguished field commander to be correct.

These extracts were not written as specific comments on tactics in the Battle of Britain, but on the leadership of wings flying over enemy territory. They are however obviously an important implied criticism of Bader's leadership and of the employment of three- and five-squadron wings in battle.

Assessment of 11 Group and 12 Group Tactics

Air Chief Marshal Dowding's control of the Battle was outstanding. He was clearly the Architect and Victor of the Battle of Britain.

Air Vice-Marshal Park's tactical control of his 11 Group and his use of single squadrons and pairs has been shown to be correct.

The introduction of big wing formations by Air Vice-Marshal Leigh-Mallory of 12 Group has been shown to have been ad hoc, without planning or rehearsal, and to have been not only less effective than single squadrons but could also have been a disruptive influence in a finely tuned battle.

2

A Meeting of Shame

Introduction

By the year 1940 the Royal Navy had been in existence for centuries, during which time it had formed its character, had built great fleets and had established a structure of command with clearly defined responsibilities. It considered itself as the tried and trusted bastion of defence of Britain and her Dominions. There had been very many Admirals. The British Army had also developed and grown over the centuries establishing itself as a powerful and effective force protecting British interests all over the World and acting as a stabilising influence. Most of its battles were fought in Europe and many in Africa, Asia and the Americas. Its role was not seen particularly as defensive for our 'Sceptred Isle', that had been left to the Royal Navy, but rather as an external extension of British power. There had been very many Field Marshals and Generals over the years.

The Royal Air Force was formed in April 1918 mainly from units of the Royal Flying Corps and the Royal Naval Air Service, which explains the unusual ranks which were introduced at the time of the amalgamation. It was to be a new and independent organisation responsible direct to the Government, but smaller than the others.

Major General Sir Hugh Trenchard commanding the Royal Flying Corps was the first Chief of Air Staff and, apart from a short period, continued as the official head of the RAF for ten years, responsible to the Secretary of State for Air. In 1930 he retired and was promoted to be the first Marshal of the Royal Air Force. He was followed as CAS by Air Chief Marshal Sir John Salmond, who was also promoted to Marshal of the RAF on his retirement.

Trenchard had a tremendous influence on the development of this fledgling force in the air, and continued to do so at least until 1941. He had to establish a raison d'etre for the RAF and as a man of aggressive intent he established the doctrine that a very large bomber force could also secure Britain's Home defence from the air thus needing only a small Fighter Command with a limited range of action. Basically then, by 1937 the RAF was dominated by the Trenchard Bomber Doctrine and its supporters, Dowding and Fighter Command were fighting for their existence well before the Battle of Britain commenced.

It is worth recording that the RAF was the only service in the War in which senior officers took no part in battle action, nor were at direct risk from enemy attack other than those experienced by civilians. The only exceptions to this were a very few individual RAF officers of great character and determination. Admirals went to sea, brigadiers and major generals fought against German units, and some landed by gliders or parachuted into action with their soldiers. In day-fighter squadrons in Fighter Command, normally the highest rank in action was that of squadron leader. Occasionally a wing commander would fly with a squadron but only rarely would a group captain go out on a sortie. In 1941 experienced Battle of Britain pilots were appointed to the rank of Wing Commander to lead wings in sweeps over France.

None of the air rank officers in the Air Council or at the Air Ministry at the time had had any operational experience in WWII and most of them could not fly a modern operational aircraft. AVM Park was an exception to this limitation and flew his own Hurricane to visit his squadrons at their airfields. In a time of rapidly changing strategies and tactics, the senior officers at the Air Ministry were soon out of touch and were still relating to WWI tactics that were a generation out of date. The speed of change after the German advance into France on 10th May had left them behind.

CHAPTER 8

The Cabal

The Impact of the Year 1919

If we are to understand the behaviour of some of the senior officers involved in the machinations, then it will be of help to return to the year 1919 when permanent commissions were being awarded in the RAF after WWI had ended.

Portal, Leigh-Mallory, Park and Douglas had all been squadron commanders in World War I. Portal and Leigh-Mallory were granted commissions with the rank of squadron leader. Although having an excellent record as a fighter pilot, Park received his permanent commission with the lower rank of flight lieutenant. The reason for this difference may have been that Park, a New Zealander, was not a public school or university man as were the others, but had started his adult life as a purser on a passenger line, and had served at Gallipoli as an ordinary soldier, where he had been wounded. In 1919, and for many years after, the correct social background was an important factor in service and civil service appointments. Social status by birth has become far less important now but other restrictive social dogmas have replaced it.

This difference in rank between Park and Leigh-Mallory stayed with them until 1940 when Park was promoted by Dowding to equal rank as Air Vice-Marshal, and with the more important status of commanding 11 Group.

Douglas left the RAF for a short time but was encouraged by Trenchard to return with a permanent commission with the rank of squadron leader. From then on he could be considered to be a Trenchard man. Portal had been a reconnaissance pilot in WWI, and Leigh-Mallory had led an army co-operation squadron and later specialised in this field.

Dowding had commanded a fighter Wing in WWI and Park had led a fighter squadron. They both believed that fighter aircraft were more important as the first line of defence for Britain, as if we could not defend our home base then our bomber strength was of no avail. This belief in the importance of fighter squadrons for defence would put Dowding at odds with Trenchard and others who were dedicated to bombers as the main strength of the Royal Air Force.

Emphasis on such a force was established RAF policy for many years with Dowding battling with the Air Ministry for more resources. However, in the event, it was Fighter Command, led by Dowding and Park, and not Bomber Command that saved Britain from invasion in 1940. The Trenchard Bomber Doctrine had been exposed by Dowding to have failed the Royal Air Force and the Country.

Secret Intrigue, Political Clique or Faction

There was a powerful cabal of RAF officers and politicians in 1940 who were hostile to Dowding and wanted him removed from the Service. A cabal is described in the *Concise Oxford Dictionary* as a secret intrigue, and political clique or faction. Cabals rarely exist as formal gatherings and membership information and records of action are naturally difficult to obtain. Different people have different contributions to make and with different interests.

Dowding was 'his own man', stubborn and resolute, and held firmly to his principles. He was not a man who made friends easily, and there would without doubt be senior officers who would regard him with disfavour, and his retirement would be welcome, not least to open up promotion for younger officers. He had already been passed over for appointment as Chief of Air Staff. If this position is regarded as essentially a political one, then probably Dowding would not have been first choice. If high intelligence, loyalty, and the courage to fight for what was best for the RAF is the criterion, then Dowding would have been best suited for the post.

My work has brought me to the conclusion that the Cabal certainly included the Marshals of the Royal Air Force – Lord Trenchard and Sir John Salmond, who although no longer holding active appointments in the RAF still represented a powerful influence on the senior active RAF officers such as Air Chief Marshal Sir Cyril Newall, the Chief of Air Staff, and on successive Secretaries of State for Air.

With four previous attempts to remove Dowding by retirement, the Air Ministry had clearly shown their intention to take him off the active list. In 1940 the recently appointed Secretary of State for Air, Sir Archibald Sinclair, a very close friend of Winston Churchill, had only a formal relationship with Dowding who at this critical time should have been his most important commander.

In 1938 listed among the Air Vice-Marshals were Portal, Douglas, Evill and Nicholl with similar seniority. At that time Leigh-Mallory was an Air Commodore and Park was a Group Captain. By October 1940 Portal was an Air Marshal, and had served for six months as Commander in Chief of Bomber Command. He had been nominated to take over later in the month as the next Chief of Air Staff with the rank of Air Chief Marshal. Douglas was Deputy Chief of Air Staff and still an Air Vice-Marshal. Leigh-Mallory had been promoted to Air Vice-Marshal, and Park had been promoted first to Air Commodore and then in 1940 to Air Vice-Marshal, with command of 11 Group, the most highly prized appointment in Fighter Command. Nicholl and Evill were also serving in Fighter Command and still at the same rank, Evill as Senior Air Staff Officer, and Nicholl as Senior Administration Officer.

With Dowding's support Park had achieved a double jump in rank to match the others and was centre stage with his crucial part in the Battle of Britain. This loss of promotional opportunity and other disagreements in the past could have been grounds for bad feeling on the part of Leigh-Mallory against Dowding.

Marshal of The Royal Air Force Lord Trenchard

As early as 1916 in WWI, Dowding had crossed swords with Trenchard over the resting of his pilots, and the installation of a new suspect propeller for one of his squadron's aircraft. Trenchard regarded him as not hard enough, but still respected him and used his abilities with ultimate promotion to Air Chief Marshal. The sudden change of appointment of Newall over Dowding as Chief of Air Staff effectively blocked Dowding's chances of becoming a Marshal in peacetime. Is that what Trenchard was concerned to achieve? Was Newall really so much more fitted for the position of Chief of the Royal Air Force or was he just more malleable?

Trenchard has been fairly described in the past as the 'Father of the Royal Air Force', and in the many years since its founding in 1918, he exerted a great influence on its growth and survival. In his autobiography published after the war, Douglas recounts that Portal as CAS told him that Trenchard, after the Battle of Britain was over, said to him that it was time for our fighter squadrons to start a campaign of 'leaning forward' against the Luftwaffe over occupied France. This was later carried out under AVM Leigh-Mallory commanding 11 Group, and was very costly in casualties with little gained. This report by Douglas is very disconcerting as it shows the influence or even power still held by Trenchard in the RAF during and after the Battle.

His policy of building and maintaining a large bomber force had failed to save Britain, and his 'leaning forward' had cost us dearly. By winning the Battle Dowding had proved him and the Air Ministry dangerously wrong with their policies, and this could have been his ultimate offence. I think we can assume that with Trenchard's influence at that time as the 'Eminence Grise', that he was undoubtedly deeply involved with the Cabal even if staying in the shadows.

Marshal of The Royal Air Force Sir John Salmond

Although only one year older than Dowding, Salmond had achieved much more in WWI, and was significantly two ranks higher. He was quite different in temperament from Dowding and was an aggressive man of action. He was antagonistic to Dowding and opposed to his appointment to be a Marshal of the Royal Air Force.

A personal attack was perpetrated in September by Salmond against Dowding's status which is most revealing. By 7th September, the day when the Germans started the day and night bombing of London, Fighter Command was at its lowest strength. Dowding needed all his energies and all the help he could get to fight on to save Britain from invasion by day. Only by 15th September could it be seen that victory might be at hand. On 16th,17th, and 18th September Salmond chaired a meeting at the Ministry of Aircraft Production, his base with Lord Beaverbrook, to consider Britain's night defence against the German bombers. But the Germans had only radically stepped up their night bombing programme on 7th September and these night attacks could have no immediate effect on the potential for invasion. The meeting had been planned when we were in crisis with our day defence, and before we had achieved victory in the day battle, which had to be Dowding's crucial concern.

Why did Salmond, no longer active in the Royal Air Force, take it upon himself to set up and chair a Committee away from the Air Ministry, but with their acceptance, to discuss night tactics against the Luftwaffe? Everyone knew that we would have no effective defence until we had our new Beaufighters and improved AI equipment, but the responsibility for the availability of this crucial re-equipment was in the hands of the Ministry of Production. Dowding had not been consulted and this action by Salmond was an unwarranted attack against his professionalism and service status. It is reported by John Ray that Salmond was prepared, if necessary, to appeal to HM the King to have Dowding removed.

Sir Archibald Sinclair, Secretary of State for Air

There is evidence to indicate that Sir Archibald Sinclair was less than friendly to Dowding and he must have been a member of the Cabal when Dowding was dismissed from his post. When Leigh-Mallory independently set up his first three-squadron Wing and then his five-squadron Wing, his friends at the Air Ministry were extremely pleased with the reported results. On the basis of his greatly exaggerated claims they gave him full support. Messages of congratulations arrived for 242 Squadron from the Chief of Air Staff and the Secretary of State. Later the Under Secretary of State made a special visit to 242 Squadron to listen to complaints about the control of the battle by Squadron Leader Bader. No senior member of Fighter Command staff was present or even knew about the visit, an unprecedented act of disloyalty by AVM Leigh-Mallory and the Air Council to the Commander-in-Chief. By the middle of October it had become obvious that the Big Wing was ineffective in a defensive battle, but Leigh-Mallory and his colleagues in the Air Ministry were locked into the Big Wing Philosophy. It was a crucial part of the plan to remove Dowding.

Air Vice-Marshal W S Douglas

Air Vice-Marshal Douglas was one of Trenchard's selected officers who had had fighter experience in World War I. He had moved steadily up the ladder of promotion and by 1938 was holding ground with his contemporaries with the rank of Air Vice-Marshal. In 1940 he was Deputy Chief of Staff to Newall, due to retire, and he held a position of some influence. Although he was involved in Fighter Command matters, like many of his contemporaries he had limited knowledge of modern aircraft and tactics, and based his views on his own experience with slow biplane fighters with no interception techniques. He must have been feeling in late 1940 that it was now time for his promotion, which could have been helped by Dowding's early retirement.

With his strong link with Trenchard and a close relationship with the Secretary of State for Air, it would be surprising if he were not one of the active members of the Cabal.

CHAPTER 9

Planning

A Meeting to Discuss Fighter Tactics

A meeting of air marshals and other senior officers was called by the Air Ministry for 17th October 1940 nominally to discuss fighter tactics, by which time the immediate danger of invasion had passed. I can find no war-progressive reason why this high-powered meeting was called at this time. As very short notice was given to Dowding and Park there was little time for them to prepare a presentation. They were unaware that S/Ldr Bader, the leader of the Duxford Wing, would be present, not merely as a witness, but as a full member with his own place at the table and later to receive a copy of the minutes. There can be no doubt that the meeting was a political ploy. It does not make sense for 10 officers of air rank, most of them chair-bound, to discuss a change in fighter tactics without even a defined strategy as a basis on which to plan such tactics.

Of course the *strategy* for Dowding of 'staying in being until 30th September' now needed revision or replacement. What was really needed from the Air Ministry was a new strategy to deal with combat through the winter months, and also defensive and offensive strategies for the Spring of 1941. These could then be used as the basis for Fighter Command to discuss new tactics. The Luftwaffe fighters were commanded by men who were well informed about modern combats and who were qualified to discuss and set new tactics for changing battle conditions.

The Meeting was chaired by AVM Douglas in his capacity as Deputy CAS. With his presence in this position he must be considered as a leading force in the attack on Dowding. Air Chief Marshal Newall, the Chief of Air Staff, did not attend because, as Douglas reported to the meeting, he was indisposed, although he was well enough to attend a meeting of the services Chiefs of Staff the following day. Discretion was wisely the better part of valour. Newall was well aware of his own imminent retirement with his promotion to Marshal of the Royal Air Force, and of being replaced by Air Marshal Portal.

It is already clear that this meeting was more than unusual. It may be thought reasonable that Portal, the Chief of Air Staff designate should attend, as the meeting had apparently been approved by Newall, the current CAS, who could not or would not attend. Quite what the CAS designate could have contributed to a meeting on fighter tactics is difficult to imagine. As previously a Bomber Command man, he would have little to offer on the special techniques of defensive day fighter tactics over Britain in 1940 and 1941. Advice on strategy perhaps, and the need for more squadrons and better equipment would concern him, but these were not on the published agenda. Did Portal know what was going on? Was he there in fact to support the anti-Dowding group to denigrate and remove him? He must have known and possibly supported it. He must have known that Bader was going to be present. Douglas would surely not have dared to invite a junior officer to a place at such a high table without his new chief designate being informed.

Portal was generally considered to be the most intelligent man in the RAF at that time. How was he associated with this Meeting of Shame, attacking the professional competence of the most senior officer in the RAF in front of a junior officer? To have been appointed firstly to be the Commander in Chief of Bomber Command, and then six months later to be selected as CAS in time of war, he must have had the full support of Trenchard and Salmond. If not an active member of the Cabal at that time he must have been one of the associated lobby anxious to see Dowding removed. His support for the Big Wings could be expected.

The fact that Squadron Leader Bader had a formal place at the table shows that he was expected to be present by Douglas and certain other senior officers, but certainly not expected by Dowding, Bader's Commander in Chief, and the other officers from Fighter Command. This was an insulting breach of Service protocol by both Douglas and Leigh-Mallory, and presaged the further humiliation that was yet to come at the Meeting. As Douglas obviously had the support of most other officers at the meeting, it confirms that the Meeting was essentially political with the intention of denigrating Dowding. As Dowding and Park had no knowledge that Bader, one of his 12 Group squadron commanders, would be present in his own right, they had brought none of their experienced squadron leaders to put forward opposing views. Nor had they been invited to do so.

Normally at such high powered meetings, a junior squadron leader, however experienced in his field, would have been kept waiting in another room until he was called to speak. For him to be present full time when Dowding and Park were being challenged on their professionalism confirms that this was indeed a meeting of infamy. Bader had been granted four days leave from 15th October, covering the date of the meeting on the 17th. More than a coincidence surely.

Purpose of Meeting

Who decided that the Conference should be called and who should attend?

Nominally Newall called the conference at the Air Ministry, but it is most unlikely that he would have *initiated* such a meeting. His retirement as CAS with promotion to Marshal of the Royal Air Force was imminent, and his indisposition, real or imagined, covered his absence. Douglas, even as deputy CAS, did not have the independent status or authority to have invited officers so senior to him on his own initiative. Was it one of the Cabal such as MRAF Sir John Salmond? It could have been the brainchild of Douglas supported by Salmond and other members of the Cabal. With documents dated 14th October 1940, Air Commodore DF Stevenson, the Director of Home Operations, invited Dowding and Park to attend a conference at the Air Ministry on 17th October to discuss *major day tactics* in the fighter force. Although he criticised Park for not giving information about the work of his squadrons, he took no action to distribute Park's report of his defensive actions up to 1st October. He submitted Leigh-Mallory's report on the first five-wing squadron engagements up to 15th September and refers to their great success in shooting down 105 aircraft at a cost of 14 of our own fighters. Examination of official German Luftwaffe casualties shows that in fact the real figure was close to 35. It should be borne in mind that in making assessments and judgements more than 60 years later, the real and significantly lower numbers were not known at the time. However, it seems that Stevenson had no doubts about the apparently superior performance of Bader's relatively inexperienced pilots compared with the 11 Group veterans. Dowding by contrast had already expressed grave doubts about the validity of some of the claims.

Stevenson presented the Big Wing philosophy as highly successful and superior to Park's tactics. His case was based on over-claiming by the Wing pilots. Strangely he stated: 'At present it seems that our fighter defence has defeated the German Air Force in their attempt this year to gain air superiority over this country.' Presumably he admitted that we had won, but would later claim that we didn't win well enough. This is describing one of the most wonderful achievements in British history as almost a non-event. Surely this victory merited a special mark of approval and commendation at the least. I have always felt that to beat back the Luftwaffe and prevent the invasion of Britain against overwhelming odds was victory, and that it was a chalice to be honoured and cherished and not tarnished by inferior men.

He failed even to hint that the Invasion in 1940 had been prevented, as this would have meant victory for Dowding. Surely Dowding's policies and Park's tactics must have been effective and deserving of praise, not criticism. He also referred to the change in Luftwaffe attacks to mainly fighter action with harassing bombing which need 'the vectoring of single squadrons or flights to intercept'. This must refer to the whole of October when the Duxford Wing failed to make one interception. But the Meeting had been specifically set up to consider, or rather to enforce, the employ-ment of wings of five or six squadrons for defence. As the Meeting was to discuss major day tactics in the fighter force, for what purpose was this force to be used? What changes were to be expected in enemy strategy or tactics? It becomes increasingly obvious that the Meeting was never planned as a serious discussion on the use of the fighter arm, which would have needed preplanning with circulation of proposals well beforehand for sensible appreciation. Can tactics be planned if the strategy had not been formulated?

In October the Big Wing with 4 or 5 squadrons sat at readiness and was totally ineffective with the 15 sorties failing to intercept even once. To publish the real performance of the Big Wing up to the date of the Meeting would have shown that it had only been effective against major raids directed at London, with a long approach, and in conditions of fine weather. He also failed to consider and emphasise the difference between defensive tactics to be employed against attacking enemy formations, and those needed for offensive sweeps against fighters over France. These were serious omissions.

At such a high-powered meeting it is astonishing that no significant reference was made to future plans, especially with the coming of winter and its attendant poor flying weather. The only reference to the future was: 'We must have regard to the possibility that more determined, better organised and heavier attacks may be made in the Spring of 1941, if not before.' Hardly 'before' with our average English weather in November, December, January and February, which would be much more suitable for high speed, low level attacks. It is difficult to accept that the Germans could have mounted heavier attacks before the Spring of 1941. If this really was Air Ministry thinking however, then the efforts should have been on the planning of a major increase in the supply of pilots and aircraft and vital improvements in the quality of our aircraft. Of special importance was greater power, speed and climb and the fitting of heating to our guns, windscreens and cockpits. There was also the urgent need for the replace-ment of cannons which had failed in August 1940 and which we needed to compete on equal terms with the existing Me109s.

The examination of squadron tactics was surely a matter for Fighter Command with the benefit of its battle experienced leaders to call upon. It was not for a meeting of senior 'non-piloting' officers who had last been in combat with the enemy in WWI biplanes. The certainty was that in the next four or five months of British winter weather, Dowding's tactics were going to be far more effective than Leigh-Mallory's Big Wings. The great irony of these machinations is that after Douglas took over as Commander in Chief of Fighter Command in late November, wings with 3 or more squadrons were never again used in the defence of Britain.

It is impossible to understand why this Meeting was called except for the specific political purpose of denigrating the work of Dowding and Park by putting forward Leigh-Mallory's September report as the panacea of fighter defence. Dowding was unaware of all who were to be present at the Meeting and had no time to prepare his defence, even if he had been aware of a need to defend himself.

When Park replied to Stevenson on 15th October, he referred to Leigh-Mallory's experience of five occasions when he had engagements. He adds that 11 Group had used wings of three squadrons in May, June, July, August and September. The results with wings of three squadrons in 11 Group over Britain in July, August and September could not have been impressive; if they had been they would have been extended!

How was it possible for the Chief of Air Staff and his deputy to call a conference to discuss squadron-fighting tactics without first formulating and promulgating the strategy for the next period of activity? All services administer and operate their forces on a basis of approved procedures. In the Meeting of Shame there appears to be a serious absence of approved procedures.

In his book *Fighter*, Len Deighton refers to the conference on 17th October as 'Alice in Wonderland'. Anyone with a knowledge of service procedures reading the documents relating to the Meeting would have no difficulty in concurring with this definition. 'Alice in Wonderland' indeed, but frightening in that these were our senior leaders of the Royal Air Force in a time of great crisis for our Country.

CHAPTER 10

Reports

Leigh-Mallory's Report on Duxford Wing

In his presentation of the work of the Duxford Wing, Stevenson used only Leigh-Mallory's report of the five actions up to and including 15th September 1940, the heyday of the Big Wing. The exceptionally high figures were accepted with approbation by the Big Wing supporters, and Leigh-Mallory's explanation for the melee that often resulted from being 'too late and too low' was equally accepted as a justifiable complaint against the controllers. There was no reference to the fact that 4 or 5 squadrons had been held at readiness for weeks, and that only two interceptions had been made in the 30 days after the report, with none at all in the first 2 weeks of October. During this period 11 Group were still fighting to the death. No one had investigated and analysed the effectiveness of the Big Wing, or if they had the results were suppressed.

The Air Ministry did not understand the mechanics of a defensive battle against an enemy so close. They did not understand the need for our pilots, including those in Big Wings, to be at readiness at the flight dispersals all day, subject to weather. With Big Wings this was a poor use of aircraft and pilots, with additional logistical problems. By contrast, with 5 separate squadrons some of them could be at '15 minutes readiness' in the Mess with easy access to food. With a Big Wing the pilots would be required to be at the same level of readiness all the time. It would have been almost impossible for 11 Group to have operated a five-squadron Wing in the Battle. There could only have been the 12 Group, five-squadron Wing in the Battle – and it is hardly possible to build an effective defence policy against several raids a day with one 'Balbo'.

Stevenson's Proposals on Use of Fighter Wings

The Air Staff Note submitted by Stevenson appears to have been written by someone who had little up-to date knowledge of the subject. He seems

173

to be unaware of the fact that Park had been fighting a defensive battle, which with the speed of change and uncertainty of information, required control of the highest order. His opening comment that *on some occasions* our fighters had been meeting the enemy on unequal terms, is evidence of his lack of experience of the battle conditions. Our pilots were always meeting the enemy on unequal terms, and rarely was height in our favour. No. 11 Group were always outnumbered as Fighter Command was fighting an enemy nearly three times as large. Only 40 % of its squadrons could be used to beat off the enemy aircraft concentrated mainly against 11 Group territory with our other squadrons spread over the rest of England, Scotland and Wales. The purpose of the note was given as: 'to examine the circumstances in which fighter units of more than a single squadron should be operated and to make general principles for their employment'. As pairs of squadrons were already being used in 11 Group with success, and extensively on 15th September, then the meeting was effectively concerned only with wings of three or more squadrons as already undertaken by 12 Group.

The opening paragraphs set out a clear criticism of Park's control of 11 Group Squadrons, and Dowding's principles. Without backing from the Air Ministry, Stevenson would not have been so foolhardy as to do this, especially after he had conceded that the German Air Force had already been bested; the Luftwaffe was battle experienced and a very professional fighting force. Without further discussion, he goes on to recommend a Wing of 3 squadrons as the minimum fighter unit to meet large enemy formations. But in his report Leigh-Mallory had already specified five squadrons as the minimum for Duxford Wings. Stevenson does not quantify the large enemy formations as to their numbers, speeds or heights or types. Would they be standard twin-engine bombers at 15,000 feet or fast high-flying Me109 bombers at 20,000–25,000 feet?

He states that to ensure superiority, when necessary, a force of two of these fighter wings would be required to operate as a tactical defensive unit over the south-east of England. Where would they be located, or where would they come from, who would decide to send them? Could we afford to have 6 squadrons sitting at readiness all day with the pilots at dispersal, waiting for the occasional chance of being sent off? A wing of 3 squadrons is 36 aircraft at most and a Balbo of 6 squadrons is 72 aircraft at most. In the Battle the Luftwaffe sent over formations of 100–400 aircraft and sometimes very much larger. How could even a Balbo Wing achieve guaranteed superiority in numbers? The Balbos would consist of two types of aircraft – the second wing would consist of Hurricanes with a climbing speed of 140mph, hardly a high-speed, dynamic attacking force.

There is a great deal of comment about R/T control. Esprit de Wing is mentioned, but this requires the same squadrons flying and fighting together. The third Duxford Wing contained only one flight from the two original wings and Bader and his No. 242 Squadron were not involved. Stevenson did not realise that fighter pilots fought as a squadron or flight units. He appeared not to realise that some of the enemy formations stretched for 10 miles in each direction and with some 10,000ft difference in height between the lowest and the highest. This meant that the concentrated Balbo attack would only affect a small part of the enemy formation, leaving the rest to fly serenely on to the target. The Balbo would of course have been broken up with their attack and they would have been queuing up to attack the bombers individually, as happened on 15th September when the Duxford Wing arrived.

Finally, Stevenson makes the daydream recommendation that the wing with the higher performance aircraft should take on the enemy fighters, and the wing with the lower performance should take on the bombers, if any. Bader had learned to his cost that this absurdly simple philosophy failed in practice. Until you arrive at the interception the leader has only a rough idea as to how many enemy aircraft he can expect to engage. He has no knowledge of the relative positions or heights of the bombers and fighters and how many of each. It is doubtful if Hurricane-led Balbos could catch or intercept Me109 formations with Me109 bombers, flying above 20,000 feet. Whereas squadrons or pairs could ensure adequate height from standing patrols, the impossibility of having big wings on standing patrols shows their inflexibility. One thing is certain and is known to any fighter pilot with significant experience in the battle, that the crucial factor is *height*. The most important functions of controllers and flight leaders is to see that their pilots arrive above the enemy, if necessary avoiding action until they have the height. Beyond that each leader must take instant action to deal with any formations as they appear.

Anyone with a knowledge of the practical aspects of fighting a defensive battle against the Luftwaffe in 1940 will almost certainly come to the conclusion that Air Commodore Stevenson was seriously out of touch with what was really happening in the air in the battle against the Luftwaffe, and was presenting a case to support the Air Ministry in their plans to remove Dowding and Park. A conference of politics – not tactics.

CHAPTER 11

The Meeting of Shame

Meeting of 17th October 1940

I always understood that the Air Ministry sets strategy and that Commands and Groups set tactics. As far as I can discover the Air Ministry never held meetings to advise or instruct Dowding in fighter tactics when the Battle of Britain was taking place, not even when invasion threatened. Why should the Air Ministry suddenly decide to take over responsibility for fighter tactics after the Battle? The use of Big Wings was surely a matter for Fighter Command to decide after they had been properly evaluated, and a strategy had been approved into which they could be fitted.

I am concerned that Fighter Command appeared to have had no authoritative officer or team of senior pilots with battle experience who were charged with the responsibility for our battle tactics, and who had also studied Luftwaffe tactics. Surely if such a team existed then immediately after 15th September they would have seriously investigated the wider use of Big Wings, and could have been present to support Dowding. There may well have been a Group or Command tactics team but we didn't see them at dispersal at Digby, Duxford or Hornchurch. Squadron tactics were essentially a matter for each individual squadron.

If, as I believe, it had already been planned by certain members of the Cabal that Douglas should take over Fighter Command with Leigh-Mallory commanding 11 Group, then there was no need for the meeting. Dowding could have been formally retired with promotion to Marshal of the Royal Air Force and with public recognition. Park could have been knighted, and sent on long leave to recover his health. Douglas and Leigh-Mallory could then have set up their Big Wings and Balbos without hindrance. For this to happen, however, the public would have to be told that we had won a great victory and that there would be no invasion in 1940.

Reluctantly I am forced to conclude that not only had the Cabal been determined to remove Dowding from the RAF for some years, but that they were now determined that he was to go without honour. It seemed that the Meeting had been set up for the denigration of Dowding's professional standing. His winning of the battle was a problem for them as it proved that his fighter defence campaign had been right and that the Trenchard and Air Ministry bomber defence policy had failed the Nation. The victory had to be played down, and it was necessary for his part in it to be disparaged. There appears to have been an element of animosity by members of the Cabal in their dealings with Dowding over the years, which is hard to explain. It seems that under no circumstances would Dowding be allowed to join the small and exalted group of Marshals including HM King George VI. Why should they wish to do this to him? I submit that the decision in 1937 to appoint Newall to be CAS instead of Dowding, as promised, destroyed his direct and certain promotion to be a Marshal of the Royal Air Force. It also ensured that he would never be in a position where he could seriously challenge the Trenchard inspired policy of Bomber Command supremacy in the Royal Air Force.

Those Attending

A Meeting held in the Air Council Room
on October 17th 1940 to discuss Major Day Tactics
in the Fighter Force

(Reference Air Staff Notes and Agenda Dated 14.10.40)

Present:

Air Vice-Marshal W. S. Douglas.	D.C.A.S.
Air Chief Marshal Sir Hugh C.T. Dowding	A.O.C.-in-C. Fighter Command
Air Marshal Sir Charles F.A. Portal	C.A.S. (Designate)
Air Marshal Sir Philip P.B. Joubert de la Ferte	A.C.A.S. (R)
Air Vice-Marshal K.R. Park	A.O.C. No. 11 Group
Air Vice-Marshal Sir C.J.Q. Brand	A.O.C. No. 10 Group
Air Vice-Marshal T.L. Leigh-Mallory	A.O.C. No. 12 Group
Air Commodore J. C. Slessor	D. of Plans
Air Commodore D.F. Stevenson	D.H.O. (Home Operations)
Air Commodore O.G.W.G. Lywood	P.D.D. of Signals
Group Captain H.G. Crowe	A.D.A.T.
Squadron Leader D.R.S. Bader	O.C. 242 Squadron
Wing Commander T.N. McEvoy}	Secretaries
Mr J.S. Orme}	

The Agendas

A copy of the Agenda is included in the Appendices.

I believe that it is highly unlikely that Dowding had seen a list of those attending before the Meeting, but if he had not he must have been severely shocked and hurt at what he saw when he entered the room. It is difficult to believe that Air Chief Marshal Sir Arthur Harris of Bomber Command would have stayed without protest after he had seen a junior squadron leader sitting alongside a difficult group commander, attacking his professionalism as a Commander-in-Chief. Dowding stayed at the table. His character as always was that of a gentleman and this could well have been a handicap in the corridors of power.

I have found it disturbing to describe the incompetent and unprofessional memoranda from Stevenson. It is difficult to accept that officers of air rank, including the designated Chief of Air Staff, allowed themselves to be associated with the published agenda.

Five out of the ten items of the agenda distributed before the Meeting start with or include 'is it agreed that' followed by a predetermined statement about the use of squadron wings. This was a clear endorsement of Leigh-Mallory's Big Wing without discussion of Park's successful techniques and results. This conference was clearly to be a trial with the defence ignored. Indeed, I feel that the minutes could have been printed before the conference took place. It gives the aura of a session of a Communist Politburo in Russia in the 1930s. The meeting had been set up for the Cabal by Douglas to emphasise the achievement of Leigh-Mallory and his Big Wing, thereby denigrating the victory of Dowding and Park. After having read the agenda, Dowding and Park must have had serious concerns about their futures.

Nine of the ten items dealt with Wings and Balbos. Item 10 required a short report by the Commander in Chief on night fighting defence. His adverse but realistic views on single-engine night fighting were later to be given as a major reason for his dismissal.

What supports the 'Alice in Wonderland' assessment is that when Douglas opened the meeting he did so, not with the agenda that had been circulated to Dowding and Park, but with an entirely different one which Dowding and Park had not seen. Who else attending the meeting was aware of the new additional agenda with its priority of presentation? Was this action just casual behaviour or was it an intended deceit? It is not surprising that the CAS was indisposed.

The Chairman

The Deputy Chief of Air Staff explained that he was presiding at the Meeting as the CAS was unable to be present owing to indisposition. This statement made it clear that the meeting had the full authority of the CAS who, this implied, had intended to be the Chairman. Douglas ignored the original agenda and instead first outlined three propositions that he wished the meeting to consider:

1. We wish to outnumber the enemy formations when we meet them.
2. We want our superior numbers to go into the attack with a co-ordinated plan of action, so that the protecting fighters are engaged by one part of our force, leaving the bombers to be engaged by the remainder.
3. If possible we want the top layer of our fighter formation to have the advantage of height over the top layer of the enemy formation.

Surely the only way to ensure that you can outnumber the enemy when you meet them is simply to have significantly more aircraft than they have. The Luftwaffe had 2,350 bombers and fighters and we had 750 fighters.

Crucially in their discussions to dominate the enemy formations with numbers and big wings, Dowding's enemies had forgotten the importance of the relative aircraft performance of the opposing forces in their fighting in WWI. In 1917, with the introduction of a new superior single seat fighter, the German aces dominated the skies over the Western Front for many months, inflicting heavy casualties on the Allied squadrons. Superior numbers were not in themselves the panacea for victory. Quality in men, machine, and tactics was more important than sheer numbers.

What is disturbing is that these questions were being posed by someone who was apparently out of touch with the use of fighters in aerial combat in 1940, and yet within five weeks would be promoted to take over as C-in-C of Fighter Command, replacing the very experienced Dowding. Perhaps it was felt at the Air Ministry that his World War I fighter experience would still stand him in good stead.

Minutes of The Meeting

A copy of the official minutes is given in the Appendices. I find that the minutes were only brief extracts and, as Park was told in a letter from the Air Ministry, are only to be regarded as aide-memoires. Was this the standard practice for minute taking at high-level Air Ministry policy making meetings? As the Air Ministry refused to accept letters from Dowding, Park and Brand, dissenting from the minutes, the total validity of the minutes must be in some doubt.

When the Chairman opened this august meeting with these totally unexpected propositions, Dowding and Park must have wondered what had happened. They must have searched in vain for these propositions in the official agendas sent to them, and for which they might have had time to prepare answers. But these basic tactical questions had been put to the meeting without warning. Dowding had no senior squadron commander with him to put forward the crucial experience of 11 Group which, after all, was where the battle had been mainly fought. He must have quickly realised that this was to be no ordinary meeting on tactics. The three propositions above are quite unrelated to the published agenda. There was no reference in the original official agenda to the need to outnumber the enemy, or of plans for attack, or the advantage of height. This shows either professional incompetence by Douglas, or confirms that the agenda was part of the charade disguising the political and real intentions of the meeting. I have selected a few points from the minutes for comment.

Park defended the use of two squadron formations, which compared favourably with wing sorties.
Dowding said that the great problem was to obtain early knowledge. Technical improvements expected soon could help them.
Leigh-Mallory welcomed opportunities of using wing formations to help 11 Group.
If this type of counter attack intercepted a big formation only once in 10 times, the effort would nonetheless be worth it. (This illustrates Leigh-Mallory's unsuitability for operational command in his acceptance of 5 of his best squadrons being tied up for 10 days, a total of 50 squadron days, for one wing interception against an enemy formation of undefined size and squadron content.)
Park very sensibly asked for more squadrons so that he could always have 20 squadrons at readiness. (This was the simplest and most effective way of putting more fighters against the enemy.)
It was agreed that additional fighter support would often be advantageous. (It required a meeting of 10 officers of air rank to come to this momentous conclusion. Surely additional controlled fighter support would *always* be advantageous.)
Bader said that from his practical experience, time was the essence of the problem. If enough warning could be given to have a large number of fighters in position, there was no doubt they would get most effective results (truism of the first order).
Portal wisely enquired how such a local concentration might affect the responsibility of a Group Commander for the defence of all the area of his Group.

Some 21 minutes were listed on the three propositions and then finally the nine items of the original agenda dealing with the Balbo were discussed.

Item No. 10, the last of the original agenda, was 'Short report by C-in-C Fighter Command on present position regarding night interception'. In view of the sudden importance to the Air Ministry of the night bombing attacks on London and other cities, it is surprising that so little emphasis was placed on this aspect. This was a current, immediate and growing problem, whereas the decision on Balbos could be of little importance for months.

Dowding explained that the new fighter and AI equipment which were the only really effective means of defence against the night bombers were not yet ready, either technically or in sufficient numbers at present to have a significant effect. (The Air Ministry were well aware of this.)

Douglas and **Stevenson** referred to the grave problem of maintaining civil morale in London in face of continuing attacks. They recommended that in the meantime a temporary wing of two Defiant and two Hurricane squadrons be formed to operate on the 1914–1918 system, and gave Dowding a preliminary draft of their scheme.

Dowding agreed to this temporary wing and the use of controlled clumps of searchlights.

Dowding and **Brand** both expressed their views that the new Beaufighter night fighters with their improved AI equipment would be the only really effective method of fighting the German night bombers. (This was later proved to be correct.)

It is interesting that Douglas and Stevenson had arrived at the meeting with a preliminary draft of their scheme for a new night fighter defence to be operated on a World War I system using a Wing of day-fighter squadrons. Rather late in the day! The Air Ministry, having failed to defend Britain by day with its Trenchard bomber force, were now trying to meet their responsibilities for night defence by the belated use of tactics from the war of 20 years ago. As the last item to be dealt with it seems that it was introduced to impose the plan on Dowding rather than to receive his report.

CHAPTER 12
Review of the Meeting

Effectiveness of The Meeting

As regards day fighting, from a strictly operational view this was a meeting of no significance except to state formally that, when conditions were suitable, three-squadron wings and six-squadron Balbos could be used to attack large German formations in defensive operations. In the event this never happened. Dowding accepted, under duress, that it would be arranged for 12 Group Wings to participate freely in suitable operations over 11 Group area. This was a final humiliation, particularly as there was little chance of large enemy formations flying over England during the next four months. The meeting had finally dealt with the official agenda, but failed to resolve the three unreal propositions put forward by Douglas at the beginning.

The Big Wing Philosophy had prevailed as had been intended, but how do you outnumber enemy formations of more than 400 aircraft? Only with a larger number of fighters than the total enemy aircraft of the German formations. The Luftwaffe had all the initiative and Fighter Command resources had to be spread. This was valid only provided that our fighters could all intercept at precise planned positions, not known until the interception.

Effectively the Meeting had made no serious recommendations for future operations of any kind, but had presented the Big Wing Philosophy as crucial for defensive operations, thereby demeaning Dowding and Park as commanders. At no time was it said simply that now we have prevented the invasion in 1940, we must prepare for more vigorous attacks against Britain in 1941. How shall we do this? That surely should have been the task before the Meeting. As previously stated, Dowding, Park and Brand refuted the published minutes and sent in their amendments; these were all rejected. There was to be no defence to the adverse claims – the only evidence that was admissible in this political exercise was that of the prosecution.

At this meeting Douglas had highlighted Dowding's reluctance to support Big Wings which had then been officially approved as effective for defensive operations. Dowding's reluctance to use his day squadrons to defend London at night for political reasons was met by a plan from

Douglas, using day-fighters and searchlights. The scene was being set.

If the meeting had really been called to consider day-fighter tactics over Britain then it must have been the most useless meeting ever held at the Air Ministry. It had no effect whatsoever on our future combats with the Luftwaffe over Britain by day.

If in fact it had been called as a political meeting to denigrate Dowding's status and professionalism to prepare for his dismissal, then it was highly successful and deeply dishonourable.

Pre-Agenda Propositions

I have repeated the propositions put forward before the original agenda by the Chairman, AVM Douglas, to show how far the Air Ministry were detached from reality and the actual war in the air.

What prompted Douglas and his colleagues to add these three propositions, or hide them until the last minute, and then to deal with them first?

1. *We wish to outnumber the enemy formations when we meet them.*

Is it necessary to outnumber the enemy when you meet them in order to win? Not if you are above them, not if you are faster, not if you are better armed. The prime purpose is to beat the enemy, not merely to outnumber them as the Luftwaffe had already found to their cost. This is a pious and unrealistic hope. What are the numbers of enemy aircraft to be out-numbered? What is the mix? In the Battle of Britain the largest enemy formation was some 960 aircraft. Would we expect larger formations to attack us in the future, or would an increase in the number of raids be more likely? How would we know how many aircraft there were in a raid? We would always have to send off excessive strength to be sure. On occasions we would need to be able to put up 1,000 fighters at a given time at a given place. Are these to operate as squadrons, pairs, or Balbos? What about the defence of the rest of Britain – another 500 serviceable fighter aircraft? They will need to be available at readiness from dawn till dusk. This could raise the total numbers required to more than 1,500 serviceable fighter aircraft. Twice our existing size? How soon could we train the pilots? Could these numbers be effectively serviced on the ground and controlled in the air?

Douglas and his advisors missed the fundamentals. Of course we needed many more fighter squadrons in Fighter Command, but what we also needed was better performance and efficiency with our aircraft. We needed heating in our aircraft. At 30,000ft we often froze up and we might as well have stayed on the ground. We needed improved Spitfires and

Hurricanes with cannons to match the Me109s. We needed faster aircraft to match or exceed the new German aircraft that were due to come into the skies in 1941 and would outclass our squadrons.

We needed quicker and more accurate plotting of the enemy aircraft to give us more time to get into position at the right height – above.

It is not a practical proposition to outnumber 900 attacking aircraft in formation over 11 Group, nor is it necessary. Co-ordinated attacks with 20 pairs of squadrons, 500 aircraft, across the enemy formation would give freedom of action, would allow Me109 protection to be fought off and would cause havoc with the enemy bombers.

Another 10 pairs of squadrons would need to be immediately available from reserves or other sectors to deal with second waves if they attacked again, before our first line had landed and refuelled.

A Balbo is not a fighting formation, it is merely a number of squadrons being led to one specific place. To attack the enemy it must break down into smaller effective fighting units, either 2 three-squadron wings or 3 two-squadron pairs depending on the preplanning. This will give greater flexibility in the attack and faster opening of fire on the enemy. A major Luftwaffe formation can be more than 10 miles long. An RAF formation of 72 aircraft could be seen many miles away. Attacking at one point could only lead to confusion, queuing, and inevitably – collisions. Most of the raiding squadrons would be left untouched or even undisturbed.

What would we plan to do if the Luftwaffe decided to make a major increase in the numbers and performance of their attacking squadrons? To stay in being we should need a system of temporary airfields and sector control units north of the Thames from which to operate.

2. *We want our superior numbers to go into the attack with a co-ordinated plan of action so that the protecting fighters are engaged by one part of our force, leaving the bombers to be engaged by the remainder.*

In the world of military conflict all co-ordinated plans are perfect until the battalions meet up with the enemy who already have their own perfect co-ordinated plans of defence.

This second proposition shows that it was put forward by someone who was out of touch with the reality of war by interception in the air. If he had studied the reports of the Big Wing he would have realised that it is not possible to have co-ordinated plans to attack formations of up to 1,000 mixed aircraft. The Me109 defending fighters can be in any position, height and numbers and with many of them not immediately visible. Some of the squadrons may divert to an alternative target. Until the interception is made the leaders are unable to make a decision as how best to attack. They may already be fighting for their lives against marauding Me109s in front of the main formation.

In land warfare, where the positions of enemy forces are known, and are likely to be there when the attack is made, a co-ordinated plan of attack can be envisaged. When an interception is made in the air it is done at approaching speeds of up to one mile in 10 seconds, and the best and only information available to the Leader is '100 or 400 bandits at 15,000 feet ahead of you'. Until you get there and see them you will not know what aircraft you have to fight, how many bombers, at what different heights, on what course, how many Me109 fighters there are, and crucially where they are, provided you manage to see them in time. Are they in front of the bombers, above, behind, off to one side? Are there any Me110s present on this sortie to be aware of? Instant awareness followed by instant decision is vital.

3. *If possible, we want the top layer of our fighter formation to have the advantage of height over the top layer of the enemy formation.*
(The Me109s would have the same intention of course).

To be sure of meeting *Proposition 3*, we would need to know which was the top layer of the fast approaching enemy formation, normally the fighters, and to know the height they were flying, and with time to get there. This again displays a lack of understanding of defensive war in the air. As the German fighters were sometimes at 30,000ft and had a higher operational ceiling, this could rarely be a practical possibility. The only way to guarantee this would be to have selected squadrons of RAF fighters scrambled and in position at 30,000ft ready to intercept.

To be effective it would need at least a further wing of Spitfires, if not two, operating separately from the Balbos. It must not be forgotten that the Battle of Britain was won by our pilots attacking very large formations; with single squadrons or flights, always seriously outnumbered. If the Air Ministry members on 17th October had been battle hardened in the air, they might have realised that it was not only numbers that mattered but also the performance of the pilots and their aircraft, their tactics and the quality of the interception information. Height would always be crucial.

The use of large wings was not significant and the use of Balbos would have been fatal.

17th October Confirmed as Political

The Meeting chaired by Douglas at the Air Ministry was of great significance. It was formally proposed as a conference to discuss fighter tactics. There is adequate evidence to show, however, that the meeting was essentially a political gathering to attack the professionalism of Dowding and Park, to initiate their removal, and to raise the status of Leigh-Mallory and his Big Wing Philosophy. I list the following facts in support of this.

1. Although solely concerned with Fighter Command matters, the Meeting was called without prior consultation with Dowding and Park who were unaware of all the personnel who would be present.
2. Out of the 10 items to be discussed in the formal printed agenda, 9 items concerned the setting up of Big Wings and Balbos. When the meeting was opened, however, quite different items were first introduced and discussed, and some 21 points were minuted before the 10 original items of the official agenda were dealt with.
3. Stevenson, the Director of Home Operations, wrote notes for the conference and an air staff note on the operation of Fighter Wings on 14th October. Dowding and Park were not given reasonable time to consider them and to present their response.
4. It is clear from Stevenson's writing that he was ignorant of the problems facing Fighter Command in a defensive battle and was not qualified to present proposals on his own.
5. He bases most of his arguments on Leigh-Mallory's report of Wing successes from 7th to 15th September. The battle continued for another month to 17th October and then finally to the 31st October. No report on the period after the 15th September, when the Wings only went into action on two further occasions, was presented or discussed.

Deliberately reporting on only the first 9 days of the Wing at readiness out of 40 days up to the meeting, presented a distorted, misleading and dangerous bias. The report gave highly inflated figures and there was no serious analysis of performance and effectiveness.

Why did no one at or before the meeting ask for a report on the total wing performance to date? Leigh-Mallory, Douglas, Stevenson and Evill, the SASO at Fighter Command, must have known the results, and Portal and Sinclair should have been concerned, as it was the substance of this important Air Ministry meeting. Dowding should have been kept informed by his SASO Evill who received daily reports of Group actions and casualties. Certainly members of the Cabal would not have wanted it to be disclosed.

I believe that the deliberate ignoring and withholding of the later reports showing the failure of the Big Wings before the meeting, typifies the standards of behaviour of those involved in the dishonour of a great man in British history. It was indeed 'a Lion brought down by Jackals'.

6. Apart from Fighter Command representatives, none of the officers of air rank at the meeting had any practical experience of air tactics since WWI. Such a high-powered gathering would never have been assembled simply to discuss fighter tactics. But there was no discussion of strategy either, which could have justified their attendance.

This fact again shows clearly the political intent of the Meeting. Newall, the CAS, was well advised to claim to be indisposed and to stay away, although as previously noted, he was fit enough to attend a meeting of Chiefs of Staff the following day. According to the Air Force list he had seniority as Marshal of the Royal Air Force with effect from 4th October 1940, but this does not appear to have been publicised.

7. The presence of Bader, a junior squadron leader, with his own place at the table in the Air Council Room for the whole meeting was unprecedented. The meeting was clearly intended to attack the past tactics of the Commander-in-Chief and the 11 Group Commander, and to make the case for Big Wings.

Douglas knew that Bader was going to be present and it must have had his and higher approval to happen. This was done without the knowledge or consent of Bader's own C-in-C, although he had been invited by Leigh-Mallory his Group Commander. Dowding was denied the opportunity of presenting one of his own very experienced squadron leaders to explain the battle problems. After the meeting Bader received a copy of the minutes confirming his privileged position.

8. After the draft minutes were circulated, Park, Dowding and Brand wrote criticising them and sending their amendments to the Air Ministry. Their amendments were not accepted and were not included in the final minutes. The Air Ministry prosecution case was preserved and recorded intact.

9. Anyone who reads Stevenson's memoranda, the Air Staff note, the Agenda, the Minutes, and Leigh-Mallory's Wings report of 17th September, can only be bewildered by the content and presentation. The Air Ministry was seriously lacking in an understanding of battle conditions and tactical requirements. The presentation and chairmanship of the meeting by Douglas was of an unacceptable standard, humiliating to some members, and obviously totally biased in favour of the Big Wing Philosophy.

10. The reference given to the meeting of 17th October as 'Alice in Wonderland' by author Len Deighton in his book *Fighter* could be accepted as a humorous and very apt description, if only it had not been describing such a key discussion on the tactical use of our fighters. The only reason for it being held must have been political. It is frightening in retrospect that Portal, to be the Chief of Air Staff only three days later, and reported to have been outstanding in this role throughout the war, allowed himself to be associated with such a political and infamous meeting. Perhaps he found the political pressure by his seniors to be too great at the beginning of his new appointment and promotion. With the impersonal and ruthless removal of Dowding from office so soon after his appointment as CAS, it can be considered that Portal was closely associated with the Cabal.

11. With his failure to mention the meeting in his autobiography and with his distortion of the events surrounding it, Douglas confirms his efforts to be publicly dissociated from this dishonourable event, which he had programmed, chaired and carried through.

CHAPTER 13

After the Meeting

Wing Activities after 17th October

At the Meeting the defensive use of Big Wings and Balbos was approved but was never once put into action.

On 19th October 242 Squadron under Bader was finally ordered to move as a complete squadron unit to Duxford, presumably to help implement the Wing decisions of two days previously. It proved to be a wasted journey. For the whole of September and the first half of October, 242 Squadron had flown almost daily to Duxford and back home again in the evening. It was difficult to understand why, for several weeks, the lead squadron of the established Wing stayed overnight at another airfield 68 miles from the Wing base. Is it possible that Bader needed to receive treatment with his artificial legs? Whatever the reason, this need to return to a separate base every evening could have affected the efficiency of the Wing, and would not have helped the Esprit de Wing. In the first half of October the Wing flew 6 sorties without action. After the meeting on 17th October, the Wing flew 9 sorties without action. They saw enemy aircraft on the last sortie, but as Bader's radio was reported to be useless no action was taken. Another example of Bader's poor leadership and airmanship? The Big Wing had fizzled out and presumably was now obsolescent, if not obsolete, for defensive action.

On 26th October, the Secretary of State visited Duxford. Rather late in the day! On 5th November Bader reported on a *two-squadron patrol* with 19 Squadron when they intercepted Me109s above them. No. 242 Squadron claimed one Me109 and lost two aircraft. Up to the end of 1940 Bader reported no other patrols.

The meeting of 17th October had served no tactical purpose. It had, however, achieved its political purpose and Dowding was dismissed in November, and Park in December, to be replaced by Douglas and Leigh-Mallory.

Evill – Man of Mystery

Since my early research I have always been puzzled by the behaviour of the Senior Air Staff Officer at Fighter Command. Evill had been an Air Vice-Marshal since January 1938, when Leigh-Mallory was an Air Commodore and Keith Park was a Group Captain. As the SASO at Fighter Command, he was Dowding's deputy and senior in the Air Force List to the 11 and 12 Group Commanders. He was an Air Vice-Marshal contemporary of Portal, Douglas and Nichol, also at Fighter Command. Evill had been Assistant Commandant at the RAF College at Cranwell when Cadet Bader graduated, and signed his logbook with an above average assessment. There were links in Fighter Command with the Cranwell brotherhood. Dowding's promotion of Air Commodore Keith Park to Air Vice-Marshal commanding the top Group in Fighter Command would hardly have been warmly received.

In 1937 Air Commodore Evill was appointed SASO in Bomber Command, the most important Command in the RAF, and continued in this position after his promotion to Air Vice-Marshal in January 1938. Prior to that he had served in Bomber Command as Air Officer in Charge of Administration. It is likely that he was committed to the Trenchard Bomber Doctrine. After service in France he was posted to Fighter Command to replace Air Commodore Park as SASO to Dowding.

Evill's behaviour in the Battle sometimes appears to be inexplicable. In the early phase of the Battle he was clearly aware of the problems between Park and Leigh-Mallory and must have realised the dangers these represented to the effectiveness of Fighter Command. Although it is reported that he had in fact advised Dowding of the dispute, he appeared to have failed to take any effective action himself to minimise this harmful dissension between the two Commanders. When questioned about the relative merits of squadrons versus wings, he managed to sit comfortably on the fence by supporting both tactics.

As the SASO at Fighter Command he received daily group returns on casualties and claims and so he must have been aware of the failure of the Big Wings after Leigh-Mallory's report in mid September. Did he advise Dowding of this crucial information or did he maintain a discreet silence? He was aware of Dowding's distrust of the Wing's claims in a minute from him, referring to claims some of which were mere thoughtful wishing. He could and should have warned Dowding about the obvious failure of the Big Wings in late September and October.

I hold the view that he supported Leigh-Mallory and Douglas but obviously avoided open commitment. In his book *The Battle of Britain*, author John Ray expresses the view that Evill had sympathy with the Big Wing Philosophy, and in a reference to an 'interesting enigma', implies that he passed a copy of Leigh-Mallory's Big Wing report direct to the Air Ministry before being instructed to do so by Dowding.

3

Dismissal of Dowding

Introduction
How the Battle is won

Great battles are not won by gung-ho leaders 'seeking the bubble reputation even in the cannon's mouth'. They are won by ordinary young men who continue to fight on and on against heavy odds, in great danger, and without thought of personal glory.

It is tragic that the lives of these gallant fighting men are even more endangered by commanders who, safe from the dangers of the conflict, are diverted from the real battle in pursuit of their own personal and political causes.

CHAPTER 14

Reasons Considered for Dismissal

Victory and its Aftermath

After 30th September there were no more major day raids by twin-engine bombers over Britain, although the fighting continued against formations of high flying Me109s and Me109 fighter-bombers with significant casualties on both sides. Britain had been saved from invasion in 1940. Dowding and his pilots had met the charge.

On 13th November 1940, and apparently without previous discussion, Air Chief Marshal Dowding was advised by the Secretary of State for Air that he was to be removed from office as Commander-in-Chief and replaced by Air Vice-Marshal Douglas from the Air Ministry, who was then promoted to Air Marshal. The exchange of office took place on 24th November. Dowding was not retired, as he might have expected, and although he had been awarded the Knight Grand Cross of the Order of the Bath on 8th October 1940, he received no public recognition as the Architect and Victor of the Battle of Britain. Instead he was quietly sent to the United States of America, for an appointment, which he did not want and for which he was not really suited, and effectively into exile well away from the scene of the Battle. Why?

Air Vice-Marshal Keith Park, Commander of 11 Group, which took the brunt of the bomber and fighter attacks by the Luftwaffe, was replaced one month later after only nine months as Group Commander and relegated to a Training Command appointment. Why? A significant purpose of this book has been to find out the answers to these questions.

Possible Reasons for Dismissal

A number of reasons which might explain Dowding's dismissal, have been listed by various authors including the following:
1. Failure to use Big Wings effectively
2. Failure to provide adequate defence against night bombing after 7th September

3. Not collaborating with Air Ministry Personnel
4. He was a difficult man to work with
5. He was due for retirement
6. He was tired and needed a rest
7. He had lost the confidence of the Politicians and the Air Ministry.

Even if true, charges 3–7 are hardly good enough reasons for the abrupt and covert dismissal without national recognition of the man whose leadership had saved Britain from invasion. They could all have been dealt with by honourable retirement with public acknowledgement of his great achievement. Indeed charges 4, 5 and 6 could have been made at times against Winston Churchill. This leaves only charges 1 and 2 as worthy of serious consideration.

His refusal to accept 12 Group Big Wings as the panacea for Victory has been shown in Part One to have been a very wise decision. The Big Wing Philosophy of Leigh-Mallory has been shown to be without substance. Without doubt Dowding and his pilots won the Battle, apparently with little assistance from the Air Ministry and with a harmful lack of loyalty from one of his commanders. This only leaves the criticism of Dowding's handling of our night defences to be considered.

Failure of Night Defence

It has been proposed by many writers that a major reason for Dowding's dismissal was his failure to provide an adequate defence against bomber attacks at night.

Dowding won the daylight battle which prevented an invasion, but he could not have been charged with responsibility for the defence of the Country against bomber attacks by night from bases so close to the English coast. It was not until 7th September that Hitler unleashed his nightly terror attacks on London from French and Belgian airfields. This was not foreseen or seriously contemplated by the Air Ministry in their planning from 1935 onwards as they were relying on Bomber Command to defend Britain from attacks across the North Sea with a 400-mile crossing each way. These German terror raids, helped by their advanced radio bombing beam, caused high civilian casualties and damage to buildings, but did not, and could not, have helped their invasion plans unless they broke the morale of our people.

As the night bombing of London and other cities continued, the casualties mounted. Churchill and the Air Staff put pressure on Fighter Command to put up single-engine day-fighters, including Defiants, in suitable conditions with searchlight support, to boost the morale of the people of London who were being bombed night after night. Dowding reluctantly agreed to do this. His honest views and reluctance to risk pilots for political purposes disturbed Churchill and were used by his enemies to discredit him. However, the use of our day-fighter pilots on ineffective night patrols would have endangered Dowding's daytime defence system, and added to the stress of his already tired pilots, with additional aircraft servicing problems and overload for the ground crews. Waiting at readiness for a night scramble or flying night patrols precludes adequate sleep, so essential to resist the daytime raids. To take out day fighter squadrons for night duties only would have weakened our defence against the main thrust of the German attack.

Spitfires with poor forward visibility were not at all suitable for night operations, as I know from some ineffective night patrols over the North Sea in 13 Group in 1941. The transfer and use of Hurricane day squadrons from 12 and 13 Groups, specifically and only for night readiness and patrols, might have provided the aircraft although training would have been necessary for this specialised work. As the ability to see and identify the enemy aircraft depended on the pilot's eyesight, pilots should have been specially selected on the inherent quality of their night vision. This varied from pilot to pilot and was made less efficient by tiredness. To be effective the fighters needed to work in co-operation with the searchlight teams and A/A guns. This would take time and Dowding was opposed to panic plans before we had won the day battle.

The Air Ministry knew that our existing night fighters and poor RDF equipment were quite inadequate to make any significant impact on the German night bomber raids. They knew that our few night fighter squadrons equipped with Blenheims and single-engine Defiants achieved their limited results only because of the courage and tenacity of their crews. These squadrons flew in all weather conditions and sometimes even when they could see the enemy they had insufficient power to catch up with them. The Air Ministry and Douglas knew as well as Dowding did, that until these squadrons were re-equipped with the new Beaufighters, with greatly improved interception radar, no serious defence could be made against the German night bombers.

Although some limited successes were achieved with Hurricanes and Defiants under special weather and moon conditions and with searchlight co-operation, Dowding, always concerned about his pilots, felt that risking their lives for minimal return was not justifiable. The importance of defending against night bomber raids had expanded suddenly on 7th September with attacks on London when, according to many, Fighter Command was close to being beaten. Dowding was sufficiently worried about our ability to meet the day attacks that, on that day, he had called a meeting to discuss Fighter Command 'going down hill'. This involved grading and relocating squadrons to ensure that the most experienced were kept in the front line, and others were used for training reinforcements. His priority at that time was to defeat the day attacks at all costs.

If at that particular time it was true that defeat was a possibility, then it would have been far more important to convert the Defiant squadrons into Hurricane day fighters in order for us to stay in being, than to take hard pressed Hurricane squadrons out of day fighting into searchlight co-operation. It could have been a simple conversion with the battle-ready Hurricanes available in the depots. It was only because of Dowding's success against the Luftwaffe by day, and Hitler's sudden emotional revenge decision, that night defence became a major issue at that time. If Dowding had lost the day battle, night fighters would not have mattered. Surely it was winning the day battles that would decide the future. I believe, however, that in the weeks of panic in the 'corridors of power' over the unexpected heavy night bombing of London, Dowding could have shown more concern to help progress the temporary makeshift defences put forward by other parties, although Marshal of the Royal Air Force Sir John Salmond at the Ministry of Aircraft Production had already taken action on his own with the support of the Air Ministry.

I am astonished that some writers should consider that Fighter Command's failure to contain the German night bombing in 1940 should be used as an attack against Dowding's professionalism. At my fighter station in Digby in early 1940, we served with No. 46 Hurricane Squadron commanded by Squadron Leader Kenneth Cross, and No. 229 Blenheim Night Fighter Squadron commanded by Squadron Leader Harold Maguire. The night-fighter pilots were held in the greatest respect by us, for their tenacity in flying night after night in poor weather and with so little to show for their courage. They, and we, knew then that there was no hope of an effective defence against the German bombers until improved aircraft and AI equipment could be delivered to the squadron. If we knew it then, Dowding also knew it then. Douglas and the Air Ministry, who were responsible for the plans for our defence, most certainly knew.

From pre-war days the policy of the Air Ministry was to protect Britain against enemy attack by the Trenchard philosophy of maintaining a powerful offensive bomber force with priority budgets allocated to do so. Bomber Command failed to provide this defence in 1940 and without our much smaller Fighter Command all would have been lost. Although Bomber Command made bombing attacks against French ports and German troop barges, these had no significant effect on the fight between Fighter Command and the Luftwaffe on which Britain's survival depended. As long as Fighter Command was kept in being as an effective fighter force we were safe. Was the unfair and unsubstantiated attack by the Air Ministry and others of the Cabal against Dowding for not containing the Luftwaffe bombers at night, a cover up for the total failure of their Trenchard Doctrine of bomber defence to protect our Island? Dowding was to be used as the scapegoat for their failure!

CHAPTER 15

Dowding and Park Removed from Office

A Lion brought down by Jackals

Dismissal of Air Chief Marshal Sir Hugh Dowding

It had been agreed with the Air Ministry in July 1940 that Air Chief Marshal Dowding would retire on 31st October 1940. Dowding had accepted this as the last in a series of four dates set for his retirement, although this was later changed again. It was a peculiar decision to set such a date, as the country was faced with imminent invasion by the Germans, which could only be prevented by Fighter Command with Dowding as Commander-in-Chief, responsible for defending the Realm. He was the only man in Britain qualified to ensure victory, if victory was indeed possible.

By the end of September and certainly by 17th October the threat of invasion by the Germans in 1940 had passed. Britain would be protected from invasion and major daylight bombing attacks for the next four months by the winter weather over England and the Channel. Dowding had served his purpose. He had many enemies at the Air Ministry who influenced the politicians. There is correspondence to show that Marshals Trenchard and Salmond were active behind the scenes to have Dowding removed. The Secretary of State for Air, Sir Archibald Sinclair, was at best neutral. The proponents of the Big Wing philosophy had won a political victory at the Meeting of Shame and commanded the heights. By the end of October, later regarded as the official date of the ending of the Battle, Dowding had few friends in high places, except perhaps Lord Beaverbrook, the Minister of Aircraft Production, who had played a crucial part in ensuring a continued supply of fighter aircraft. After his victory, his promotion to Marshal of the Royal Air Force could have followed naturally. All great victors of national battles have been honoured. Honour would then not only have been paid to Dowding, but by association also to Park and all the pilots.

I am forced to the conclusion that Marshals Trenchard and Salmond and other members of the Cabal were not only jealous of Dowding's victory, but were angered that by his victory he had exposed the failure of the Trenchard Bomber Defence Strategy. If Dowding were to be publicly declared the RAF commander who had beaten off the invasion, then his promotion would be inevitable and getting rid of him would have been most difficult. To retire Dowding with promotion to Marshal of the RAF with the grateful thanks of the Nation would not have been acceptable to the Cabal. By removing Dowding from office and finding him quite unsuitable employment abroad such a situation was averted.

On 13th November Sinclair interviewed Dowding and told him that he was to be replaced as Commander-in-Chief of Fighter Command, and that he would go to the United States on a mission relating to the supply of equipment. He was told that Air Vice-Marshal Douglas would be taking over from him as Commander-in-Chief. Dowding was reluctant to accept the proffered appointment, realising that it was not his forte. He had been specially requested for this overseas work by Beaverbrook, the Minister of Aircraft Production. Was MRAF Salmond involved in this unusual appointment? In an interview with Churchill the next day, which he had requested, he accepted the appointment but only out of a sense of duty. His replacement at Fighter Command was delayed until 25th November, as Douglas was unable to take over before then. His chagrin at being replaced by Douglas and then sent into exile must have been difficult to bear. It had indeed been the culmination of 'A Lion brought down by Jackals'.

On 30th November, five days after the ignominious removal of Dowding from office, Churchill authorised the ringing of church bells on Christmas Day as the imminence of invasion had greatly reduced. On the day when the victory of the Battle of Britain was to be celebrated across the nation, Dowding, the Architect of Victory was not in Britain to receive his rightful honour. Churchill knew that Dowding had won the Battle but gave him no promotion or public praise. This compares ill with the acclaim awarded to General Montgomery after the Battle of El Alamein in North Africa. One can only suppose that Churchill, who had previously held Dowding in the highest regard, had suddenly been heavily influenced by the Cabal with its senior Marshals, the Secretary of State and politicians. The report of the Meeting of Shame would have implied blame on Dowding for not using big wings, charging him with greater casualties and providing an excuse not to give him due acclaim. This Meeting has been proved to be a conspiracy of a Cabal based on incorrect information and uninformed opinion to destroy Dowding's personal and professional standing. It succeeded at the time but the infamous behaviour of those involved is now documented in this book.

The termination of Dowding's service as the Victor of the Battle and Saviour of the Country was reported in the *Daily Telegraph* simply as 'Fighter Command New Chief.' This must question the integrity of the press release by the Air Ministry.

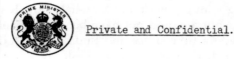

Private and Confidential.   10, Downing Street,
                                             Whitehall.

July 10, 1940.

My dear Archie,

          I was very much taken aback the other
night when you told me you had been considering
removing Sir Hugh Dowding at the expiration of his
present appointment, but that you had come to the
conclusion that he might be allowed to stay on for
another four months. Personally, I think he is one
of the very best men you have got, and I say this
after having been in contact with him for about two
years. I have greatly admired the whole of his work
in the Fighter Command, and especially in resisting
the clamour for numerous air raid warnings, and the
immense pressure to dissipate the Fighter strength
during the great French battle. In fact he has my
full confidence. I think it is a pity for an officer
so gifted and so trusted to be working on such a short
tenure as four months, and I hope you will consider
whether it is not in the public interest that his

10, Downing Street,
Whitehall.

- 2 -

appointment should be indefinitely prolonged while
the war lasts.   This would not of course exclude his
being moved to a higher position, if that were thought
necessary.   I am however much averse from making
changes and putting in new men who will have to learn
the work all over again, except when there is some
proved failure or inadequacy.

Yours always,

The Right Hon. Sir Archibald Sinclair, Bt., C.M.G., M.P.

Private

10, Downing Street,
Whitehall.

10 August 1940.

My dear Archie,

I certainly understood from our conversation
a month ago that you were going to give Dowding an in-
definite war-time extension, and were going to do it at
once. I cannot understand how any contrary impression
could have arisen in your mind about my wishes. Let me
however remove it at once, and urge you to take the step
I have so long desired. It is entirely wrong to keep
an officer in the position of Commander-in-Chief, con-
ducting hazardous operations from day to day, when he is
dangling at the end of an expiring appointment. Such a
situation is not fair to anyone, least of all to the
nation. I can never be a party to it.

I do hope you will be able to set my mind at
rest.

Yours ever,

W.

In 1941 after the Battle, the Air Ministry published a booklet on the Battle of Britain and its victory, which made not one single reference to Air Chief Marshal Sir Hugh Dowding. This action by the Air Ministry seems to indicate that they were still in a conspiracy to hide Dowding's achievements in the Battle. Was Portal aware of this? Churchill found out about it and ordered the booklet to be reprinted with due honour accorded to the former Commander in Chief.

At the height of the Battle, Dowding was the only man. After the battle was won – he was of no importance. Something similar happened to Prime Minister Winston Churchill with the election of a new Parliament and a new Prime Minister at the end of the war in 1945. These happenings could not in any way diminish their achievements for Britain.

HM The King and Winston Churchill

I would have thought that the two men of greatest standing in Britain in 1940 who could have had the authority or influence to effect the promotion of ACM Sir Hugh Dowding to the status of Marshal of the Royal Air Force were His Majesty King George VI and Prime Minister Winston Churchill. The King, himself a Marshal of the Royal Air Force, wanted it to happen and was ready to welcome Dowding into this very select group of senior Royal Air Force officers. He felt that Dowding's achievements merited such status. A letter dated 17th July 1942 from Sir Alexander Hardinge, the King's Private Secretary to Sinclair, the Secretary of State for Air, presented the case. But, by the next day, the matter had been quickly, firmly and finally disposed of. Peter Flint in his book *Dowding* writes that, after discussing it with Portal, Sinclair answered that a serious objection to such promotion was that Dowding had already retired once. He promised that when rewards came to be made at the end of the war, Sir Hugh Dowding's name might be considered along with those of other senior officers of the RAF who had rendered outstanding war service. The King accepted this response. However, the promise did not materialise. To have promoted him to MRAF would have brought him back to the RAF with significant influence! The Air Chief Marshal had now been safely retired and the reputations and honour of Trenchard and the Air Ministry were no longer in danger.

In July 1940 Churchill held Dowding in the highest regard and assuredly on 15th September when he was in the 11 Group operations room during the decisive raids on London. He was fully aware of Dowding's great contribution before and during the Battle. What was the power of those men in the Cabal that they could have resisted the King's request for Dowding's promotion, and had distorted or minimised his contribution to keeping Britain safe from German invasion? Following 15th September with the day battles coming under control, the heavy night bombing attacks, which had started a week before, now became a major political issue for Churchill. With his instinctive concern for the protection of the people, his fear was of the danger of the cracking of their morale, which could lead to us suing for peace. Dowding, while militarily correct with his reluctance to use single-engine fighters and to protect his pilots, was politically unwise not to offer more help. His attitude was exploited by the Cabal.

By July 1942, when the King's views were made known to the Secretary of State for Air, Germany was locked in a great battle with Russia. By then Sinclair and the Cabal knew for certain that Dowding had won the Battle of Britain, and that the threat of invasion had gone. Churchill's letter to Sinclair on 10th July 1940 illustrates his high opinion of Dowding, referring to him as being 'an officer so gifted and so trusted' and expressing his full confidence in him.

Newall was CAS for the years 1937/1940. I would suggest that Dowding's contribution to Britain in that period more than equalled that of Newall. This despicable conspiracy took place while the people of Britain were making great sacrifices in their fight to stay a free and honourable Nation.

Churchill had further thoughts about the failure to give public honour to Dowding for his great achievement in the Battle of Britain, and on 2nd June 1943 Dowding was honoured with the Barony of Bentley Priory.

Dismissal of Air Vice-Marshal Keith Park

The dismissal of Air Vice-Marshal Keith Park after Dowding had been removed was inevitable, and it took place on 18th December 1940. He was replaced by Air Vice-Marshall Leigh-Mallory of 12 Group who had been closely associated with Douglas in the Big Wing controversy and the meeting of 17th October.

Park had loyally and efficiently carried out his C-in-C's defensive philosophy and had played a major part in the victory. He had battled with Leigh-Mallory over the use of 12 Group squadrons – both on tactical grounds and as part of the deep-rooted animosity that had existed between them. Although Park was a superior tactician to Leigh-Mallory, the latter had the support of powerful people at the Air Ministry and won the battle at the 17th October meeting, which in the event proved more important than the Battle of Britain as regards Park's immediate future.

Park's transfer to command a training group was unjustifiable, although not as dishonourable as the ill treatment meted out to Dowding. This could have been interpreted by some that Park had failed as an operational commander, quite the opposite of the truth. In spite of his unique experience as a fighter commander over Dunkirk and throughout the Battle, he was ungenerously removed from the operational scene. It has been argued that Park was very tired after his exhausting experience. This is probably true but what he needed was rest, not humiliation. Although I am sure that at first Park resented his appointment to command 23 Training Group, he soon realised that he had a most important task in hand. The Group was still living in the past and operating at peacetime outputs. He knew only too well that shortage of pilots was a major problem and that he could still make a major contribution and bring his flying training stations to full efficiency.

His ability as a fighting commander was not employed again until his appointment as Air Officer Commanding Malta in July 1943, at the most dangerous time in the defence of the island. Who can doubt the justification for his anger and contempt for his and Dowding's dismissal, and for those air marshals responsible for such infamous behaviour.

In January 1944, after his achievements at Malta, Park took over as Air Officer Commanding in Chief Middle East with promotion to air marshal. His next appointment occurred with a strange twist. Air Chief Marshal Leigh-Mallory had been appointed as Air Commander in Chief South East Asia Air Command but was killed when flying over the French Alps to take up his position. It is ironic that Park was appointed to replace Leigh-Mallory in this very senior position with promotion to Air Chief Marshal.

Air Vice-Marshal Keith Park's Personal Views

On 23rd October 1956, at the age of 64, Park wrote a letter to F/Lt Hunt OBE who worked at the Air Ministry, describing his thoughts, memories and emotions about the dismissal of Dowding and himself after the Battle.

Park had refrained from writing his account of the Battle before, as he did not wish to hurt friends and relatives of some very high-ranking officers still very much alive. His gentlemanly instincts had served to hide the depth of feeling he had retained for 16 years of his shameful treatment by the Air Ministry and other senior officers, two of whom immediately replaced him and Dowding.

In this letter Park clearly shows his anger and feelings about Leigh-Mallory and others in relation to the dismissals. He had no doubt that he and Dowding were removed by a cabal of senior RAF officers and politicians, and that the meeting on 17th October was essentially political, and an attempt to justify Leigh-Mallory's criticism of the way the battle had been fought.

I had not seen a copy of this letter until after my major research had been completed and my book has therefore been written without any

AIR CHIEF MARSHAL SIR KEITH PARK, GCB, KBE, MC, DFC, DCL.

P.O. BOX 2340, AUCKLAND, N.Z.

October 23rd, 1956.

Flight Lieutenant J. L. Hunt, OBE
Air Ministry,
Adastral House,
LONDON, W.C.1,
England.

My Dear Hunt,

      Thank you very much for your letter of October 10th, and for the Press Cutting about the book written by Group Captain Johnson.

      You said that many ex 11 Group chaps have wondered why I have not written my own account of the Battle of Britain. For your personal informa- tion, my reply is that I do not wish to hurt the friends and relatives of some very high-ranking officers still very much alive.

      During the Battle of Britain there were two Air Marshals at Air Ministry who very much wanted Lord Dowding's job at H.Q. Fighter Command. At the same time Dowding was very unpopular with the C.A.S., Newall, who was very friendly with the aspiring Air Marshals at Air Ministry. Dowding was so highly thought of by the Cabinet that his position appeared to be unassail- able, until the conspirators at Air Ministry discovered an Air Vice Marshal in No. 12 Group who badly wanted my job commanding 11 Group. Consequently, in October, when the Battle had been won, it was brought to the attention of the Air Secretary that Air Vice Marshal Leigh Mallory claimed that the tactical handling of 11 Group Fighters had been faulty, and that the mass formation tac- tics of his Group would have been more successful. The trouble was that neither Dowding nor I took seriously this criticism of my fighter tactics, because we were so confident that we had been right in the method of winning the Battle.

      Imagine the surprise and anger of Dowding when, in October, 1940, he was summoned to attend an Air Council Meeting with me, to justify my fighter tactics in the face of critics from 12 Group. This Meeting was arranged without the knowledge or approval of Dowding, and I was asked to explain to the Meeting the reasons for my fighter tactics. As will be seen from the Official History of the R.A.F., this criticism after the event was used by the retiring C.A.S. and his Air Marshals, as an excuse for getting rid of Dowding. Of course, being his First Lieutenant and his tactical commander throughout the Battle of Britain, I was banished to a Training Command. The result was that Air Marshal Sholto Douglas, from Air Ministry, replaced Dowding in Novem- ber, 1940, and, shortly after, I was replaced by his close friend, Leigh Mallory from 12 Group, whose malicious criticism had been used by the ambitious Air Marshals at Air Ministry.

      Should I pass on before I have had an opportunity of writing a book, then I give you full permission to publish this letter so that ex- 11 Group Members will know why a small section of the Air Ministry listened to the criticism of 11 Fighter Group, after the Battle had been well and truly won.

With kind regards.
Yours sincerely,
Keith Park

influence which it might have had. I now present this letter as a crucial document on page 204. I am content that my own work is supportive of Park's interpretation of events, and that his letter is supportive of my own analysis. Park, in his letter, gave F/Lt Hunt permission to publish it, and I hold full written authority from F/Lt Hunt to do so here. It can only serve to confirm the sad and almost unbelievable behaviour of certain senior RAF officers, 'Men of Ambition', against our valiant and loyal Commanders.

The emotion expressed in this letter by Park was almost certainly felt equally by Dowding. I am sure that Dowding and Park were aware of the extreme affection that the Battle of Britain pilots held for them. This may have been their only consolation – but certainly one of inestimable value.

CHAPTER 16

Elevation of Conspirators to High Office

Promotion of Air Vice-Marshal Douglas

In his autobiography *Years of Command*, published in 1966, Douglas writes:

> The Battle of Britain was fought against the immediate threat of a German invasion and the Germans were defeated. As a great air battle, it was an event that is unique in military history and winning it was for us a great triumph.

His words 'it was for us a great triumph' could be taken to imply that he had played a significant part in the battle, which was quite untrue. What a missed opportunity to make an honourable record of gratitude to Air Chief Marshal Dowding. How different these words sound from his attitude to Dowding and Park in 1940.

Although totally involved in the management of the meeting on 17th October, he makes no mention of this exceptional high level conference at the Air Ministry. This was a conference that resulted in the denigration and removal of Dowding, his own promotion, and the elevation of Leigh-Mallory to a command for which he was not best suited, and eventually to a status he did not deserve. Douglas obviously did not want to be associated with this dishonourable meeting, although it certainly led to his own promotion, and in theory to a significant change in Fighter Command tactics. He expresses his great surprise at this unexpected appointment to be the new C-in-C of Fighter Command. This can hardly be true. Surely if the plan was to remove Dowding, then the Air Ministry must have had someone already selected for the post. As an established Deputy Chief of Air Staff serving the CAS, and with nearly three years service as an Air Vice-Marshal, Douglas must have known who this was to be. Perhaps this statement was a further ploy to distance himself from Dowding's removal from office.

He describes Leigh-Mallory and Park as both very able commanders and writes that each was right in his own way, thus suggesting that he was a neutral observer. After 17th October 1940, it would have been difficult to convince Park of this description.

Douglas also writes:

> So far as we on the Air Staff were concerned his [Dowding's] relinquishment of his command was an honourable one in every conceivable way.

Dowding would have had grave difficulty in accepting this. The statement bears no relationship to the reality and could only be true if Dowding had been retired with due honour and public acclaim.

Douglas refers to Leigh-Mallory's appointment to replace Park as Air Officer Commanding 11 Group, still the most sought after appointment in Fighter Command, as 'I was quite happy about having him as one of my senior officers'. This presumably is intended to prove that he had no hand in the removal of Park and the appointment of Leigh-Mallory in his place. However, he then describes Leigh-Mallory as self-opinionated, with the habit of raising the hackles of other people. There was no comment on his experience and ability for this crucial appointment. It might seem from this denigration of Leigh-Mallory that he had in fact used him in the machinations simply to further his own ambitions.

After his political manoeuvres in 1940 had led to his appointment as C-in-C of Fighter Command, Douglas went on to further high office, followed by post-war promotion to Marshal of the Royal Air Force and then ennoblement. Douglas was indeed a 'Man of Ambition'. One cannot doubt his ambition and his success.

Having retired after the war, Douglas took his seat in the House of Lords on the Labour bench. The Labour Party was in power with a massive majority. In the Spring of 1949 he was rewarded with the chairmanship of British European Airways.

Air Vice-Marshal Leigh-Mallory to 11 Group

With his transfer to command the prestigious 11 Group, the ambitious Leigh-Mallory was now back on the promotion road again, later to become Commander-in-Chief of Fighter Command with the rank of Air Marshal. He went on to high honour as Air Chief Marshal, commanding all the air forces involved in the D-Day landings in the invasion of France in 1944.

Despite his political battles in 1940 for five-squadron Wings and six-squadron Balbos, when commanding 11 Group Leigh-Mallory never once used a wing formation as a defensive unit over Britain. He didn't even use wings with more than three squadrons in his offensive battles with Me109s over northern France. In early 1941, as 11 Group Commander, he set up an exercise over the coast to test the effectiveness of Big Wings as a defensive formation. The results showed that the Big Wings were too slow in operation to serve as protective formations at readiness. He had proved that Dowding and Park were right, but too late for honour to be restored.

In his sweeps over France, in 12 months he lost 426 pilots in air battles in which he had superiority in numbers and had the advantage of being the attacking force. At Dieppe, he had sent up wings of 3 squadrons to defend our soldiers and naval forces taking part in the landings. However, he was soon advised by Group Captain Broadhurst, patrolling over the beaches, to send up the fighters in simple pairs of aircraft instead. Much better results were immediately achieved. In the fighting over Dieppe we lost 88 fighters compared with only 48 enemy losses.

Whatever his special virtues may have been, few historians could describe Leigh-Mallory as a great aerial fighter commander. The German Military Intelligence assessment of him as 'a pedantic worker with a preference for administration' would seem to be much nearer to the truth.

In October 1944 Leigh-Mallory was appointed to be C-in-C of the South East Asia Allied Air Forces. On 14th November, L-M, his wife and his staff boarded an Avro York aeroplane to fly out to the Far East to take up his new command. The aircraft crashed in the Alps in bad weather and all aboard were killed.

CHAPTER 17

The Final Judgement

Men of Honour

The Battle of Britain was either to be won or lost. There was nothing in between. The Luftwaffe bombers flew back to their bases at the end of September 1940 as a very disillusioned force, never to return by day as a serious threat to our freedom. We had won. How well we cannot judge, but it had to be a Great Victory – the alternative is too dreadful to think about.

Sometimes our Leaders and Commanders made judgements and took decisions that could be criticised. After the surrender of France, Dowding should have designated 12 Group to become an active reserve to support 11 Group and to share the load. He should have changed his philosophy, that each Group fought its own battles, to one giving greater flexibility. A decision to remove Leigh-Mallory would have been challenged by the Air Ministry, but he could have been given revised instructions for new responsibilities to ensure disciplined behaviour. Bearing in mind the breadth of all his responsibilities and the rapidly changing scene, I suggest that Dowding really needed a deputy of Air Marshal rank to be responsible for co-ordinating all aspects of the operational work of the Command, including disposition of squadrons, tactics, intelligence and aircraft performance His SASO Evill was not the man. But was there a man in the RAF who could have taken over in the middle of the Battle and who would have been acceptable to Dowding?

As a pilot I believe that Park's most serious error was in not realising in time that his policy of always attacking the bombers with a direct inter-ception even with a height disadvantage put our pilots in even greater danger. Too late he remembered that the sky is three-dimensional and that height would always be crucial. The pilots took their own action to level the odds.

These criticisms should not be allowed to diminish their achievement, and it is vital to stress that the Battle was fought under conditions that had never been met before. The epicentre of the fighting had radically changed, there was the unexpected need to fight Me109s over England, there were the huge formations involved, and the speed of interceptions – these were all a far cry from what we had anticipated in 1939. Overcoming all these unexpected factors only made the victory even greater.

In honouring Dowding and Park, we must also pay tribute to the battles fought by 10 Group pilots under AVM Sir Quintin Brand in the south of England, and the ready support given to Park and his squadrons in the hard pressed 11 Group. Also to the pilots in 13 Group in the north, commanded by AVM RE Saul, who continued to carry out their responsibilities with little glory but with total dedication and loyalty. We must also remember the pilots of 12 Group, commanded by AVM Leigh-Mallory, who fought hard against the Luftwaffe whenever they had the opportunity.

During the Battle it seemed that Dowding had few friends. However, one close friend was Lord Beaverbrook, our Minister of Aircraft Production. They both had sons serving in squadrons in action in the Battle, which gave them a common bond. At all times during the Battle our squadrons were able to replace the aircraft that they had lost. Beaverbrook had a significant responsibility in this.

Men of Shame

There is little doubt that there was a conspiracy at high level to remove Dowding from the Royal Air Force. It started in the early days of 1937 with only a small group of persons involved, but once the Battle had started the numbers increased. The depth of involvement varied and it seems that only two people made tangible personal gain out of Dowding's removal. These were Air Vice-Marshals Douglas and Leigh-Mallory, who were immediately given enhanced status and set on the road to high office. These officers had played a very active part in the fight to humiliate Dowding and to attack his professionalism. However the Cabal had a great covert success which is discussed later.

In his book about Dowding, *Battle of Britain: Victory and Defeat*, J.E.Dixon presents extracts of letters between MRAFs Trenchard and Salmon in September and October 1940. These show that they were almost certainly the initiators of the plan to remove Dowding from the Royal Air Force. Trenchard wrote to Salmond on October 4th stating that although they were working for the same cause (to sack Dowding), he never mentioned that he and Salmond were working in agreement on this matter. From the correspondence it appears that while Trenchard remained in the shadows, it was Salmond who was the activist. With his appointment at the Ministry of Aircraft Production, he was well placed to contact people in the Air Ministry and the Government. This information must place Trenchard and Salmond at the heart of the Cabal against Dowding. The first act of aggression against Dowding took place in 1937 when, although promised that he would be the next CAS, in fact ACM Newall was appointed in his place. With the continued setting of dates for Dowding's retirement, his dishonourable treatment after his victory in the Battle and the refusal to meet the request of HM the King for him to be promoted to MRAF, the aggression continued until July 1942. For this period, the only members of the Cabal considered in this book who were continuously in a position of authority or influence to act against Dowding were Trenchard and Salmond.

I have set out to find the common factor, so powerful and disturbing that it caused a number of senior RAF officers and politicians to bond together over a period of years, however loosely, to attack and dishonour the C-in-C of Fighter Command in order to have him removed from office. Apart from any clash of personalities, or his natural independence, the major cause of conflict with Dowding over some years was undoubtedly his opposition to the Air Ministry plans for Home Defence. MRAF Trenchard had initiated and maintained a doctrine of defence based on his belief that Britain could best be protected from attack by a very powerful bomber force. This Trenchard Doctrine was accepted and upheld by the Air Ministry as its main function, and indeed as its raison d'etre, and a large bomber force was built up and became the mainstay of the Royal Air Force in size and commitment.

Dowding was opposed to this doctrine and battled continuously with the Air Ministry for a stronger Fighter Command. He propounded the view that unless you can defend the home base you cannot operate the bomber squadrons. In order to protect the Trenchard Doctrine it was essential that Dowding, the most senior officer in the RAF, should be prevented from becoming Chief of Air Staff, followed by promotion to Marshal, which would have given him great influence over Air Ministry policies.

I believe that it was decided by Trenchard and the Air Minister, Viscount Swinton, well before the Battle of Britain, that Dowding should not be appointed as CAS as promised, but would be replaced as the next CAS by Air Chief Marshal Newall. He would then be retired from the RAF as soon as possible. Successive dates of retirement were set on four occasions, but in the event this plan was frustrated and by July 1940 Dowding still commanded Fighter Command, although under the threat of retirement at the end of October. In the Battle of Britain he then won a great defensive victory with his fighter squadrons over the attacking Luftwaffe armadas. Bomber Command by contrast were unable to make any significant contribution to defeating the attacking squadrons. The Trenchard doctrine for defence had been shown to have been a total failure. In fact in 1939, 1940 and 1941 Bomber Command failed to make any significant impact as an aggressive and effective bomber force over Europe. It was only Dowding's continued battles with the Air Ministry and his professional brilliance that had saved Britain. Dowding had proved Trenchard and the Air Ministry to have been dangerously wrong. To the Cabal it was now even more important to have Dowding removed from the scene. To have to announce to the Country that Dowding and his Fighter Command alone had saved Britain, and then to promote him to MRAF was something that the Cabal could not contemplate. The Air Ministry would be exposed as having failed the Nation twice with its Trenchard Bomber Doctrine. Dowding's standing had to be attacked.

Already in September 1940 MRAF Salmond had set up a conference under the auspices of the Ministry of Aircraft Production, and with the support of the Air Ministry, to consider methods of protection against German night bombing. This was clearly a serious attack against the professionalism of Dowding who had not been consulted. The high level Meeting of Shame on the 17th October was set up at the Air Ministry, with little regard for the validity of the evidence, to denigrate Dowding's competence. Dowding was later unfairly accused of failing to give protection against the night-bombers although the responsibility for inadequate aircraft and poor AI performance lay clearly with the Air Ministry and the Ministry of Aircraft Production. The Big Wing Controversy and the Night Defence failure were not the *reasons* for Dowding's dismissal but were used as *excuses* to justify and implement a decision that had been made some years before.

After September the Cabal were able to influence Churchill against Dowding who was then discreetly relieved of his command and posted to the United States into exile without public honour. He had been removed to a position where he was no longer a threat.

Trenchard's power in the Royal Air Force up to 1941 was such that even the most senior officers came under his influence. Marshals of the RAF Trenchard and Salmond would also have had access to politicians to put forward their views. Dowding did not have this access nor do I believe that he would have taken such action.

The Cabal had triumphed with their shameful and dishonourable attack on a man of honour and great achievement.

When Dowding finally retired from the RAF in 1942, His Majesty the King proposed to Sinclair, the Secretary of State for Air, that he should be promoted to Marshal of the RAF for 'performing a really wonderful service to this country'. With their rejection of the proposal, the Air Ministry had finally blocked his last chance to be promoted to Marshal of the Royal Air Force. The power of this dishonourable Cabal had extended to Buckingham Palace.

Dowding not only defeated the Luftwaffe, but over the years he had also fought a great battle to defend his Fighter Command against the Cabal of the defenders of the Doctrine. He had been denied his promotion to Chief of Air Staff, which would have led to elevation to MRAF. Following his

COPY.

Confidential.

Buckingham Palace.

17th July, 1942.

Dear Sinclair,

Thank you for your letter of July 14th about Air Chief Marshal Sir Hugh Dowding. I telephoned before luncheon today to say that, on his return from North Wales, The King had this morning signed the submission which included the retirement of Sir Hugh Dowding. At the same time His Majesty wished me to raise with you the question of his being promoted to Marshal of the Royal Air Force on retirement. There may be all sorts of difficulties of which The King is not aware; but it has always seemed to him that Dowding performed a really wonderful service to this country in creating, and putting into practice, the defence system which proved so effective in the Battle of Britain. His Majesty would be grateful if you would give this suggestion your consideration; and let me have your views on it in due course.

Yours sincerely,

(Sgd.) Alexander Hardinge.

The Rt. Hon. Sir Archibald Sinclair, Bt., KT.,CMG.,MP.,
Secretary of State for Air.

successful defence of Britain with Fighter Command the Cabal executed a plan to denigrate his achievements and to have him removed from office. This behaviour on the part of some senior commanders and politicians serves to confirm the adage that 'power corrupts, and absolute power corrupts absolutely'.

It is difficult to believe that such vindictive behaviour within the RAF should have been carried out, not to defend our Country, but to defend treasured doctrines even when they have been proved wrong.

When I started to write this book, I regarded Dowding as a great man who was the leader of our fighter squadrons who had challenged and turned back the Luftwaffe, defeating the German plan to occupy Britain. My research has shown that, not only was he fighting the Luftwaffe squadrons that heavily outnumbered Fighter Command, but he was also having to battle with the Trenchard and Air Ministry Doctrine and the related Cabal. This made his task so much harder and his achievement even greater. He was indeed a man of great vision, courage, tenacity and honour and should be remembered as such.

I hope that my book will be a further contribution to the call by many for the Nation to know that Air Chief Marshal Sir Hugh Dowding was the Architect of Victory of the Battle of Britain whose Fighter Command successfully defeated the German aerial armadas in 1940 to keep Britain a free, democratic, and independent Nation.

CHAPTER 18

The Case Against the Cabal

So are they not all, all honourable men?

Dowding Against the Trenchard Bomber Doctrine

In the previous chapter I expressed my views that, from 1937 onwards there was formed a cabal of MRAFs, senior RAF officers and politicians responsible for the dishonourable treatment and dismissal in 1940 of Air Chief Marshal Dowding, C-in-C of Fighter Command. This is a very serious indictment of highly respected figures from the past and needs justification, but if honour is to be restored to Dowding then it can only be done if the evil machinations of those responsible are exposed.

The Air Ministry doctrine of building and maintaining a powerful Bomber Command, which would provide Britain with its defence against enemy attack, has been shown to be a failure. I claim that Dowding was removed from office, not because of any professional deficiency, but to protect the reputations of the Air Ministry and others who had allowed themselves to be committed to a policy which was based on an adage that the best method of defence is attack.

My assessment of the pattern of dishonour has been based on events, the behaviour of those involved and official documents. If my findings can be refuted by factual evidence I shall be relieved, as I have always had great pride in the prestige of our Royal Air Force. However the reference to the Meeting of Shame as 'Alice in Wonderland' by Len Deighton in his book *Fighter* must make the reader wonder, with some trepidation, what was happening at the Air Ministry in 1940 when hundreds of Luftwaffe warplanes were flying over England. We know what our fighter pilots were doing but what were our Air Ministry commanders doing?

In support of this Trenchard doctrine policy in 1938 there were 51 regular bomber squadrons and 21 regular fighter squadrons. The bomber squadrons were mostly twin-engined with 3–5 crew members compared with the single-engined fighters mostly with just a pilot. The cost of building and maintaining such a bomber force was many times that of Fighter Command. It is easy to understand Trenchard's pride in his big battalions.

During my research I have noted a number of events, which I could not understand, including the behaviour of specific people. The Cabal was not going to be easy to define, as those likely to have been involved were part of a group with amoebic-like characteristics. I was unable to find any logical reason for the continued policy over several years to remove Dowding, which was not only dishonourable behaviour but which I felt contained a significant degree of hostility. Did Dowding have a personal failing which had been kept secret? What was this terrible thing that he had done, or could do, to members of the Cabal that merited such awful treatment? The following pattern of events and dates may explain their fear.

14th July 1936. Air Marshal Sir Hugh Dowding appointed C-in-C of Fighter Command.

In 1936 Dowding had been told by the CAS, Air Chief Marshall Edward Ellington, that he was to be the next CAS.

October 1936. Sir Thomas Inskip appointed as Minister of the Co-ordination of Defence. He opposed the principle of the Trenchard Bomber Doctrine and recommended increasing the numbers of our fighter squadrons to provide for a better defence of Britain.

1st January 1937. Dowding promoted to Air Chief Marshal, the most senior officer in the RAF.

1st April 1937. Air Marshal Newall promoted to Air Chief Marshal.

1st September 1937. ACM Newall appointed the new Chief of Air Staff instead of Dowding. Newall represented no threat to the Doctrine

22nd December 1937. The Inskip report changing the RAF philosophy of Defence had the approval of Neville Chamberlain, the Prime Minister, and was accepted by Parliament, in spite of the most powerful objections from Trenchard and the Air Ministry.

August 1938. Dowding was advised by the Air Ministry that it would not be possible to employ him after the end of June 1939.

Although Dowding had battled for a more powerful Fighter Command, as an Air Marshal he did not did not have the individual status to have an impact on the Trenchard Bomber Doctrine. But with Minister Sir Thomas Inskip, supported by the Cabinet, now holding similar views, the balance of power was shifting. Although it had been planned for Dowding to take over as CAS, Trenchard and his supporters realised the dangers of such an appointment to their Doctrine and indeed the control of the RAF. His traditional promotion to MRAF would be even more disastrous. Under no circumstances could Dowding be promoted and he must be retired as soon as possible.

I decided to review the illogical events and behaviour that had given me concern. I could find only one explanation that answered all the anomalies; they were all part of a pattern indicating either antagonism against Dowding or a failure to give him the assistance he so desperately required. Those involved were either Trenchard men or were powerful supporters of the Trenchard Bomber Doctrine. It seemed that they must have been part of, or associated with, a cabal determined to bring down Dowding. The behaviour of Leigh-Mallory was strictly personal to help his own ambition, but it proved to be of great help to the Cabal in their campaign of denigration. Dowding's dismissal was not due to his so called failures in the Battle, but was the result of his continued fight for Fighter Command against the Trenchard Bomber Doctrine. Sadly his victory over the Luftwaffe merely made more certain his own destruction.

His valiant and successful defence of Britain against the Nazi Luftwaffe with Fighter Command alone had exposed the unforgivable failure of the Air Ministry policy based on the Trenchard doctrine. To save the face of the Air Ministry Dowding had first to be denigrated and then removed from the public eye.

The Campaign

I detail below a number of those events which I could not comprehend at the time, but which now highlight the activities of those who were determined to remove Dowding.

Why was the decision to appoint Dowding as CAS in 1937 revoked, with his replacement by AVM Newall who was junior to him? The decision would have been made by Viscount Swinton, Secretary of State for Air, almost certainly working closely with Lord Trenchard. They were both members of the House of Lords.

On 30th March 1940, Dowding was told he would be retired on 14th July. CAS Newall waited until 5th July to tell Dowding of a change of policy and to ask him to stay on until 31st October. This was callous treatment of such a senior officer in the RAF. Why had they not found, within the three months available, a suitable replacement for the man they most wanted to get rid of?

Why on 4th July, just as the Battle of Britain was about to start, did CAS Newall advise Dowding that he would be retired on 31st October? How could he give Dowding, the most important fighting commander in the RAF at that time, a specified period of some 3 months' notice to fight the Battle. Was he more concerned with getting rid of Dowding on this fourth attempt than in ensuring the defence of Britain? Churchill was seriously disturbed when he heard of this and had the date of retirement set aside immediately.

Why was Dowding sent out of Britain immediately after his dismissal, on the recommendation of the Ministry of Aircraft Production, to do work for which he was not suited and did not want? Exiled to the USA he was then no longer a threat. Was Salmond at the MAP party to this?

Why did MRAF Salmond initiate a conference for defence against German night bombers from the Ministry of Aircraft Production with the connivance of the Air Ministry and without consulting Dowding?

Why was MRAF Salmond prepared to approach to HM the King if necessary to get rid of Dowding?

Why did Secretary of State for Air Sinclair fail to provide the replacement pilots desperately needed by Fighter Command, earning a rebuke from Winston Churchill?

Why was CAS Newall conveniently indisposed for the meeting at the Air Ministry on 17th October yet was fit enough to attend a meeting of the Chiefs of Staff the next day?

Why did Portal, former Chief of Bomber Command, and CAS Designate, attend a meeting called solely to discuss Fighter tactics? Was not the real reason for his presence political? It could have been to advise on strategies, but strategy was not on the agendas.

An analysis of the Big Wing performance up to 17th October showed that the Wing had failed after the first seven days out of 42. Why was this not reported by Stevenson in his Air Staff note circulated for the meeting?

Why did Douglas fail to report these crucial results during the Meeting?

Why was Dowding not invited to bring with him an experienced 11 Group squadron commander to state the case for single squadrons to balance the presence of Wing Leader Bader?

Why did Chairman Douglas re-orientate the meeting to deal first with three broad unpublished questions, which, in the event, could not be satisfactorily answered?

Why were 9 out of the 10 items on the original agenda concerned only with Big Wings for a meeting called to discuss fighter tactics?

Why was Bader, a junior Squadron Leader, given a formal place at such a high level meeting and later received a copy of the minutes?

Did Portal, as well as Douglas and Leigh-Mallory, know that Bader would be present? (Dowding and Park, of Fighter Command, certainly did not.) Was he aware of the political intent of the meeting? If so then he must be considered to be closely associated with the Cabal.

Why did the Air Ministry refuse to accept any of the drafts from Dowding, Park and Brand disputing some of the minutes, which the Air Ministry claimed were published basically as aide-memoires? (Minutes at a meeting of this level should surely be a clear statement of record and intent especially with the two secretaries present.)

Why was AVM Evill, previously Air Officer in Charge of Administration and then Senior Air Staff Officer to Bomber Command as an Air Vice-Marshal, posted to a lower status at Fighter Command? There is a reference by John Ray in his book *The Battle of Britain* to Evill's sympathy for 12 Group Big Wings. Was this posting a political appointment?

Why did Evill, as Dowding's deputy, fail to take positive action himself to deal with the harm caused by the bad relationship between two of the group commanders, and was satisfied with just referring the matter to his C-in-C?

Did Evill advise Dowding of the failure of the Big Wings? He had daily knowledge of this and such information could have transformed the Meeting of Shame.

All of these 20 queries can be answered by the existence of a campaign to denigrate and to remove Dowding from office, in order to protect the reputation of the Trenchard Bomber Doctrine. No doubt a few of the items listed could have a simple and honourable justification, but I can find no other single reason to explain all the examples of the behaviour of these people that I have considered as members of the Cabal.

The List

Below are listed some of the officers and politicians who had an involvement in the machinations to remove Dowding from office and the Royal Air Force.

Marshal of the Royal Air Force Lord Trenchard

Dowding had battled with Trenchard since 1916 and his outspoken views were not welcome. Dowding's strong fight for the safety of Britain to be maintained by a powerful Fighter Command must have been anathema to Trenchard. If Dowding were to become CAS and then promoted to MRAF, Trenchard's continued influence in the Royal Air Force could be greatly diminished. He had very good reason to get rid of Dowding and worked behind the scenes with fellow MRAF Salmond to this end. After the Battle had been won, Trenchard told Portal, the CAS, that it was time for the fighter squadrons to start 'leaning forward'. If not still a man of power, he was certainly a man of considerable influence. This authority exercised by Trenchard and Salmond over the RAF for so many years, both on the active list and when retired, is a disturbing factor in its history.

Marshal of the Royal Air Force Sir John Salmond

Salmond was an aggressive and successful man of action. He had always been linked closely to Trenchard and was certainly involved with him in the plans to get rid of Dowding in the late 1930s and in 1940. Although I have found no direct evidence of conflict between them, there are examples of antagonism against Dowding. In September when at the Ministry of Aircraft Production, he set up a conference to consider emergency tactics to defeat the German night bombers with the approval of the Air Ministry. This was clearly an attack on Dowding who was not invited to take part. Certainly he was in the Cabal and one of the leaders.

Sir Archibald Sinclair, Secretary of State for Air

Sinclair did not take office until 1940 and by then the Cabal was already established; and it would not be difficult for him to relate to the Marshals and the CAS. He soon had a close relationship with AVM Douglas, the Deputy CAS, who was a Trenchard man. I am sure that Sinclair was part of the Cabal. He was an old and close friend of Winston Churchill, but in July he was rebuked in writing by him over his treatment of Dowding, who was held in high esteem by the Prime Minister. Sinclair may have been partly responsible for Churchill's change of heart about Dowding after September. In 1942, with Portal, he was unable to acquiesce to the proposal of HM the King that Dowding should be promoted to MRAF for 'a really wonderful service to this country'.

Air Chief Marshal Sir Cyril Newall, Chief of Air Staff

Newall had held similar ranks to Dowding, although slightly junior, from World War I until 1937 when Newall was promoted to CAS over him. I have read nothing that indicates any direct conflict between them, but Newall, under Trenchard's influence, would have had to be a supporter of the Cabal. He would certainly have felt easier in his position if Dowding were to be retired. With his own imminent retirement and move to New Zealand as Governor-General, it seems probable that he avoided open involvement on 17th October by being indisposed.

Air Marshal Sir Charles ('Peter') Portal, Chief of Air Staff (Elect)

In his biography *Trenchard – Man of Vision* Andrew Boyle writes that among those selected for Trenchard's special brand of favouritism were Portal and Slessor, who were already being groomed for stardom in the early '20s. Later in the book Boyle makes note of Trenchard's reference to Portal, by then CAS, as his 'favourite disciple'. With this evidence of Portal's very close relationship with Trenchard then some of the peculiar behaviour patterns already outlined can be explained.

With his appointment as Commander in Chief of Bomber Command in 1940 followed six months later by promotion to CAS, we must assume that he had the full approval of Trenchard, and was a supporter of the Bomber Defence Strategy. His presence at the meeting on 17th October 1940 is clear evidence that the meeting was political. He had nothing to offer on tactics about day defence. As he did not chair the meeting he cannot be proposed simply as a replacement for Newall who was unable to be present as Chairman. It is easy to understand that as the young and new CAS elect he would need to follow the party line and defend the Doctrine. No doubt he felt that his future appointment would be less difficult if this elderly, very senior and difficult Victor of the Battle was removed from active service in the RAF, and replaced by a younger and more malleable officer.

Air Vice-Marshal William Sholto Douglas

With his duties as Deputy CAS, Douglas had been closely involved with the CAS and the Secretary of State for Air. Whatever his personal feelings were as an ex fighter pilot about the Trenchard Bombing Policy, he would have needed to be involved with the Cabal. His chairmanship and planning of the Meeting of Shame shows clearly his opposition to Dowding and his determination to bring him down.

Douglas knew from his very privileged position and his relations with Fighter Command that, if Dowding were to go, he would be a front-runner to replace him. He had a high stake in the outcome.

Douglas, a 'Man of Ambition', had given Leigh-Mallory his fullest support with the Big Wings. His attacks on Dowding and his support of the Cabal, eventually led him to a senior promotion to replace the great leader he had helped to dishonour.

Air Vice-Marshal Trafford Leigh-Mallory

Although Leigh-Mallory did great harm to Dowding, I do not believe that he was an inner member of the Cabal. Whatever he did, he would do in his own interests. He would probably have carried out his own disloyal plans even if there had been no Cabal, but he must have welcomed their support and reward.

Although I do not see Leigh-Mallory as an inner member, his disloyalty to his Commander-in-Chief and his support of the irresponsible and even dangerous activities of Bader, qualify him for a seal of dishonour.

Flight Lieutenant Peter McDonald M.P., Adjutant to No. 242 Squadron

McDonald, a Canadian, had been with the Squadron in France earlier in the war when it was designated as a Canadian squadron, and he still felt great loyalty towards it. He came under Bader's spell and presumably believed all his claims of victories and all his complaints about controllers. Unfortunately many of Bader's views were based on emotions rather than on facts. I believe that McDonald was misguided by his loyalty to Bader and the squadron, but the effect of his actions was to give help to the Cabal in their machinations leading to dishonour for Dowding.

Fortunately Dowding had three loyal Group Commanders who served him well. He also had the fighter pilots and aircrews of his Command whose courage and dedication ensured his victory in the Battle.

CHAPTER 19

Honour Restored

A Claim for Honour to be Restored to Dowding, the Architect of our Great Victory, and for the British Nation of today to be told of the courage and sacrifice of our Citizens in 1940

It is too late for the circumstances of the infamous dismissal of Dowding and Park to be formally investigated and their honour restored. To achieve it would mean formally attacking the honour and reputations of senior figures of 60 years ago. However, I have tried to show that there is adequate evidence to confirm that Dowding's victory was well established, that the ineffectiveness of the Big Wing Philosophy has been proved, and that the political machinations of the Air Ministry and Air Marshals have been exposed. The Battle of Britain was won by the young fighter pilots who day after day, in squadrons of twelve aircraft and often in flights of six, attacked overwhelming numbers of German bombers and fighters. It was not won, nor could it have been won, by a loose cannon of three squadrons of Hurricanes protected by two squadrons of Spitfires roaming uncontrolled over 11 Group skies. The discussions and decisions of the Meeting of Shame, denigrating Dowding's policy, dishonour all the pilots and aircrew who fought in the Battle.

It is right that the 'high commanders' involved in the machinations of dishonour should be exposed. The honoured reputation of the RAF has been built up over the years by the courage, tenacity and the sacrifices of its pilots and aircrews, fighting the enemy and the elements high in the sky. No machinations by desk-bound officers at the Air Ministry could ever tarnish the honour of the Royal Air Force.

But it is not too late to put on public record recognition equal to that given to other great military leaders of the past. When young people are told about the Battle of Britain, they should know that it was won by Dowding and Park and 2,936 extraordinary young men of whom 544 sacrificed their lives for our Freedom, supported by the ordinary people of Britain who stood firm against the horrendous German attacks and refused to surrender.

Honour must be restored.

References and Documentation

In my years of research I have read many excellent books on the Battle of Britain. Within the National Archives I found many documents to be examined, giving a wide and deep penetration of events before 1940, during and after. The activities of a cabal will never be easily recorded with precision, but I have tried to present my book as a simple and honest reconstruction of the critical events and to draw reasonable and sometimes forceful conclusions.

My chart of the daily record of the total Big Wing sorties on page no.149, and its concealment from the Meeting of Shame, is enough to expose the dishonourable behaviour of Leigh-Mallory, Stevenson, and Douglas.

For any reader who wishes to research the activities described in this book, I would recommend the following documents, which I have found provide the evidence to show that the meeting at the Air Ministry on 17th October 1940 was indeed a Meeting of Shame. They can be examined at the National Archives at Kew and photocopies can be purchased. There are of course a wealth of other relevant documents there which can be searched to give a fuller insight into the Dismissal without due Honour.

Documents at The National Archives (PRO):

Air 16/281, Report on Wing Patrols sent up by No 12 Group, 17/09/40
Air 16/735, Conference to discuss Major Day Tactics in the Fighter Force.
Air 16/735, Air Staff Note on the Operation of Fighter Wings, 14/10/40
Air 16/735, Agenda, 14/10/40
Air 16/735, Minutes of a Meeting on Tactics on 17th October 1940, Not dated

Bibliography

I gave my first lecture on the Battle of Britain in 1942 when I was a flight lieutenant student in the newly formed Empire Central Flying School at Hullavington, attended by officer pilots from all Commands in Britain and from flying establishments from our Dominions overseas. My lecture was based on my own experiences in the Battle and my interpretation of events. I clearly remember stating that the only real practical benefit obtained from the Duxford Wing was its psychological value when, as a formation of 50/60 Spitfires and Hurricanes, it suddenly appeared ready to do battle with the main German bomber formations twice on 15th September. After my research, reading and analysis of the Battle over many years I still hold to that view.

I believe that in writing a book on such an immense subject as the Battle, each work is a stepping-stone to add to those we ourselves have walked on. I hope that *Honour Restored* will prove to be another, well based, if controversial stone.

Over the past nine years I have talked to some of the authors of the great books that have been written since the Battle, discussing their interpretation of events. My sincere thanks to them for their willing assistance which has made my work more effective.

The following are some of the publications that helped shape the book.

Angelucci, Enzo and Matricardi, Paulo, *World Aircraft. Origins – World War I,* Sampson Low, 1977.

Aeroplane Monthly, *Alcorn Combat Analysis,* Sept 1996, Pub: Stephen Curtis.

Aeroplane Monthly, *Alcorn Update,* July 2000, Pub: Stephen Curtis.

Boyle, Andrew, *Trenchard. Man of Vision,* Collins 1962.

Brickhill, Paul, *Reach for the Sky. The Story of Douglas Bader* Collins, 1954

Bungay, Stephen, *The Most Dangerous Enemy. History of the Battle of Britain,* Aurum Press, 2000.

Churchill, Winston, *The Second World War, Volume II, 'Their Finest Hour',* Cassell, 1949.

Collier, Basil, *Leader of the Few. The Dowding Story,* Jarrolds, 1957.

Collier, Basil, *The Battle of Britain,* Batsford, 1962.

Cross, Kenneth ACM with Orange Vincent, *Straight and Level,* Grub Street, 1993.

Deighton, Len, *Fighter: The True Story of the Battle of Britain,* Cape, 1977.

Dixon, JEG, *The Battle of Britain: Victory and Defeat*, Woodfield, 2003.

Douglas, Sholto with Wright, Robert, *Years of Command*, Collins, 1966.

Dunn, Bill Newton, *Big Wing: The Biography of ACM Leigh-Mallory*, Airlife Publishing Ltd, 1992.

Flint, Peter, *Dowding and Headquarters Fighter Command*, Airlife Publishing Ltd, 1996.

Franks, Norman, *Air Battle Dunkirk*, Grub Street, 2000.

Gelb, Norman, *Scramble: A Narrative History of the Battle of Britain*, Michael Joseph, 1986.

Gelb, Norman, *Dunkirk: The Incredible Escape*, Michael Joseph, 1990.

Gilbert, Martin, *Finest Hour: Winston S. Churchill 1939–1941*, Minerva, 1989.

Hough, Richard and Richards, Denis, *The Battle of Britain: The Jubilee History*, Guild Publishing, 1990.

James, T C G, *The Battle of Britain*, Frank Cass, 2000.

Jenkins, Roy, *Churchill*, Pan Books, 2002.

AVM Johnson, 'Johnnie', *Wing Leader*, Air Data Publications, 1995.

Lucas, 'Laddie', *Flying Colours: The Epic Story of Douglas Bader*, Wordsworth Editions, 2001.

Mason, Francis K, *Battle over Britain*, Aston Publications, 1990.

Orange, Vincent, *Sir Keith Park*, Methuen, 1984.

Price, Alfred, *Spitfire*, PRCL, 1991.

Price, Alfred, *Battle of Britain Day*, Sidgwick & Jackson, 1990.

Probert, Henry AC, *Air Commanders of the Royal Air Force*, HMSO, 1991.

Ramsey, Winston G, *The Battle of Britain – Then and Now*, Battle of Britain International Ltd (7th impression), 2000.

Ray, John, *The Battle of Britain. New Perspectives*, Brockhampton Press, 1999.

Ross, David, *Richard Hillary*, Grub Street, 2000.

Terraine, J, *The Right of the Line*, Wordsworth Editions, 1997.

Turner, John Frayn, *The Bader Wing*, Airlife Publishing, 1990.

Winterbotham, FW, *The Ultra Secret*, Orion, 2000.

Wood, Derek and Dempster, Derek, *The Narrow Margin*, Pen & Sword Military Classics, 2003.

Wynn, Kenneth G, *Men of the Battle of Britain*, CCB Associates, 1999.

Diary of Events

1916	Lt Col Hugh Dowding commanded a Fighter Wing in France. Dispute with Major General Trenchard over Dowding's request to rest one of his squadrons with high casualties. Soon after, Dowding posted back to England for training appointment finally attaining the command of a training brigade. He was replaced by Lt Col Newall.
1932/1936	Air Marshal Sir Hugh Dowding as Director of Research and Development was responsible for the introduction of monoplane fighters and RDF development.
14th July 1936	AM Sir Hugh Dowding appointed Air Officer Commanding in Chief of Fighter Command.
1st January 1937	Dowding promoted to Air Chief Marshal, making him the most senior serving officer in the Royal Air Force.
1st April 1937	Newall promoted to Air Chief Marshal.
1st September 1937	Newall appointed Chief of Air Staff.
August 1938	Air Council advised Dowding that he would be retired in June 1939.
20th March 1939	The CAS advised Dowding that he would be retired at the end of March 1940.

At War

3rd September 1939	Britain and France declare war on Germany.
30th March 1940	The CAS advised Dowding of his new retirement date as 14th July 1940. Dowding requested the name of his successor. This was not provided.
10th May 1940	Germany invades France and Low Countries and sweeps through to the Channel ports.
26th May 1940	Beginning of evacuation of retreating British Army through Dunkirk, the last remaining open port available.
4th June 1940	The evacuation ends with the transfer of 330,000 Allied personnel across the Channel to England,

but without their heavy weapons and vehicles. This great escape was aided by British Hurricanes, Spitfires and Defiants fighting the Luftwaffe high over the beaches and losing 80 pilots and 106 aircraft, a quarter of the aircraft taking part.

18th June 1940	France surrenders leaving England to face the military might of Germany completely alone. Luftwaffe units will be based on airfields across the Channel and with some less than 40 miles flying distance from the English coast.
5th July 1940	Dowding was advised of a further delay in his retirement. On this occasion the CAS gave the extended date as the end of October 1940. After intervention by the Prime Minister this date was cancelled.
10th July 1940	Germany plans to invade England. Fighter Command must be destroyed first and Goering plans to do this with more than 2,000 operational bombers and fighters against Fighter Command strength at that time of some 650 Hurricanes and Spitfires.
13th August 1940	On Goering's Eagle Day, German massed formations started their bombing attacks on the British mainland. In the seven days of fine weather, Fighter Command shot down 317 Luftwaffe aircraft and lost 148 fighters, a win to our fighters by 2:1.
19th August 1940	The weather changed to poor and halted the German massed attacks.
24th August 1940	With the start of a long period of fine weather the Luftwaffe recommenced their heavy attacks on airfields ports, and factories with serious casualties on both sides.
1st September 1940	Hitler confirmed that the Luftwaffe must destroy Fighter Command by 17th September or the Invasion in 1940 would be cancelled.
4th September 1940	Hitler announced that as British bombers had bombed Berlin at night he would retaliate with a series of terror raids of night bombing on London and other cities. Goering would now also be free to bomb London by day.
7th September 1940	The first major daylight raid on London took place on this date with heavy casualties and major damage to the Capital. The first night raid on London followed with further very heavy damage. The Duxford Wing of 3 Squadrons first flew together on this day.
15th September 1940	Goering planned two major raids against London, each with hundreds of bombers and twice as many Me109 fighters to protect them. The German formations were attacked all the way to London

by 11 Group squadrons and the Duxford Wing of 5 squadrons. The same treatment was given to the afternoon raid. The Germans lost 56 aircraft during the raids and many more were damaged.

On this day, later to be known as Battle of Britain Day, the Luftwaffe suffered not only a defeat in the air, but they now knew that the invasion could not take place in 1940

17th September 1940	Hitler cancelled the invasion for 1940.
19th September 1940	The German soldiers and Channel barges started to leave the invasion ports for Germany.
30th September 1940	The last major bomber raid on London. Heavily defeated. This had no tactical value and it could have no effect on the invasion.
1st October 1940	The weather changed to poor throughout the month. There were no massed bomber attacks but the Germans sent high-flying Me109s, some with bombs. The fighting was heavy and the Germans lost 293 aircraft against Fighter Command operational losses of 156 aircraft.

The Duxford Wing flew 15 sorties in the month but made no contact with the enemy.

8th October 1940	Dowding awarded honour of Grand Companion of the Order of the Bath.
31st October 1940	Some time later the Battle was officially declared to have ended on 31st October although fighting with Me109s still continued over south-east England after this date.

The Meeting of Shame

4th October 1940	Air Chief Marshal Newall, the CAS was promoted to Marshal of the RAF.
17th October 1940	A meeting was called by the Air Ministry to discuss fighter tactics to be used after the Battle had been won. It was chaired by AVM Douglas, the Deputy CAS in the absence of the CAS due to indisposition.

Those attending included 10 officers of air rank. The agenda was basically concerned with the use of one-, four-, five-, or six-squadron formations. An additional agenda on how to outnumber and outmanouevre the enemy formations was presented by the Chairman for first discussion followed later by the original agenda which had been circulated prior to the meeting.

It was decided that five- and six-squadron wings were to be part of the tactical defence philosophy for Fighter Command in the future.

There was no planned discussion on strategy.

24th October 1940	MRAF Newall relinquished his appointment as CAS.
25th October 1940	Air Marshal Portal was promoted to Air Chief Marshal and appointed Chief of Air Staff.
13th November 1940	Dowding was interviewed by the Secretary of State for Air, who told him that he was to be replaced as Commander in Chief, but that he was not to be retired. He was to go to the United States on a mission related to the supply of equipment. He was told that AVM Douglas would be taking over as Commander in Chief.
25th November 1940	Dowding relinquished his position as Commander in Chief of Fighter Command.
	Dowding's termination of his great service to Britain and Europe was reported in the press simply as 'Fighter Command New Chief'.
18th December 1940	AVM Park was removed from his position as Commander of 11 Group, which had borne the brunt of the fighting, to a Training Command Group, effectively a demotion. He was replaced by AVM Leigh-Mallory of 12 Group whose Big Wing Philosophy had played a significant part in Dowding's dismissal.
25th December 1940	Church bells were rung to celebrate the victory. Dowding was on duty in the USA.
1941	The Air Ministry published a booklet for sale about the Battle of Britain. It contained no reference to Air Chief Marshal Sir Hugh Dowding. Winston Churchill ordered the book to be rewritten and republished with recognition of the part played by Dowding.
10th January 1941	First Fighter Command offensive sweep ordered over France by AVM Leigh-Mallory. None of the wing formations in the sweep had more than 3 squadrons.
22nd June 1941	German forces commenced their invasion of Russia.
14th July 1942	Last day of his service with the Royal Air Force following his decision to take voluntary retirement.
17th July 1942	Through his secretary, Sir Alexander Hardinge, HM The King raised with Sinclair the question of Dowding being promoted to Marshal of the Royal Air Force on retirement, which the King obviously felt was merited. The following day it was minuted at the Air Ministry that the King would not wish to pursue this suggestion.
2nd June 1943	Dowding honoured with the Barony of Bentley Priory on the recommendation of Winston Churchill.

Appendices

Agenda for meeting set for 17th October 1940

Secret Agenda

<u>Item1</u> Is it agreed that the minimum fighter unit to meet large enemy formations should be a Wing of 3 Squadrons?

<u>Item 2</u> Is it agreed that a larger fighter formation than a Wing should operate as a tactical unit? If so, is it agreed that this unit should consist of 2 Wings?
By what name should such a unit (referred to in this Agenda as a 'Balbo') be known?

<u>Item 3</u> Are any surmountable obstacles foreseen in operating all the squadrons of a Wing from the same aerodrome?

<u>Item 4</u> Is it agreed that the Wing and Balbo should be controlled by a squadron commander from one of the squadrons composing the formation?

<u>Item 5</u> Are there likely to be any difficulties in co-ordinating the operations of the two Wings of a Balbo?

<u>Item 6</u> In weather conditions which enable the enemy to operate in mass formation, it is likely that the fighter leader may be able to dispense with sector control. Is it agreed that in these conditions he should inform the sector controller and take over control of the Wing or Balbo, being informed by the controller of the location, size, speed, course and height of the enemy mass?

<u>Item 7</u> Has the conference any comments on the method of R/T control of Balbos described in paras 12 to 15 of the attached Air Staff Note?

<u>Item 8</u> Can Wings be regarded as permanent units and moved complete when necessary, from one sector station to another?

<u>Item 9</u> Is it agreed that Wings should be deployed at stations from which they can gain advantage in height over the enemy, without having to turn?

<u>Item 10</u> Short report by C-in-C Fighter Command on present position regarding night interception.

<u>14/10/40</u>

Minutes of a Meeting Held in the Air Council Room on October 17th 1940 to Discuss Major Day Tactics in the Fighter Force.

(Reference Air Staff Notes And Agenda Dated 14.10.40.)

Present:-

Air Vice-Marshal W. S. Douglas.	D.C.A.S.
Air Chief Marshal Sir Hugh C.T. Dowding	A.O.C.-in-C. Fighter Command
Air Marshal Sir Charles F.A. Portal	C.A.S. (Designate)
Air Marshal Sir Philip P.B. Joubert de la Ferte	A.C.A.S. (R)
Air Vice-Marshal K.R. Park	A.O.C. No. 11 Group
Air Vice-Marshal Sir C.J.Q. Brand	A.O.C. No. 10 Group
Air Vice-Marshal T.L. Leigh-Mallory	A.O.C. No. 12 Group
Air Commodore J. C. Slessor	D. of Plans
Air Commodore D.F. Stevenson	D.H.O. (Home Operations)
Air Commodore O.G.W.G. Lywood	P.D.D. of Signals
Group Captain H.G. Crowe	A.D.A.T.
Squadron Leader D.R.S. Bader	O.C. 242 Squadron
Wing Commander T.N. McEvoy}	Secretaries
Mr J.S. Orme}	

----

1. D.C.A.S. explained that he was presiding at the meeting, as C.A.S. was unable to be present owing to indisposition.

2. There was three propositions that he would like the meeting to consider.

(1) We wish to outnumber the enemy formations when we meet them.

(2) We want our superior numbers to go into the attack with a co-ordinated plan of action, so that the protecting fighters are engaged by one part of our force, leaving the bombers to be engaged by the remainder.

(3) If possible we want the top layer of our fighter formation to have the advantage of height over the top layer of the enemy formation.

3. This was the ideal, but it was obviously not always possible of attainment. For instance, the time factor might not allow us to do what we wanted. It might be necessary to engage the enemy before he reached some vital objective, and in such cases there might not be time either to collect a superior force or to obtain superior height. D.C.A.S. then invited comments on the propositions he had outlined.

4. A.O.C. No. 11 Group said that with the factors of time, distance and cloud that were often involved in the operations of No. 11 Group it should not be laid down as a general principle that the 'Wing' of fighters was the right formation with which to oppose attacks, even those made in mass. He felt that the satisfactory use of the 'Wing' by No. 12 Group related to ideal conditions when the enemy bombers were in retreat, separated from their escort. No. 11 Group, using formations of one or two squadrons had, on the other hand, quite recently obtained results against bombers on their way in, which compared not unfavourably with those of the 'Wing' sorties from No. 12 Group.

5. The A.O.C. outlined to the meeting the principle that applied in No. 11 Group for operations against a large force of escorted enemy bombers with a fighter screen; this involved the use of squadrons in pairs at different heights to engage separately the top fighter screen, the close escort and the bombers.

6. A.O.C.-in-C. Fighter Command said that the great problem was to obtain early knowledge as to which of perhaps many raids was the major one. The Observer Corps did good work but were often baffled by the extreme height of enemy formations. He therefore attached great importance to the development of the G.L. and L.C. organisation; Kent and Sussex would be covered by the end of November. This beam control had, of course, the disadvantage that the plot of only one formation at a time could be brought through into a Sector Operations Room, but it would be a big help when a big raid was known to be coming in.

7. A.O.C. No. 11 Group referred to experiments he had been making with reconnaissance Spitfires, which in favourable conditions were useful for obtaining early reports of big formations. The general installation of V.H.F. would give better results from this reconnaissance work.

8. Incidentally, there had been two recent occurrences of experienced pilots on reconnaissance being shot down at over 25,000 feet by raids of which the R.D.F. had given no indication.

9. Experience showed that this reconnaissance work was not suitable for young pilots whose commendable keenness led them to engage, rather than shadow, the enemy.

10. Reverting to the general question of fighter tactics, the A.O.C. 11 Group said that to meet the present 'tip-and-run' raids he felt that the only effective system was that now employed in No. 11 Group. The reconnaissance Spitfire section was always backed by one or two strong Spitfire squadrons patrolling on the Maidstone patrol line at 15,000 feet, as soon as the first R.D.F. warning was received these squadrons went up to 30,000 feet and then to 35,000 feet, so as to cover the ascent of other squadrons; one of these was always at instant readiness and, generally, the present situation demanded an exceptionally high degree of readiness throughout the Group.

11. A.O.C. No. 12 Group said that he would welcome more opportunities of using the 'Wing' formation, operating, say, from Duxford and coming down to help No. 11 Group. He could get a 'Wing' of five squadrons into the air in six minutes and it could be over Hornchurch at 20,000 feet in thirty-five minutes. If this type of counter-attack intercepted a big formation only once in ten times this effort would none the less be worth it. On two recent occasions good results had again been obtained, once against fighters alone.

12. A.C.A.S. (R) drew attention to the shortness of some of the warnings that Groups had recently received.

13. A.O.C.-in-C. Fighter Command said that he had recently given written orders that an 'arrow' should go down on the Operations Table on receipt of the first 'counter'; it must be realised that the enemy's approach at great height presented a difficult problem.

14. A.O.C. No. 11 Group said that he could face the problem when it was a large bomber raid coming in.

15. Discussion followed on this question and it was generally agreed that additional fighter support would often be advantageous, since the more we could outnumber the enemy, the more we should shoot down. The A.O.C.-in-C. said that he could, with his Group Commanders, resolve any difficulties of control involved in sending such support. The other main difficulties to be met, it was agreed, were those involving the time factor, though in this connection it was mentioned that the Me109 carrying bombs had not, so far, been found over 22,000 feet.

16. Squadron Leader Bader said that from his practical experience time was the essence of the problem; if enough warning could be given to bring a large number of fighters into position, there was no doubt they could get most effective results.

17. Air Marshal Portal enquired how such a local concentration might affect the responsibility of a Group Commander for the defence of all the area of his Group. A.O.C. No. 12 Group said that satisfactory plans were prepared to meet the possibility of other attacks coming in; he was satisfied that the concentration of a 'Wing' was not incompatible with his general responsibility as Group Commander.

18. This raised the question of whether some of No. 12 Group's squadrons might be moved to No. 10 Group, which was, the C-in-C. agreed, at present somewhat weak should any concentrated attack develop in the West. On the other hand, the protection of the Midlands and of the East Coast convoys was a big commitment for No. 12 Group. Though it was a serious limitation he had, as C-in-C. to keep in mind the necessity of meting every threat with some force.

19. Further discussion followed in which the importance of a long warning from the R.D.F. was stressed. A.C.A.S. (R) said that everything was being done to get the south-east coast R.D.F. stations back to full efficiency following the damage suffered from enemy attacks. He mentioned the recent example when a twenty-five minute steady R.D.F. warning had not been received without delay in No. 11 Group. It was decided that No. 11 Group should have the services of a certain member of the Stanmore Research Station who had previously been of assistance to them.

20. D.C.A.S. said that he thought the views of the meeting could be summarised as follows:

    The employment of a large mass of fighters had great advantages, though it was not necessarily the complete solution to the problem of interception. In No. 11 Group, where the enemy was very close at hand, both the methods described by A.O.C. No. 11 Group and those of A.O.C. No. 12 Group could, on occasion, be used, with forces from the two Groups co-operating.

21. The A.O.C.-in-C. said that it would be arranged for No. 12 Group 'Wings' to participate freely in suitable operations over the 11 Group area. He would be able to resolve any complications of control. In reply to D.H.O. the C-in-C. said that co-operation of this kind could, in the present circumstances, hardly be employed generally throughout the Command as similar conditions seldom arose elsewhere.

22. With reference to the formal Agenda prepared for the meeting, the following observations were made.

Items 1 and 2
Items 1 and 2 formed the subject of general discussion as shown above.
    It was agreed that, where conditions were suitable, Wings of three squadrons should be employed against large enemy formations and that

where further forces could be made available without detriment to other commitments larger fighter formations than Wings should operate as tactical units.

It was agreed that it would, on occasion, be convenient to operate two Wings together as a unit and that, for want of a better name, such a unit should provisionally be known as a 'Balbo'.

Item 3   It was agreed that it would not always be practicable to operate the combined squadrons of a Wing from the same aerodrome, particularly in winter when aircraft might be confined to the runways. It was, however, agreed that all the squadrons of a Wing should operate from the same Sector.

Item 4   It was agreed that, as was now the practice, the Wing or 'Balbo' should be controlled by the Sector Commander. It was considered undesirable for a squadron Commander from one of the squadrons to control such a formation.

Item 5   No major difficulty was foreseen in co-ordinating the operations of the two Wings of a 'Balbo'; it was agreed that one Sector Commander should control the two Wings, and that when possible the two Wings of a 'Balbo' could work on a common frequency.

Item 6   It was agreed that, in the conditions, which enable the enemy to operate in mass formation, the fighter leader of a Wing could dispense with sector control and that if he was given information about enemy movements he should be responsible for leading his formation to the Battle.

Item 7   It was agreed that all squadrons of a 'Balbo' could operate effectively on the same frequency with H.F. R/T up to a theoretical maximum of seven 'Balbos'. It was agreed that when V.H.F. R/T was introduced the method of working suggested in paragraph 13 of the Air Staff paper would be satisfactory.

Item 8   It was not thought that Wings could be regarded as permanent units to be moved complete, but that whenever possible the same squadrons should operate together as a Wing.

Item 9   It was agreed that where practicable, Wings should be deployed at stations from which they could gain advantage in height over the enemy without having to turn.

Item 10

23. A.O.C.-in-C. Fighter Command, in amplification of his earlier reports, gave the meeting an interim account of the development of the A.I. Beaufighter. As yet, troubles with the Mark IV A.I., the Beaufighter, and

its engines were causing much unserviceability, but he was satisfied that the system was sound in principle.

24. The method of using searchlights in clumps promised good results and was about to be developed in the South.

25. D.C.A.S. and D.H.O. referred to the grave problem of maintaining civil morale in London, in the face of continued attack, over the two or three months that might be expected to pass before the system outlined by the C-in-C was practically efficient. To bridge the gap during the intervening period it was suggested that a temporary Wing of two Defiant and two Hurricane squadrons should be formed to specialise in night fighting on a 1914-1918 basis. C-in-C. Fighter Command said that continual experiments had been made on these lines, many of them by the A.O.C. No. 10 Group who had, since the last war, been a specialist in night interception, but with the height and speed of modern night raids the old methods had not so far proved effective. He felt certain that now the only sound method would be a combination of A.I. and G.L. (or L.C.); he was not averse, however, to his Defiant squadrons being employed temporarily on night interception; with great reluctance, he would agree to the diversion of a Hurricane squadron; these, he felt, would show reasonable results when the controlled clumps of searchlights began to work round London towards the end of November, but a real solution to the problem would only be found through the logical development of a system based on the two new radio aids to interception.

26. A.O.C.-in-C said that he would be prepared to experiment with a 'Fighter Night' over London, but this was not a course he could recommend. As people heard the fighters over London they would imagine that the noise represented so many more enemy aircraft.

27. A preliminary draft of the scheme, which D.C.A.S. and D.H.O. had explained to the meeting was handed to the C-in-C. Fighter Commander who undertook to examine it.

APPENDIX III

Operation Seelöwe (Sealion)
DIRECTIVE No. 16

The Fuhrer and CINC of the Wehrmacht   Führer Headquarters
OKW/WFA/L #33 160/4O g. Kdos   16 July 1940
Secret   Office Courier only

Concerning preparations for an amphibious operation against England.

Since Britain still shows no sign of willingness to come to an agreement in spite of her hopeless military situation, I have decided to prepare and if necessary carry out an amphibious operation against England.

The purpose of this operation will be to eliminate the English mother country as a base for continuation of the war against Germany and, if it should become necessary, to occupy the entire island.

To this end I order as follows:

1. The amphibious operation must be carried out as a surprise crossing on a broad front extending approximately from Ramsgate to the region of the Isle of Wight, with Luftwaffe elements assuming the role of artillery, and naval units assuming the role of engineers.
Each individual branch of the Wehrmacht will examine from its own viewpoint whether it appears practicable to carry out subsidiary operations, for example to occupy the Isle of Wight or Cornwall County, prior to the general crossing, and will report its findings to me. I reserve the decision to myself.

Preparations for the overall operations must be completed by mid-August.

2. These preparations will include the creation of conditions which will make a landing in England possible:
a) The English air force must be so far neutralized, both actually and in morale, that it will offer no appreciable

resistance to the German crossing operation;
b) Lanes must be cleared of mines;
c) Both outlets of the Straits of Dover, and the west entrance to the English Channel in a line approximately from Alderney to Portland, must be sealed off by a dense belt of mines;
d) The coastal areas must be commanded and covered by the fire of heavy coastal artillery;
e) It is desirable that all British naval forces should be tied down in action, both in the North Sea and in the Mediterranean - here by the Italians - shortly before the crossing; efforts must be made now already by means of air and torpedo attacks to weaken as far as possible the British naval forces presently in those waters.

3. Organization of Command and Preparations.
Under my command and in accordance with my general directives the commanders in chief of the three branches of the Wehrmacht will direct the operations of their forces employed in the operation. From 1 August on, the operations staffs of the commanders in chief of the Army, the Navy, and the Luftwaffe must be within the area with a maximum radius of 30 miles from my headquarters at Ziegenberg.
To me it appears advisable for the most vital elements of the operations staffs of the commanders in chief of the Army and the Navy to occupy mutual premises in Giessen.
The commander in chief of the Army will thus have to establish an army group headquarters to conduct the operations of the landing armies.

The operation will be given the designation Sea Lion (Seelöwe). During preparations and in the execution of the operation the missions of the three branches of the Wehrmacht will be as follows:
a) Army. Preparation of plans of operations and of a crossing plan initially for all units to be shipped in the first wave. The units accompanying the first wave will remain under Army control (under the individual landing groupments) until it is possible to subdivide their mission into responsibility for (1) support and protection for the ground forces, (2) protection of the ports of debarkation, and (3) protection for the air bases to be occupied. The Army will also allocate shipping space to the individual landing groupments and will define the points of embarkation and debarkation in agreement with the Navy.

b) Navy. Procurement and assembly of the required shipping space at the points of embarkation designated by the Army and in accordance with nautical requirements. As far as possible use will be made of ships from defeated hostile countries.
The necessary naval advisory staff, escort ships, and other protective naval units will be provided by the Navy at each crossing area. In addition to the protection afforded by the air units employed, naval forces will protect the flanks of the

entire movement across the Channel. Orders will be issued
regulating the chain of command during the actual crossing.

Another mission of the Navy is to direct the uniform disposition
of coastal artillery, namely, of all naval and Army batteries
which can be used against naval targets and to generally organize
the control of fire.The largest possible number of the heaviest
artillery units will be so placed that they can be brought into
effective action as speedily as possible to protect the flanks of
the movements against hostile naval attack. For this purpose all
railway artillery, reinforced by all available captured guns but
minus the K-5 and K-12 batteries earmarked for counterbattery
fire against shore-based hostile artillery in England, will be
withdrawn from present positions and emplaced on railway
turntable mounts.

In addition to the above, all platform guns of the heaviest types
will be so emplaced under concrete protection opposite the
Straits of Dover that they will be proof against even the
heaviest air attacks. They will be so sited that they will
command the Straits under all circumstances as far as their
ranges permit.The technical work involved will be carried out by
Organization Todt.

c) Luftwaffe. The mission of the Luftwaffe will be to prevent
interference by hostile air forces. In addition airpower will be
employed to neutralize coastal fortifications which could deliver
fire in the landing areas, to break the initial resistance
offered by the hostile ground forces, and to destroy reserves
during their forward movement. These missions will require
extremely close contact between the individual air units and the
landing forces of the Army.

It will also be important for air units to destroy roads which
could be used by the enemy to move reserves forward, and to
attack naval units approaching the areas of operations while
still far distant from the crossing routes.I request
recommendations on the use of paratrooper and glider and other
airborne forces. The question must be examined together with the
Army whether it would be wise to withhold paratrooper and other
airborne forces during the initial stages as a reserve force
which could be moved quickly to critical areas in the event of an
emergency.The Wehrmacht chief signal officer will ensure that all
necessary preparations are made to establish communications
between France and England.Preparations will be made in
cooperation with the Navy to lay what is still available of the
48 miles of marine cable taken up from the East Prussian canal.

4. Preparations to ensure the necessary communications between
France and the English mainland will be
handled by the chief of the armed forces signals

5. I request the commanders in chief to submit to me as early as possible:

a) The measures planned by the Navy and the Luftwaffe to create the conditions necessary for the Channel crossing operation (Item 2, above);

b) Details on the disposition of the coastal artillery batteries (Navy);

c) A survey of the shipping to be employed and of the methods of concentration and equipment. All civilian agencies participate? (Navy);

d) Plans for the organization of air defense in the areas of concentration for troops and for equipment to be used in the crossing operation (Luftwaffe);

e) Channel-crossing schedule and plan of operations of the Army, and organization and equipment of the first attack wave;

f) Organization and action planned by the Navy and the Luftwaffe for the defense of the crossing movement itself, for reconnaissance, and for support during the landing;

g) Recommendations concerning the commitment of paratrooper and other airborne forces and concerning the command of forces after an adequately large area has been brought under control in England (Luftwaffe);

h) Recommendations for the location of headquarters for the command echelons of the commander in chief of the Army and the commander in chief of the Navy;

i) Comments by the Army, the Navy, and the Luftwaffe as to whether and what partial operations are considered practicable prior to the general amphibious operation;

k) Recommendations by, the Army and the Navy concerning the chain of command during the crossing, while seaborne.

[Hand-initialed]
J[odl]
K[eitel]

(signed)
Adolf Hitler

Distribution:
Commander in Chief,
Commander in Chief,
Commander in Chief,
Wehrmacht Operations,
National Defense Branch

Army Ribbon Copy
Navy Second Copy
Luftwaffe Third Copy
Office Fourth Copy
Fifth to Seventh Copies

Index

Index